T0368115

THE HANDBOOK OF TRANSFORMATIONAL EDUCATION

by Helen Purgason Vaughan, PhD

WESTBOW
PRESS®
A DIVISION OF THOMAS NELSON
& ZONDERVAN

WestBow Press books may be ordered through booksellers or by contacting:

WestBow Press
A Division of Thomas Nelson & Zondervan
1663 Liberty Drive
Bloomington, IN 47403
www.westbowpress.com
844-714-3454

ISBN: 978-1-6642-7878-3 (sc)
ISBN: 978-1-6642-7895-0 (e)

Library of Congress Control Number: 2022917851

Print information available on the last page.

WestBow Press rev. date: 11/09/2022

Soli Deo Gloria

Such is the confidence we have through Christ before God. It
is not that we are competent in ourselves to claim anything as
coming from ourselves, but our adequacy is from God.

—2 Corinthians 3:4–5

CONTENTS

ACKNOWLEDGMENTS

Thanks to my husband, Ellis, who supported me in every way imaginable, even when writing this book seemed like a bad idea for us personally.

Thanks to our ministry partners who prayed, encouraged, and financially provided for the missional experiences in the schools for whom this book originated and hopefully will benefit.

Thanks to my children who unknowingly prompted this project.

Thanks to the many writers, composers, artists, bloggers, and preachers who have shaped my faith.

And most importantly, I acknowledge Dr. George Durance with appreciation and indebtedness for all he did to foster this project. George is the key player in every aspect of the book, from graciously receiving my resignation from a position in the mission to pursue writing, to editing, to providing a platform to introduce it to others. I think George should have written the book due to his deep understanding of transformational education and his excellent writing ability. However, George's choice was to equip, encourage, and provide for me to follow what I believe God called me to do. That's just what George does. I am grateful and indebted.

HOW TO USE THIS BOOK

Silly me. Trying to tackle transformational education when the whole idea is for transformation to tackle me. What can I possibly contribute to a work that scripture clearly states, and I honestly observe, is not something *I do* but something that the *Holy Spirit does*? Yet Jesus refers to us, His followers, as colaborers in this task of transforming lives. He gives us duties, such as teaching, loving, discipling, encouraging, practicing hospitality, bearing testimony, carrying one another's burdens, disciplining, rebuking, correcting, and more. So, the way I understand it, the Holy Spirit engages us in this work of transforming lives.

The Handbook of Transformational Education and its accompanying *Facilitator's Guide* represent an invitation to the Christian educator to think, experiment, question, pray, and discuss how teachers can effectively partner with the Holy Spirit in changing lives through education. It is more than information; it is intended to be an exercise in learning, which is why many of the discussion points end with a question rather than an assertion. Each is meant to foster reflection and further inquiry, especially with other Christians walking the same vocational pathway. In the end, the enduring benefit may be the unexpected discoveries of the shared sojourn, rather than the passing insight for a moment at hand.

Use This as a Handbook

This book is not written as a chronological narrative or a series of sequential proofs in a persuasive essay. Understand that one chapter of the book is not dependent on having read previous chapters. Consequently, each chapter stands on its own—a hodgepodge of ideas on transformational education. This approach follows logically from an understanding of transformation as a process rather than an event, although events are an integral part of the process. The table of contents will assist in finding the chapter or section of interest. Use it as the handbook it is meant to be.

Adapt to Your Cultural Perspective

While the orienting principles in this book hopefully transcend time and culture, the applications naturally emerge from a particular experience in a particular culture in a particular time period. The strengths and limitations of this reality are well known, and the reader is reminded that the text must be read analytically in order to discern what is culturally appropriate and relevant in their time and place. Then the educator must adapt the applications for their students in their unique culture. This may be especially true for the sections of chapter 4.

Transformational Education Is for All Students

Transformation is not limited to a religious concept but rather involves every aspect of life. Although our desire is always to see students come to faith in Jesus, our desire also includes seeing God's will being done on earth. When Christians teach students the medical skills necessary to heal the sick, or teach peacemaking skills used to restore families, communities, and countries, or teach anything that restores God's kingdom plan, we are promoting God's will on earth. Hence, this handbook is not limited to the Christian school.

Teachers Teach in Many Settings Other Than a Classroom

Broadly speaking, education is a transaction that takes place between two people, usually identified as the teacher and the learner. For many, this conjures up the image of a classroom, but an educational event can occur in a variety of settings, such as when a learner engages with a ministry worker, music instructor, peer, sports coach, foreign language instructor, or even a parent. Although this book primarily refers to the classroom as the educational setting, readers should substitute their own educational setting into the narrative. Together the teacher and learner create a dynamic relationship pregnant with potential, particularly when it features prayer, service, and modeling with intentional openness to God's Spirit. Witness to its effectiveness spans the centuries.

Use This Book with the Facilitator's Guide for Professional Development

This book has an accompanying *Facilitator's Guide* for the purpose of promoting collaborative and reflective professional development among colleagues working in the same school or project. The *Facilitator's Guide* is a tool to assist small groups of educators meeting regularly to study the handbook and encouraging one another to be transformed and transformational. I refer to this experience as *sojourn*.

Of course, this handbook can also be used for quick reference and for individual study, but because Christians have the advantage of shared presuppositions and relationships, discussing the book in community is particularly effective. Furthermore, sojourn, or this group approach, is recommended in part because there is some surprising evidence that Christian educators working in environments like Christian schools have been slow to leverage the advantages associated with leaders working collaboratively and reflectively with their staff to enhance professional development (Swaner 2016). Swaner says the research indicates that school leaders are rarely trained in how to offer collaborative and reflective professional development within their own schools. Other researchers affirm Swaner's point that the better school leaders are at fostering collaborative and reflective development, the better students' learning outcomes.

The purpose, therefore, is to provide school leaders with readily available resources like this handbook and the accompanying *Facilitator's Guide* to assist teachers in their continuing effort to be transformational educators.

CHAPTER 1

DEFINING TRANSFORMATIONAL EDUCATION

Do not conform to the pattern of this world but be transformed by the renewing of your mind. Then you will be able to test and approve what God's will is-his good, pleasing, and perfect will.

—Romans 12:2

What is transformational education and what does it look like for teachers? This book is for educators who are followers of Jesus and eager to see other lives transformed by God's grace. The word *education* is used broadly to refer to any scenario having a teacher and a learner, such as the instructional relationship between a parent and a child, a coach and a player, a minister and a congregant, a musician and student, and of course all kinds of pupils in classrooms. The word *transformation* is defined in this chapter and discussed throughout the book. This book is premised on the belief that God uses teachers as agents of transformation.

Topics included in this chapter:

Section 1

Definition of Transformational Education

Definition of Transformational Education

The worthy task of being a transformational educator is best served by having an idea of what that means. I have discovered that it means a variety of things to different people, creating some interesting cross wires in communication and vision. Not to discount other meanings or understandings of transformational education, but for the sake of clarity and cohesion, the chapters that follow are based on the definition by Dr. George Durance, the founding president of TeachBeyond:

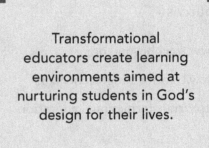

Transformational educators create learning environments aimed at nurturing students in God's design for their lives.

> Transformational education is an education that creates learning environments where a student is encouraged through every aspect of the environment to embrace wholeheartedly and in every dimension of life, God's amazing design for him or her and His empowerment for a full, rewarding, and impactful life now and in the life to come. (Durance 2019)

Notice some of the distinctions mentioned in this definition:

- the reference to *learning environments* and not only the *classroom*
- the reference to *every aspect of the environment and dimension of life* and not just the academic work
- the goal is for the student *to embrace God's amazing design for him or herself*
- the emphasis on the abundant life is *not only for eternal life but also for the here and now*
- the emphasis is having an *impactful life* not just for the benefit of oneself or securing a place in heaven

As important as it is to operationalize our topic by giving it a definition, we also, according to George Durance, "draw inspiration from the fact that transformational education communicates a rich and variegated message that is incapable of full and final definition." Hence, instead of being a treatise or final say on transformational education, this book is an invitation to explore with us what God may have us consider as those he made as educators.

Questions to consider:

1. What strikes you about this definition of transformational education? Would you add or change anything?

2. How comfortable are you with the idea of disagreeing or tossing out ideas presented in this book?

Sources:

www.teachbeyond.org

www.transformingteachers.org

http://transformational.education

George Durance

Transformational Education

- variety of learning environments
- every aspect of the environment and dimension of life
- embrace God's design for students
- abundant life now and in eternity
- impactful life now and in eternity

Section 2

Imagine Being an Agent of Transformation

Scripture is the basis of our understanding that God uses us in the transformation of others.

> "For we are co-workers in God's service; you are God's field, God's building. By the grace God has given me, I laid a foundation as a wise builder, and someone else is building on it. But each one should build with care" (1 Corinthians 3:9–10).

> "For we are God's fellow workers; you are God's field, God's building" (3 John 1:8).

> "As God's co-workers we urge you not to receive God's grace in vain" (2 Corinthians 6:1).

> Transformational educators imagine God's capacity to use them in changing lives.

Two stone cutters are asked what they are doing.

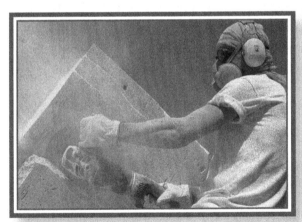

One answers, "I am cutting this stone in a perfectly square shape."

The other responds, "I am building a glorious cathedral."

Etienne Wenger (Wenger 1998, 176) uses the illustration above in his book *Communities of Practice*, to reflect two stonecutters' different assessments of what they are doing. One stonecutter imagines his contribution to the edification of a glorious cathedral, while the other imagines a simple measuring and cutting task. Both responses are technically correct yet are radically different in imagination.

The same can be applied to the transformational educator. He or she imagines teaching as a sacred collaboration with the Holy Spirit. Compare one teacher simply meeting the lesson objectives for solving quadratic equations with another teacher who envisions each lesson and student interaction as an invitation to uncover more of the fulness of God's design of His creation and for the life of the student being taught. Both teachers may be teaching a math lesson, but they are imagining their tasks in radically different ways.

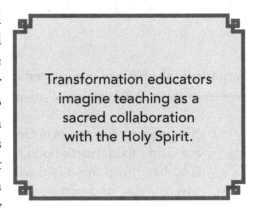

Transformation educators imagine teaching as a sacred collaboration with the Holy Spirit.

Teachers Are Agents of Transformation

Jesus refers to us, His followers, as colaborers in this task of transforming lives. Imagine yourself as the instrument God uses in the lives of your students and colleagues. Don't assume for one minute that our task is as simple as delivering a curriculum or managing a classroom of students. For reasons that remain both mysterious and motivational, God uses us to accomplish His purposes. God has commissioned His followers who are educators to accomplish His purposes on earth. We are commanded to teach, lead, feed his sheep, obey, go, tell, give, disciple, discipline, baptize, encourage, give testimony, rebuke, inspire, and unconditionally love. God uses transformed teachers in His work of transforming others.

> "For we are co-workers in God's service; you are God's field, God's building"
> (1 Corinthians 3:9).

There is a myriad of decisions a coworker teacher can make to create a transformational learning environment that the Holy Spirit can use. For example, a coworker teacher can:

- petition the Holy Spirit to guide the teacher's work
- enhance the frequency and nature of student interactions
- be mindful in methods of instruction
- imagine the physical presentation of the learning space
- be purposeful in what is assessed and how it is assessed
- help students establish habits that open them to the Spirit's work
- make time for students to reflect
- reflect on one's own teaching and student interactions
- accommodate for individual student interests and aptitudes

- assume vulnerability and reliance on the Holy Spirit
- embrace suffering from a biblical perspective
- befriend the friends of transformation
- seek to be personally transformed

Considerations for the Teacher Coworking with Christ

- Consider the teachers' prayers for the Holy Spirit to direct their work and to bring transformation to those who are taught. Isn't it easy to get in a rhythm of teaching out of our own strength, forgetting what we believe about the power of prayer?

- Consider the teachers' intentional interaction with students. Compare the difference between calling students by their names versus never addressing them by their names or never addressing them personally. Consider the impact of a teacher congratulating a student on successes outside of school or attending a funeral of the student's family member.

- Consider the teacher's mindfulness in methods of instruction, as in thinking through what might or might not be Christian about pedagogical practices. Compare the difference between regularly giving students one point of view versus several points of view for them to critique. Could this be training them in habits of critical thinking, which, when undergirded by the teachings of Jesus, lead to Godly discernment? Notice how the famous scripture for transformation, Romans 12:2, states that we will be able "to test and approve" God's will. Could teachers' selection of instructional approaches matter when coworking with the Spirit?

- Consider the physical presentation of the learning space. Compare how a clean, ordered, safe, age-appropriate, and welcoming space communicates "you are worth it" to a student, especially when they have known what the opposite learning environment is like. A well-cared for classroom, school, or learning area also demonstrates our God-given task as caretakers for the world. We restore and repair what is broken—literally and figuratively. To the contrary, can a learning environment be too over the top? Too lavish? Too expressive of a material association with quality education? Exactly what do we communicate through the learning environment?

- Consider the purpose in what is assessed and how assessment takes place. Are students set up to compete against one another or assessed by their own mastery of the instructional objective? How are individual handicaps, strengths, and weaknesses considered by the assessment process? What role does assessment have in student accountability for their own studying/learning? Is it realistic to think we can foster a growth mindset in students while recognizing that we all are fallen creatures?

- Consider how teachers can help students establish habits that open them to the Spirit's work. Are students indoctrinated by the teacher or ushered into the presence of God to nurture the student's personal relationship with Christ?

- Consider the time teachers designate for reflection. Compare the life of action without much reflection to a life of allowing times of reflection to be the seed for transformation. For the Christian, reflection is likened to listening prayer. Philippians 4:8 states, "Finally, brothers and sisters, whatever is true, whatever is noble, whatever is right, whatever is pure, whatever is lovely, whatever is admirable—if anything is excellent or praiseworthy—*think about* such things."

- Consider the teacher's responsiveness to the unique way God made each student for a purpose in His kingdom on earth. Do we cultivate this understanding of a student's unique meaning and value through a broad range of what we do through education? Think about the kindergarten teacher who changed the question from "What do you want to be when you grow up?" to "What kind of work do you think God uniquely designed you to be good at doing?" Do our curricula and instructional methods account for individual differences?

- Consider the contrast that a humble teacher brings to a student who has spiritual questions and doubts and is encouraged to share without being judged. Consider the impact of a teacher responding to spiritual questions saying, "I do not know."

- Consider the damage done by isolating scriptural promises about God healing or making things better and the experiences that are the opposite. Incomplete theology about God and suffering can be presented to students. This issue is the stated reason for numerous casualities of Christian belief. How can students really appreciate the crucifixion if they do not understand suffering themselves?

- Considering that many people who make life-altering transformations do so after experiencing a trauma, failure, or suffering of some description, is it fair to call these *friends of transformation*? Do we shield students from such friends or find ways to accompany students through difficulties?

Questions to consider:

1. How much of your thinking about your teaching reflects your deep conviction that God is using you and that your means, methods, and message are different because He is working through and with you?

2. Do you and your colleagues pray as if transformation truly depends on the work of the Holy Spirit?

3. Do any of the teacher decisions mentioned above reflect areas of your personal giftedness and professional skill?

Sources:

Smith, D. I. (2016). *Teaching and Christian Imagination.* Grand Rapids: Wm. B. Eerdmans Publishing Co.

"Teachers have a hidden vocation as an embodied messenger of God's love." (author unknown)

God uses teachers as his colaborers.

Section 3

Transformed People Are Transformational

You show that you are a letter from Christ, the result of our ministry, written not with ink but with the Spirit of the living God, not on tablets of stone but on tablets of human hearts. (2 Corinthians 3:3)

> The life of a transformed person is transformational, hence transformational educators' lives impact students' lives in an abundance of known and unknown ways.

Think of your life as a letter from Christ to students. What a high calling! This is foundational to understanding transformational education. Students may easily mistake Christianity for a set of rules regarding how to behave, a philosophy of correct precepts to believe, a tradition of rituals, holidays, or membership criteria based on baptism, christening, or joining. I've asked a lot of people if they were Christians, only to get the response, "Yes, I go to church" or "Yes, I try to be." Both responses indicate a misunderstanding of the gospel. The answer lies in the incarnation of God. Instead of just sending a text, email, written announcement, or newscast about God's love and plan for humanity, God condescended to become like us so we could know Him. God loves us beyond our imagination. Christ is with us, within us, revealing Himself to us. Our lives as a testimony to Christ and an instrument of transformation for our students is crucial to being a transformational educator.

Most of us are familiar with the story of the Sunday school teacher's lesson that used a squirrel as an object lesson for the young children. She started, "I'm going to describe something, and I want you to tell me what it is when you can figure it out." The children eagerly awaited the guessing game.

The teacher described something that lives in trees and eat nuts. She waited for the children to respond before adding, "It is gray and has a long, bushy tail." Still no hands were raised, but the children were restless and looking at one another.

Finally, one of the children tentatively raised her hand and said, "I know the answer is supposed to be Jesus, but it sure sounds like a squirrel to me."

At first, this familiar story is amusing because it reflects something we know happens. But it also reflects mindless, mechanical inauthenticity associated with rote learning and indoctrination. As well-meaning teachers, our intent is to tell students the stories of Jesus … write every line on their hearts. So then, what needs to change for us to cultivate meaning in those stories for our students? Is *writing every line on their hearts* different from *writing every line in their heads*?

"And you show that you are a letter from Christ delivered by us, written not with ink but with the Spirit of the living God, not on tablets of stone but on tablets of human hearts" (2 Corinthians 3:3). Likewise, as teachers, we show (not just tell) students that we are letters of Christ to them by touching their hearts.

Research

Research done by Barna (Kinneman 1990) measures the importance of relationships and the resiliency of faith in young adults. Data was collected during February 16–28, 2018, from a total of 1,514 US adults ages eighteen to twenty-nine who were current/former Christians. For research, Barna used the following terms to identify young adults who have grown up in Christian churches:

Prodigals, or ex-Christians, do not identify themselves as Christian despite having attended a Protestant or Catholic church as a child or teen, or having considered themselves to be Christian at some time.

Nomads, or lapsed Christians, identify themselves as Christian but have not attended church during the past month. Most nomads haven't been involved with a faith community for six months or more.

Habitual churchgoers describe themselves as Christian and have attended church at least once in the past month yet do not have foundational core beliefs or behaviors associated with being an intentional, engaged disciple.

Resilient disciples are Christians who (1) attend church at least monthly and engage with their church more than just attending worship services; (2) trust firmly in the authority of the Bible; (3) are committed to Jesus personally and affirm He was crucified and raised from the dead to conquer sin and death; and (4) express desire to transform the broader society as an outcome of their faith.

The researchers concluded that, compared to other professing Christian, resilient disciples are higher in overall relational well-being. In comparing resilient disciples to the other young adults who grew up as Christians, it's striking to see that being a resilient disciple—which is based on a set of questions about theology and faith engagement—correlates to overall relational well-being."

Data show that resilient disciples' sense of belonging correlates with intergenerational friendships and a positive emotional climate. They welcome relationships with and feedback from older adults.

In light of this research, it seems apparent that when transformational educators make the effort to show love, respect, and unconditional regard to students, it is not only valued but wins them the opportunity to speak (positive criticism) into their students' lives. Cultivating relationship must be seen as critically important in the world of transformational education.

Questions to consider:

1. On a scale of one to ten, with ten being very relational, how would you rank your effort in establishing relationships with your students?

2. Is there a polite and caring response to give to people who say they are Christians because they go to church or that they try to be a Christian?

Sources:

https://www.barna.com

Any books by Parker Palmer

Journal of Education and Christian Belief

"Following the first London performances in 1743, a patron was complimenting Handel on the 'noble entertainment' he had provided for the audience. Handel responded, 'My lord, I should be sorry if I only entertained them. I wish to make them better'" (Program for Performance of Handel's Messiah 2019)

Section 4

Are Schools a Biblical Concept?

If you have a few willing people around, discuss this question. If alone, think about it and jot down your ideas: *If the teacher is a Christian and there is prayer, weekly chapel, Bible class, biblical integration, and a biblical worldview, can we assume that the offering is transformational education? What more is there to add or leave off?*

> Transformational educators deliver the education they advertise with excellence while also rooting their offering in a Christian worldview.

For starters, what is Christian education? This section is about the education that takes place in schools that teach language arts, math, sciences, arts, and such. I hope that much of the content of this book will be helpful in churches, parachurch groups, camps, sports, and more for the purpose of spiritual formation. However, this section addressed academic schools. Unfortunately, an identity crisis often exists with Christian schools, confusing their role with that of a church or parachurch organization. This identity problem is foundational, often showing up in a school's mission statement. I took the following mission statements off the internet to illustrate the propensity to confuse the mission of an academic school with that of a church.

Samples of Actual Academic School Mission Statements

Mission Statement: To fulfil the mission statement of (name of church) by making disciples for Jesus Christ according to Matt 28:19–20.

XXX's mission is to assist Christian parents in the training of their children to conform to the image of the Lord Jesus Christ.

To advance a Christian school of excellence through Kingdom education so that the generations to come will know the truth of God's Word and not forget His works, nor be taken captive by the vain philosophies of their day.

Schools Differ from Churches

School is not a biblical concept. There are not verses about schools or teaching children how to read, do long division, or dissect frogs. Our intellect is not the way to discover Jesus, as He Himself said in Matthew 11:25–26, "I praise you, Father, Lord of heaven and earth, because you have hidden these things from the wise and learned and revealed them to little children. Yes, Father, for this is what you were pleased to do."

In his book *Piety and Philosophy*, Richard Riesen (2002, 35) states, "Education is not biblical in the sense that it can be supported by verses from the Bible. Nowhere do the words school or education (or science or history or math) appear, and nowhere is there a suggestion in either the Old Testament or New that academic training—reading, writing, arithmetic—is important, is even recommended. To try to say that it is by quoting verses is to misunderstand both the Bible and the nature of the academic enterprise."

So, if schools and the academic subjects are not direct biblical constructs, then why has Christianity been at the forefront of education almost since its beginning? Very simply, education is an excellent way to equip humankind for our role as caretakers of the world God created and to reflect God's image. As God's designated restorers of His kingdom on earth, we need to know how to care for the earth and one another, all of which may start by simply knowing how to read. Riesen calls these reasons for Christian education the practical, the ameliorative, and the *Imago Dei*.

1. *The practical:* Practically speaking, Riesen makes the argument that most of life is lived out between what the Bible specifically requires that we do and what it specifically commands us not to do. Most of our daily activities do not have a moral mandate other than the overarching injunction to love God and others and to do all things well, for His glory. Most of our daily human demands of living out life are "not enjoined nor forbidden but allowed." Just as we fix breakfast, go to work, and enjoy a movie, we also go to school, and this is simply practical participation, required by law for underaged students. As far as scripture goes, Christians are to participate in school in a manner that glorifies God. First Corinthians 10:31 states, "So whether you eat or drink or whatever you do, do it all for the glory of God."

2. *The ameliorative:* Christians engaging in educational endeavors is advisable for the *ameliorative* benefits of education. The Bible has much to say about doing good works. Educating people always tops the list of ways that people, communities, and nations can move toward a better life. Knowing that education alone is not the answer to abundant living, Christians still recognize the benefits and encourage efforts to educate the masses.

Helping people gain an education is a way of doing good and the responsibility of all Christians. Education is good in and of itself and does not need to be baptized as Christian to be of benefit for the one receiving it. That said, a transformed teacher will exude the sweet aroma of Christ with life-affirming teaching naturally radiating from a Christian worldview, whether he or she teaches in an overtly Christian school or not.

> Hebrews 13:16 says, "And do not forget to do good and to share with others, for with such sacrifices God is pleased."

> Ephesians 2:10 says, "For we are God's handiwork, created in Christ Jesus to do good works, which God prepared in advance for us to do."

> Galatians 6:10 says, "Therefore, as we have opportunity, let us do good to all people, especially to those who belong to the family of believers."

3. *The Imago Dei:* Riesen's final argument for Christians' participation in and support for education is derived from his understanding of what it means for us to be created *Imago Dei*, in the image of God. As image bearers of God, humans are uniquely able to think and create, two qualities that are honed and expressed through education. Riesen says (2002, 41), "It is not surprising that redeemed human beings should want to return in worship the talents which are God's alone to bestow." Education is an act of nurturing students to become all that God created them to be.

> So God created mankind in his own image, in the image of God he created them; male and female he created them. God blessed them and said to them, "Be fruitful and increase in number; fill the earth and subdue it. Rule over the fish in the sea and the birds in the sky and over every living creature that moves on the ground." (Genesis 1:27–28)

In summary, there is a powerful argument for Christians to serve God and humankind through education. The fact that its primary function is not the same as the church in discipleship or evangelism does not detract from the significant role it contributes to God's kingdom and His will on earth as it is in heaven. God has used schools and academics to make Himself known to people throughout history and will continue to do so through transformational educators. We simply must pursue our task with integrity to the learners we serve and faithfulness to God.

Questions to consider:

1. Do you agree that although schools are not a biblical construct, they indeed have a major role in God's kingdom on earth? If so, name a few ways.

2. The Bible really does not address the spiritual nurture of children through an institution called school but rather through the training of children by their parents. Hence, schools carry

a delegated responsibility. Keeping in mind that many Christian school parents care greatly about the spiritual formation of their children, teachers are wise to defer to or invite parents into situations where a student is considering devoting their life to Christ. Teachers respect the boundary of parent responsibility and privilege when they give parents a heads-up about their child's spiritual formation. This heads-up allows the parent to have those critical conversations and prayers with their child. Do you agree with this statement? In what situations, if any, would the above statement not be applicable?

3. How can teachers respect or honor a parent's role in the spiritual growth of their child?

Education is an excellent way to equip humankind for our role as designated caretaker of God's world.

Riesen's Reasons for Christian Education

The practical schooling fits in with the majority of life in that it is biblically not enjoined nor forbidden but allowed Most countries have laws requiring schooling for certain aged children, so it is practical for students to attend.

The ameliorative education is beneficial to individuals and communities; it is the essence of doing good works as instructed by the Bible.

The Imago Dei education. As created in the image of God, people are uniquely able to think and create. Education is all about challenging students to think and create.

Section 5

Are Transformational Education and Christian Education the Same?

Christian education is as diverse in its representation as are Christian churches, so the contrast between Christian education and transformational education must be considered with this fact of diversity in mind. However, transformational education differs from some current expressions of Christian education.

> Transformational education differs from some implementations of Christian education.

Full transformation is understood as new life in Christ and is the prayer of the transformational educator colaboring with the Holy Spirit. But transformational education also includes, for lack of a better word, *partial* transformation, which are the positive, life-affirming changes that bring humankind closer to what God intended for His creation. We believe God cares deeply about an abundant life so that the teaching of hygienic practices to promote good health; the teaching of advanced agricultural methods to feed the hungry; and the teaching of collaborative skills to foster peacemaking are also enveloped into transformational education. There is much to celebrate and ask God to change for the betterment of life on earth now.

Transformational education is also attuned to how God made each learner with a unique design for a place in our world. The teacher ascribes meaning and value to each individual as he or she helps the student imagine and prepare for their purposeful contributions in the world. The emphasis is very much on living out our identity on earth, not only salvation for eternal life.

Transformational education focuses on letters written on human hearts (2 Corinthians 3:3) and not just tablets of stone. A student can pass all the theology and Bible exams with top scores, master every argument in apologetics, share a doctrinally astute devotional in chapel, and receive a "job well done" accolade from the Christian school. In the transformational school, none of these would serve as indicators of transformation because transformation is internal change that manifests through relationships with God and neighbor. The transformed person is focused on surrendering the inner life to Christ as opposed to conquering external markers of orthodoxy.

There is a common-sense and growing recognition that Jesus was clearly concerned about the specific healing and transformation of real persons and human society "on earth as it is in heaven." The Church, more than Jesus, historically focused on doctrinal belief and moral stances, which ask almost nothing of us in terms of real change. They just define groups—often in an oppositional way. (Rohr, A New Reformation Monday from Richard Rohr's Daily Meditations 2017)

Other emphases of transformational education are listed in the chart below. Be mindful that the chart is highlighting different levels of emphases and not suggesting that the items in either column are exclusively correct or wrong.

Continuum of Transformational Education

Moving away from ...	Moving toward ...
an exclusive emphasis on orthodoxy, correct beliefs	an emphasis on orthopraxy, living out beliefs
identification as one going to heaven	identification as God's visible compassion on earth
seeking reform or external appearance	seeking transformation, change in substance
control of his or her behavior, outer life	surrender of his or her inner life
thinking in labels	avoiding labels
a focus on what is taught, info-centric	*who* is teaching and *how* students are taught
responding to God in intellectual propositions	responding to God in awe, humility, and love
asking, "What are we saved from?"	asking, "What are we saved for?"
certitude in knowing God's mind	humility in seeking to know God's mind
being a hearer of the Word only	being a doer of the Word
perceiving students as needing to be controlled, molded	perceiving students are image bearers of God
evaluating students in comparison to their classmates	seeing students as unique with purposeful design
protecting students through a spirit of fear, self-righteousness, and moral superiority	preparing students to move toward others in love
an emphasis on what we know	an emphasis on what we love

Is transformational education synonymous with biblical integration or worldview instruction?

A Christian worldview undergirds transformational education, but the operative word in this question is *instruction*. Is teaching about varying worldviews or aligning instruction so that it always points out contrasting worldviews a synonym for transformational education? No, biblical integration or Christian worldview instruction is not a synonym or definition of transformational education. Christian worldview instruction is of paramount importance in opening a learner's eyes to God's presence throughout creation and how this has been distorted by humankind. However, the information-centric nature of biblical integration and Christian worldview instruction is limited to the cognitive domain. If more knowledge of the Bible and worldviews is correlated to transformation, then where does that place Satan and his obvious knowledge of scripture? Transformational education is founded upon a distinctly Christian worldview; however, it is more encompassing than instruction in worldview assumptions or propositions or upon our gaining information about our duties and behavior. Transformation is formational—the student is changed—and that rarely happens by information alone. The teacher must live out the worldview, teach from the worldview perspective, pray for students to be transformed, and know how to shepherd students to the presence of the Transformer. It is all-encompassing.

> What if education was primarily concerned with shaping our hopes and passions—our vision of "the good life"—and not merely about the dissemination of data and information as inputs to our thinking? What if the primary work of education was the transforming of our imagination rather than the saturation of our intellect? And what if this had as much to do with our bodies as with our minds? What if education wasn't first and foremost about what we know, but about what we love? (J. K. Smith 2009)

Questions to consider:

1. Do people who know the Bible better display evidence of more transformed living? What are some of the different ways of *knowing* the Bible?

2. What is the difference in worldview instruction and teaching from a specific worldview?

3. Ponder (or if in a group, discuss) James K. Smith's question, "What if education wasn't first and foremost about what we know, but about what we love?"

Resources:

James K. Smith and David I Smith, *Teaching and Christian Practices; Reshaping Faith and Learning*

https://mindshift.school/

Piety and Philosophy by Richard Riesen

James K. A. Smith, *You Are What You Love*

Section 6

Transform, Not Only Reform

Transformational educators do not only seek compliance through external behaviors of their students but seek to nurture internal changes of their minds and hearts.

The word *reform* means to make changes in or restructure; make changes in something in order to improve it.

The word *transform* means to make a thorough or dramatic change in the form, appearance, or character of something.

We are starting from the core of what we understand about who God made us as teachers and learners to rework education, not simply make an improvement to what already exists. While working to reform/repair the broken parts of our world, transformational educators ultimately seek full transformation in their lives and the lives of their students.

The metamorphosis of a caterpillar into a butterfly is a frequently used example of transformation. The caterpillar makes a complete change in its form and structure into a butterfly. It is a new creation. Jell-O is an example of reformation. The Jell-O liquid conforms to the shape of the container. Changing the shape does not change the fact that it tastes the same, smells the same, and is digested the same, because it is the same. One can *reform* the Jell-O by using different molds, but it is not transformed. Just like Jell-O, our students may take on an appearance of Christian faith but not experience the process of transformation.

Our prayer as transformational educators is asking God to change us and our students into the likeness of Christ. It does not involve a system of manipulations that mold students into patterns of Christianly behaviors. Transformation has Christ as its focus and does not sway with the winds of cultural approval.

Scripture is the basis of our understanding of transformation:

> No one sews a patch of unshrunk cloth on an old garment, for the patch will pull away from the garment, making the tear worse. Neither do people pour new wine into old wineskins. If they do, the skins will burst; the wine will run out and the wineskins will be ruined. No, they pour new wine into new wineskins, and both are preserved. (Matthew 9:16–18)

> Therefore, if anyone is in Christ, the new creation has come: The old has gone, the new is here! (2 Corinthians 5:17)

> For we are God's handiwork, created in Christ Jesus to do good works, which God prepared in advance for us to do. (Ephesians 2:10)

> You show that you are a letter from Christ, the result of our ministry, written not with ink but with the Spirit of the living God, not on tablets of stone but on tablets of human hearts. (2 Corinthians 3:3)

> Now the Lord is the Spirit; and where the Spirit of the Lord is, there is freedom. And we all, who with unveiled faces contemplate the Lord's glory, are being transformed into his image with ever increasing glory, which comes from the Lord, who is the Spirit. (2 Corinthians 3:17–18)

> Therefore we do not lose heart. Though outwardly we are wasting away, yet inwardly we are being renewed day by day. (2 Corinthians 4:16)

Donovan Graham, in his book *Teaching Redemptively*, compellingly warns teachers of the misconstrued process of reforming children into good little boys and girls without challenging them to a Christ-filled transformation. Graham says:

> Unfortunately, it is all too possible that students are validated for their right "doing" without much concern for their "being." And ironically, we may even attribute their success in doing to God's blessing while we ignore their internal being. We (and they) do the right things, so God blesses us. Even more unfortunately, we may not fully concern ourselves with the fact that the fall has left everyone internally empty and suffering a sense of loss and lack of value. We readily focus on the outward effects of the fall and believe our duty is to do all we can to eliminate sinful outward behaviors. But if we are continually focusing on outward behaviors by affirming the positive and punishing the negative, we may never attend to the internal emptiness of the fallen broken sinner. We may never introduce our students to what *living the gospel* is all about. Instead, we teach them to *talk* about the gospel while *living under the curse of the law.* (D. L. Graham 2003, 9-10)

Don't misunderstand. Reformation is great *as long as it is not confused with salvation* through Jesus Christ. As Christians, we are to be about the business of reforming. Why? Two main reasons follow:

1. Christians serve people all over the world who may never come to faith. Jesus cared deeply about the poor, the sick, the imprisoned, and for anyone fitting the description of "the least of these" (Matthew 25). Jesus told us to do likewise by serving the disenfranchised, the abused, the brokenhearted, the ill, the hungry, the imprisoned, and the poor.

2. In the creation mandate from Genesis 1:28, God essentially gave us the task of caretaker of his creation: "God blessed them and said to them, 'Be fruitful and increase in number; fill the earth and subdue it. Rule over the fish in the sea and the birds in the sky and over every living creature that moves on the ground.'" As the salt of the earth (Matthew 5:13), we influence the culture for good.

Author Richard Pratt, in *Designed for Dignity*, claims that "God ordained humanity to be the primary instrument by which His kingship will be realized on earth." Here's Pratt's down-to-earth description of how the cultural mandate works:

> The Great King has summoned each of us into his throne room. Take this portion of my kingdom, he says, I am making you my steward over your office, your workbench, your kitchen stove. Put your heart into mastering this part of my world. Get it in order; unearth its treasures; do all you can with it. Then everyone will see what a glorious King I am. That's why we get up every morning and go to work. We don't labor simply to survive, insects do that. Our work is an honor, a privileged commission from our great King. God has given each of us a portion of his kingdom to explore and to develop to its fullness. (R. L. Pratt 2000)

Nancy Pearcey, in *Total Truth*, expands on our working definition by describing the relationship between the cultural mandate and work:

> The lesson of the Cultural Mandate is that our sense of fulfillment depends on engaging in creative, constructive work. The ideal human existence is not eternal leisure or an endless vacation—or even a monastic retreat into prayer and meditation—but creative effort expended for the glory of God and the benefit of others. Our calling is not just to "go to heaven" but also to cultivate the earth, not just to "save souls" but also to serve God through our work. For God himself is engaged not only in the work of salvation but also in the work of preserving and developing His creation. When we obey the Cultural Mandate, we participate in the work of God himself. (Pearcey 2008)

Through our school practices, are we cultivating *good* kids or kids who know they are sinners in need of a Savior? Do we inadvertently equate compliance with godly character? Do we produce young people who at least partially believe they are *more spiritual* because they memorize scripture and listen to Christian music? As educators, we want to effectively communicate the Gospel message to our students, but do we do this by being a role model of goodness or by making sure our students know that we are broken sinners saved by grace alone? Admittedly, these questions do not allow fair response choices, but hopefully they do spark some reflection on the message of *being good* we sometimes communicate in Christian schools.

I grew up in a home where there was always a pet dog. We adored our pets. As my siblings and I grew up and got pets of our own, we exchanged humor about the spiritual condition of our pets. Bad behavior certainly meant the dog had *backslid* or was a *carnal Christian*. Good behavior meant the dogs were regularly having their *quiet time*.

Some people take it even further. YouTube clips show dogs bowed in prayer before they can eat. https://www.youtube.com/watch?v=OQk23H42dxo&list=RDCMUCZSUvJTxnp 7ay48TUJAf4tart_radio=1&rv=OQk23H42dxo&t=39&ab_RQ&schannel= Not mockingly, just playfully, the pets were trained with outwardly Christian behaviors; no one believes these trained behaviors meant the dogs had a spiritual experience.

More serious is the question of whether we socialize children in a similar manner. At the school I directed, we had a guest speaker from the Red Cross. With summer vacation a few weeks away, the speaker talked about water safety. During her presentation, she asked the students a question in which her voice inflected upward at the end, as teachers often do when they think all the children know the answer and will answer in unison. She asked the children, "And who do you think trains the lifeguards?" You probably guessed their response; the kindergarteners all shouted, "God." I cringed with fear we were indoctrinating our students with "God" or "Jesus" as the answer for any question. The Red Cross speaker was a little stunned, and the other adults present had a chuckle. But think of the truth at the root of the kindergarteners' response. These young students had knowledge of the design of the universe and the foundation of knowing that God typically uses people to accomplish His purposes. The speaker could easily ask students who might God use to train the lifeguards.

Children blessed with Christian parents often spend a lot of time in church programs, parachurch organizations, and possibly Christian schools. In addition to the provision of these opportunities, parents may teach Christian living and the Bible directly to their child. In these settings, the children do the following:

- Demonstrate their memorization of scripture: "I have hidden your word in my heart that I might not sin against you" (Psalm 119:11).

- Demonstrate their learning of Bible: "Whatever you have learned or received or heard from me or seen in me-put it into practice. And the God of peace will be with you" (Philippians 4:9).

- Perform acts of service or giving: "And do not forget to do good and to share with others, for with such sacrifices God is pleased" (Hebrews 13:16).

- Repeat the sinner's prayer or are baptized: "Peter replied, 'Repent and be baptized, every one of you, in the name of Jesus Christ for the forgiveness of your sins. And you will receive the gift of the Holy Spirit'" (Acts 2:38).

We, the teachers, parents, and disciplers of the children, are pleased when children memorize scripture, learn the Bible, serve, give to others, and give testimony to their faith in Jesus Christ. The Bible identifies each of the above behaviors as worthy. There is no question that these are good goals and actions, behaviors we unapologetically want to see in our children.

We often give students a public forum to demonstrate what they learn, followed by recognition, words of praise, awards, badges, or even gifts. When there is a day of service, participants are honored by being named or shown doing the work in a video or photographs. Even baptism is often an event with much patting on the back and accolades.

The intent is clearly a desire to see a student wholeheartedly embrace Christ. However good the teacher's intention may be, the approval of an adult is enticing. Students will jump through several hoops to receive praise and appreciation from a respected adult, congregation, or peer group. I am not accusing the student of being disingenuous; he or she may simply be seeking the outcome without the substance. Sometimes the student has simply been socialized in the ways of church, the class, the family, or the school.

Cross-Cultural Challenges

Sometimes a similar pattern of behavioral acquiescence occurs in cross-cultural settings. To please or appease the foreigner, a national will say whatever the foreigner wants to hear; agreement with the expat guest is more hospitable than refusing what is being offered. People may agree to baptism or "make decisions for Christ" as a cultural expression and not an act of faith.

We give them the right stimulus of praise, and they comply. Would their choices have been the same if only God were the audience?

Questions to consider:

1. Do we inadvertently teach our students that Christianity is a way of behaving?

2. How can we celebrate scripture memory, baptisms, acts of service, and so on in a way that points students to a life devoted to Christ alone?

3. What experience(s) have you had with people of other cultures wanting to please you by complying with what they think you want?

Resources:

Nancy Pearcey, *Total Truth*

Donovan Graham, *Teaching Redemptively*

"The Bible's purpose is not so much to show you how to live a good life. The Bible's purpose is to show you how God's grace breaks into your life against your will and saves you from the sin and brokenness otherwise you would never be able to overcome … religion is 'if you obey, then you will be accepted.' But the Gospel is, 'if you are absolutely accepted, and sure you're accepted, only then will you ever begin to obey.' Those are two utterly different things. Every page of the Bible shows the difference." (Timothy Keller)

"Not by might, not by power, but by *my spirit* says the Lord" (Zechariah 4:6).

Not by teacher expertise in biblical integration or worldview dictates, but by His spirit.

Not by doing good deeds, not by following every rule, but by His spirit.

Not by creative sermons, not by liturgical recitations, but by His spirit.

Not by the old hymns, not by contemporary choruses, but by His spirit.

Not by dunking in a baptismal pool, not by confirmation, not by reciting a formulaic prayer, but by his spirit.

Section 7

The Teacher as Role Model

God warned us about whitewashed tombs—the effort to look good on the outside in neglect of the authentic self. Certainly, it is rooted in our desire as believers to honor God. Yet somehow the external applause for being good got confused with the internal outworking of the Holy Spirit. How does a teacher get across that the Gospel is not about *being good* but about the fact that you are *not good enough* and need Jesus to take care of that?

> Transformational educators communicate their brokenness and need of a Savior in Christ. They ensure students understand that their Christlike behavior is a result of Christ in their lives.

As head of a Christian school, I tried to be a good role model. To be honest, I even tried to be a role model about things I did not actually believe, quoting to myself the scripture about not offending a weaker brother or sister. Although role modelling and sensitivity to offending a weaker Christian can impact students, it is imperative to avoid the mistake of putting my goodness rather than Christ's redemption of my brokenness before the eyes of the student. The goal is to make sure there is no confusion about the difference between being good and truly following Christ. As I've wrestled with this distinction, here are a few ideas for ways to model the Gospel to our students:

- Confess to students that we have struggles and the need for Christ's power and His forgiveness in our lives,
- Consider how and why we present awards to students. Are the students responding with gratitude for what God has allowed them to achieve?
- Carefully evaluate what we are saying when we offer praise. Are we encouraging students with the concept that they are becoming who God made them to be or puffing them up?
- Ask forgiveness even when the person does not know what we did.
- Offer correction as one sinner to another, remembering 1 Timothy 5:1–2, an exhortation to treat students as our younger brothers and sisters.

> As role models, do we try to put our goodness, rather than Christ's redemption of our brokenness, before the eyes of the student?

Questions to consider:

1. How do you model for your students that you are a sinner in need of a Savior?

2. Do we inadvertently equate compliance with godly character?

3. Do we produce young people who, at least partially, believe they are *more spiritual* because they memorize scripture and listen to Christian music?

4. Apply the story of the prodigal son, Luke 15, to the idea of transformation being different from reformation.

Resources:

Donovan Graham, *Teaching Redemptively*

> "When our civility isn't rooted in something sturdy and deep, when our good behavior isn't springing from the core of who we are but is instead merely a mask we put on, it is only a matter of time before the façade crumbles away and our true state is revealed: an entire generation of people who are really good at looking good" (Miller 2019).

Section 8

Reworking, Not Improving upon, Education

As a brilliant example of transformation and not simply reformation, Smith and Shortt (2002, 13–14) retell a story about the Christianization of Ireland in AD 1004. The Irish called an assembly, the Althing, to discuss Christianity, which stood in opposition to their beliefs. In the end, they decided to sacrifice two men from each area of the country who would give their lives as a living prayer to the heathen gods, asking them to stop the spread of Christianity throughout the land. The two missionaries leading the work in

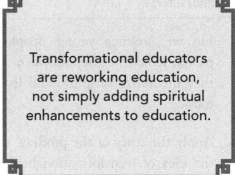

Transformational educators are reworking education, not simply adding spiritual enhancements to education.

Ireland, Hialte and Gizor, responded by similarly agreeing to resort to human sacrifice but with a profound difference. As they put it, "The heathen sacrificed the worst men and cast them over the rocks or cliffs, but we will choose the best of men and will call it a gift of victory to our Lord Jesus Christ, and we will bind ourselves to live better and more sinlessly than before, and Gizor and I will offer ourselves as the gift of victory of our quarter."

In this story, Hialte and Gizor did not choose to just do better than the heathen at human sacrifice; they changed the way the quality of human sacrifice was measured. No longer would the number of people thrown over a cliff to their death be the measure (not a Christian value), but rather consecrated lives lived out for the betterment of the community (a Christian ideal) became the measure. The Christians offered a radical change, rooted in Christian belief and practice, to change the cultural meaning of human sacrifice. This is transformation. Parallels to this story exist for education. We don't want to simply do better at what exists in terms of education or add Christian ornaments to education but rather transform the core of education, or as Smith and Shortt state, "to shape a set of practices that are as consistent as we can manage with the story of all things made new as the kingdoms of this world become the kingdoms of our God and His creation." (Smith and Shortt 2002, 13-14)

So, what if we like this idea of transformation instead of reformation? What would that look like in a classroom? The truth is it would look like thousands of teacher decisions and teacher behaviors made all through the day. It is not restricted to Bible class or clever connections of a Bible story to a history lesson, moralizing over a student's misbehavior or such. It is interwoven in personal prayer before school and throughout the school day, teacher/student relationships, teacher/teacher relationships, the methods used to assess whether learning has taken place, methods used for instruction, the physical and emotional comfort of the learning environment, and so on. It does not ascribe to an individualistic view of sin alone but includes corporate sin, emphasis on personal salvation with little regard to the call to establishing God's kingdom on earth, or focus on the soul to the exclusion of the body and matter.

Here are a few examples of how this can be cultivated in a classroom or school.

Each student is assigned to a cooperative learning group for six weeks of working with three other students they do not know well. The teacher strategically selects group placement so that students will be working with other students who are different from them. The teaching of collaborative skills and coaching when the situation calls for such are added to the simple act of a group of four people working together on academic tasks for an extended period.

Challenge active not passive Christianity by ending the lesson with the sincere question, "What do you think God would have us do with this knowledge?" As a class, act upon student suggestions whenever possible, while also allowing time for students to share about when they act upon knowledge individually. Be doers of the Word and not hearers only.

Resources:

David Smith, *Teaching and the Christian Imagination*

Not making education better but reworking what education is.

Not conforming better to the present standard of education but changing the standard of education.

The gospel is absurd and the life of Jesus is meaningless unless we believe that He lived, died, and rose again with but one purpose in mind: to make brand-new creations. Not to make people with better morals, but to create a community of prophets and professional lovers, men and women who would surrender to the mystery of the fire of the Spirit that burns within, who would live in ever greater fidelity to the omnipresent Word of God, who would enter into the center of it all, the very heart and mystery of Christ, into the center of the flame that consumes, purifies and sets everything aglow with peace, joy, boldness, and extravagant, furious love. This, my friends, is what it really means to be a Christian. Our religion never begins with what we do for God. It always starts with what God has done for us, the great and wondrous things that God dreamed of and achieved for us in Christ Jesus(Manning, 2009).

Section 9

Established Transformational Education Theory

The words *transformational* or *transformative* are commonly used in current educational literature without a universal agreement regarding what is meant by the terms. In academic circles, more than among practitioners, work has been done in terms of definition and theory development of transformational education. While this book recognizes the need for more research into the definition and philosophy of transformational education, the most urgent need is for educators to put into practice what is already known. For those interested in investigating theoretic aspects of transformational education, a brief description of seminal research follows.

> Transformational educators benefit from and build upon established theory, research, and practices in the field of transformational education.

Jack Mezirow

Columbia University sociologist Jack Mezirow was the first to research the modern concept and theory of transformation, and most work even today is either based on his ideas or a reaction to them. Central to his work was what he referred to as phases of meaning.

Mezirow's phases of meaning:

- a disorienting dilemma
- a self-examination with feelings of guilt or shame
- a critical assessment of epistemic, sociocultural, or psychic assumptions
- recognition that one's discontent and the process of transformation are shared and that others have negotiated a similar change
- exploration of options for new roles, relationships, and actions
- planning a course of action
- acquisition of knowledge and skills for implementing one's plan
- provisional trying of new roles
- building of competence and self-confidence in new roles and relationships
- a reintegration into one's life on the basis of conditions dictated by one's perspective

James Loder Jr.

James Loder offered an academic perspective on transformational education from a Christian perspective. The purpose of Christian education is to construct a Christian style of life in response to the work of the Spirit, in which each domain of human action learns to intentionally participate in the Spirit's redemptive initiative to conform human reality to the nature of Christ. James Loder presents a Christian perspective that emphasizes the work of God's Spirit in the process of transformation.

Stages of Loder's transformational education model:

- contextually situated conflict (an ongoing opposition that drives the person to find an adequate solution)
- scanning (contemplative scanning) immersed exploration of possible connections and combinations of meanings
- insight (bringing into cognitive association two factors previously thought to be unrelated)
- release and redirection of energy
- interpretation and verification
- revisit the new insight to make sure it is coherent (e.g., blogging, debate)

James Westerhoff

In his book, *Will Our Children Have Faith?*, the Reverend John Westerhoff describes four stages of Christian faith development. His stages differ from stage models that assume completion of the characteristics and needs of one stage before going to the next. Westerhoff describes stages of faith to be like rings of a tree. Just like a tree adds one ring on top of another, the needs of the earlier stages remain active even after expansion to the added rings. The faith experiences of the earlier stages are needed throughout life. Westerhoff labels the four stages of faith development: experienced faith, affiliative faith, searching faith, and owned faith.

1) *Experienced faith* grows by participating with a community of other Christians in the customs and rituals of one's faith tradition. Understanding the meaning behind the rituals is not what matters; the rituals matter because they are experienced through participation.

2) *Affiliative faith* develops by belonging to (being affiliated with) a Christian community. In Western cultures, this stage is often associated with church and parachurch ministries that focus on teenagers and activities geared to teenagers deepening their relationships with other Christians. According to Westerhoff, research shows that most adults have had their faith arrested in the affiliative faith stage.

3) *Searching faith* is the faith of questioning, doubting, and seeking that accompanies the cognitive onset of abstract thinking in adolescents. The truism of *God has no grandchildren* comes into play as adolescents assess whether their inherited faith is truly their own. Westerhoff considers searching faith a prerequisite to owned faith.

4) *Owned faith* is faith claimed as true by the believer, usually occurring in adulthood. Owned faith may appear as a great illumination or enlightenment because of the serious doubt that preceded it. Even though doubts and questions remain, those who own their faith want to witness it by personal and social action and are willing and able to stand up for what they believe in as mature disciples of Jesus Christ.

Owned faith is God's intention for everyone, even though (according to Westerhoff) most adults have had their faith arrested at the affiliative stage.

Slavish and Zimbardo (Zimbardo 2012) propose practices of teaching that may lead to transformation, although they clearly state their concept of transformation does not involve a worldview shift but rather a change in attitudes about learning. Transformational teaching involves creating dynamic relationships between teachers, students, and a shared body of knowledge to promote student learning and personal growth. The main objective of transformational teaching is to improve students' mastery of a topic in a way that also impacts their learning-related skills, attitudes, and beliefs; it is not to change a student's worldview.

Transformation is realized through:

- establishing a shared vision for a course
- providing modeling and mastery experiences
- challenging and encouraging students
- personalizing attention and feedback
- creating experiential lessons that transcend the boundaries of the classroom
- promoting ample opportunities for preflection and reflection

CATE

From *Elements of Transformational Education Theory* (Vaughan 2019):

1. The Holy Spirit initiates transformation in the life of a student.
2. The Spirit's initiative may be embraced or rejected by the student.
3. Transformation can be major or minor; repetitive, rare, or non-existent.
4. Prayer is an essential part of provoking the Holy Spirit's work and of a student being open to the transforming work of the Holy Spirit; hence prayer is key to the proliferation of transformation.

5. Transformation is not only a cognitive structure but can manifest physically, spiritually, emotionally, and socially.

6. Transformation occurs out of a love relationship with God. Practicing the spiritual disciplines is significant for cultivating a loving relationship with God.

7. Teachers are agents of transformation. They are used by the Holy Spirit for transforming purposes—or not. Teachers can do better or worse at this. Encouragement, modeling, prayer, and training are important in preparing teachers for transformational education.

8. Competency in the application of worldviews, knowing and being known by students, listening skills, critical thinking pedagogies, interpersonal skills, hospitality mindset, casting imagination, understanding differences in age cohorts are all foundational to teacher preparation in transformational education.

9. Transformational education is not taught through information-sharing (e.g., biblical integration, biblical worldview instruction, Bible class), as much as it is experienced (e.g., reflection, face-to face challenging discussions, receiving the benevolence of a transformed person, novel experiences/discussions involving a disorienting dilemma, brokenness, and suffering)

10. Transformational education moves people in the direction of understanding how God uniquely made them to contribute to the kingdom of God, preparing themselves to effectively make their contribution, and then expending themselves in the service of God, humankind, and the creation.

11. Societies are restored by the attractive outcomes of transformational people serving within God's design.

Closely Related Theories

In the pursuit of understanding transformational education, the area of spiritual formation and faith development are noteworthy contributors to practices that support the teacher as an agent of transformation. James Fowler (Fowler 1981) is a stage theorist known in academic circles for foundational work in stages of faith development. He is critiqued by Rebecca Nye (Nye 2009) for presenting children as spiritually empty, gradually being grown into adult faith. Nye and Hay propose that children are inherently spiritual. As a result of their research and determination to see their conclusions bear fruit in the spaces where children live and learn, they developed a program called Godly Play.

Questions to consider:

1. Do you think of spiritual development as happening in predictable developmental stages or as unique and variable without a pattern?

2. Do you think teachers can cause cognitive dissonance?

Resources:

Rebecca Nye, *Children's Spirituality, What It Is and Why It Matters* (London, UK: Church House Publishing, 2009).

George M. Slavich and Philip G. Zimbardo, "Transformational Teaching: Theoretical Underpinnings, Basic Principles, and Core Methods," *Educ Psychol Rev.* 24, no. 4 (Dec. 2012): 569–608.

James Fowler, *Stages of Faith: The Psychology of Human Development and the Quest for Meaning* (USA: Harper One, 1981).

David Hay and Rebecca Nye, "Investigating Children's Spirituality: The Need for a Fruitful Hypothesis," *International Journal of Children's Spirituality* 1 (1996):6–16.

CLOSING PRAYER

Holy Father,

Thank You for creating us as teachers and giving us meaningful work to do.

Transform us by Your Holy Spirit.

Create in us a desire to learn, change, and flourish according to Your purposes.

Make our influence matter in the lives of students and our entire community, and may we return in gratitude and thanksgiving for what a great God You are.

Amen.

CHAPTER 2

IT TAKES TWO, USUALLY THREE

"And we all...are being transformed into his image with ever-increasing glory, which comes from the Lord, who is the Spirit" (2 Corinthians 3:18). It takes two, the Holy Spirit's initiative and the person's yieldedness, for transformation to occur. Sometimes the Spirit works through conditions created by a teacher and/or uses friends of transformation to bring about changed lives.

By faith, experience, and God's Word, transformational educators understand that the Holy Spirit is the transformer. These educators also know that the learner's participation in the process of transformation involves an act of the will that often begins as seeking truth, appreciating beauty, and embracing goodness. The student can resist. The transformational context is often populated with *friends* who mediate, shape, or even give birth to the transformational experience (e.g., failure, suffering, overwhelming joy, experiencing another culture, conflicting thoughts, and other similar disorienting, impactful experiences). Transformational educators pray for the Holy Spirit's work and a student's yieldedness as they serve as agents of transformation amid a student's encounter with the friends of transformation.

Topics included in this chapter:

Section 1

The Holy Spirit and Yieldedness

Transformational educators recognize that the coming together of the mysterious work of the Holy Spirit and a student's yieldedness leads to a fully transformed life.

For our purposes, transformational education encompasses all the teaching and relating to a student that nurtures God's intention for that student. We seek to prepare them for their place in the respective familial, church, occupational, social, and recreational plans God designed for them. Any effort a teacher makes that moves a student toward becoming the person God made them to be is transformational. "For we are God's handiwork, created in Christ Jesus to do good works, which God prepared in advance for us to do" (Ephesians 2:10). Full transformation is realized through yielding one's life to Christ. Transformational educators follow the Holy Spirit's lead in helping students know the God who created and designed them for a purpose.

Four Key Points

- Teachers *don't* transform students.
- The Holy Spirit transforms.
- Students may resist the work of the Holy Spirit. A student may choose not to yield to God. This choice is inherent in God's nature as love. Love cannot demand or control; it must be given.
- Teachers *do* pray, practice the spiritual disciplines, create conditions that are conducive to transformation, and usher students into a loving relationship with God.

Second Corinthians 3:18 says, "And we all … are being transformed into his image with ever-increasing glory, which comes from the Lord, who is the Spirit."

In John 18:36, Jesus answered, "I tell you the truth, no one can enter the kingdom of God unless he is born of water and the Spirit. Flesh gives birth to

- Teachers *don't* transform students.
- The Holy Spirit transforms.
- Students may resist the work of the Holy Spirit. A student may choose not to yield to God. This choice is inherent in God's nature as love. Love cannot demand or control; it must be given.
- Teachers *do* pray, practice the spiritual disciplines, create conditions that are conducive to transformation, and usher students into a loving relationship with God.

flesh, but *the Spirit gives birth to spirit.* You should not be surprised at my saying, 'You must be born again.'"

First Peter 4:10 says, "Each of you should use whatever gift you have received to serve others, as faithful stewards of God's grace in its various forms."

Questions to consider:

1. Describe some ways a transformational teacher may respond to students who rebuff the Holy Spirit's work in their life.

2. If a student is not a Christian, how do you respect their beliefs in an educational setting with Christian traditions and values?

Resources:

The Bible

www.transformational.education

Section 2

Asking God for Transformation

As stated in the previous section, God initiates all transformation. Hence, the teacher's essential task in transformational education is to ask the one who transforms to be present and to do His transformative work. It means the teacher will pray with expectancy and boldness for the Holy Spirit to indwell our being, create in us a clean heart, renew our minds, have our lives bear spiritual fruit, and take the scales off our eyes to see God's work in ourselves and those in our sphere of influence. We are a conduit through which He does His redeeming work.

> Transformational educators ask God to change themselves, their students, and their communities. They pray for transformation.

Colossians 4:2 says to devote yourselves to prayer, being watchful and thankful.

The Bible affirms the importance of prayer, and here is just a sampling of those scriptures. Meditate on them.

> The prayer of a righteous person is powerful and effective. (James 5:16b)
>
> For this reason, since the day we heard about you, we have not stopped praying for you. We continually ask God to fill you with the knowledge of his will through all the wisdom and understanding that the Spirit gives. (Colossians 1:9)
>
> And pray for us, too, that God may open a door for our message, so that we may proclaim the mystery of Christ, for which I am in chains. (Colossians 4:3)
>
> I urge, then, first of all, that petitions, prayers, intercession and thanksgiving be made for all people. (1 Timothy 2:1)
>
> In the same way, the Spirit helps us in our weakness. We do not know what we ought to pray for, but the Spirit himself intercedes for us through wordless groans. And he who searches our hearts knows the mind of the Spirit, because the Spirit intercedes for God's people in accordance with the will of God. (Romans 8:26–27)
>
> I urge you, brothers and sisters, by our Lord Jesus Christ and by the love of the Spirit, to join me in my struggle by praying to God for me. (Romans 15:30)

Get Past Polite Prayer

Any quick perusal of the psalms or even a reminder of the fact the Jesus sweated blood during His prayer in the Garden of Gethsemane demonstrates the passion and earnestness of biblical prayer. Richard Foster quotes Walter Wink, "Biblical prayer is impertinent, persistent, shameless, indecorous. It is more like haggling in an outdoor bazaar than the polite monologues of the churches" (Foster, 1992, 247).

Are our prayers for ourselves, students, schools, and communities simply too tame, sometimes too apathetic? Wholehearted commitment to prayer is the essential activity of a transformational teacher. We must be in constant communication with the Father, inviting His Spirit to transform all of us and all that is in our learning environment. Transformational educators investigate opportunities to learn about and practice prayer. Prayer is the most significant thing we can do to invite the Holy Spirit to transform lives, including our own.

Questions to consider:

1. How do you nurture a rich, effective, faithful, loving, powerful, sincere prayer life?

2. Do you pray as if you wholeheartedly believe that your prayers are powerful for your students?

3. What are some prayer resources that have helped you?

Resources:

Prayer; Finding the Heart's True Home by Richard Foster

Centering Prayers: A One-Year Daily Companion for Going Deeper into the Love of God by Peter Traben Haas

CATE website at www.transformational.education

Section 3

Creating Conditions Conducive to Transformation

In addition to prayer, is there anything else that the teacher can do to invite transformation? If the Holy Spirit is the transformer, how do we fit in as teachers? The scripture is clear that God includes us in His work. Ephesians 2:10 says, "For we are God's handiwork, created in Christ Jesus to do good works, which God prepared in advance for us to do."

> The work of a transformational teacher is to create conditions conducive to transformation.

What transformational educators do is create conditions conducive to transformation. What is meant by creating conditions? The following four analogies shed light on creating conditions for something we cannot control but can nurture.

Getting to Sleep

James K. A. Smith describes the need to create conditions conducive to sleep prior to falling asleep.

> In the context of discussing this mode of intentionality between intellect and instinct, and a kind of action that is neither voluntary nor involuntary, Merleau-Ponty points to an intriguing analogy: *sleep*. I cannot "choose" to *fall* asleep. The best I can do is to choose to put myself in a posture and rhythm that welcomes sleep ... I *want* to go to sleep and I've chosen to climb into bed—but in another sense sleep is not something under my control or at my beckoned call. I call up the visitation of sleep by imitating the breathing and posture of the sleeper ... There is a moment when sleep comes, settling on this imitation of itself with I have been offering to it, and *I succeed in becoming what I was trying to be*. Sleep is a gift to be received, not a decision to be made. And yet it is a gift that requires a *posture* of reception—a kind of active welcome. What if being filled with the Spirit had the same dynamic? What if Christian practices are what Craig Dykkstra calls "habitations of the Spirit" precisely because they *posture* us to be filled and sanctified? What if we need first adopt a bodily posture in order to become what we are trying to be?

Conception and Birth

Ask anyone who has experienced infertility, and they will readily acknowledge that humans cannot make conception happen of their own will and actions. God creates life, but He uses human activity to do so.

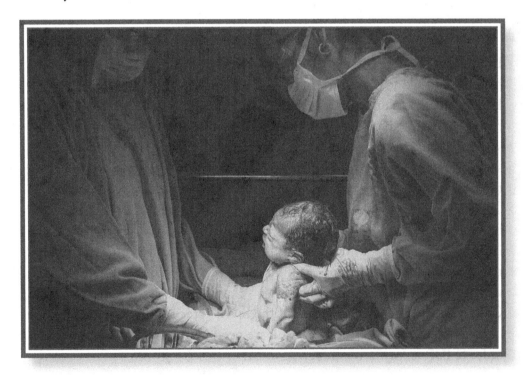

Growing Crops

Farmers cultivated soil and plant their crops, but God makes the seed germinate, grow, and bear fruit. The farmer tends the fields, but God sends the warmth, rain, nutrients, and atmosphere for the crops to grow.

Doctors Healing

Doctors cannot choose to heal. At best, they create sterile environments for healing to occur and perform operations to facilitate healing. God heals.

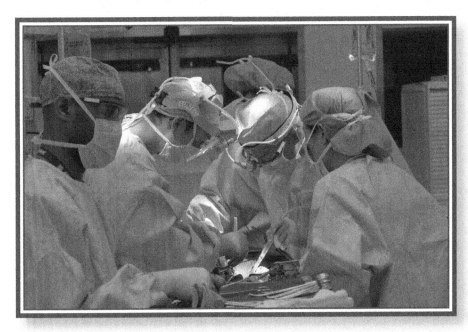

Christian teachers have a major role in creating conditions for the Holy Spirit to use in the life of a student. Transformational education is the summation of many teacher decisions and actions that create learning environments where a student may be transformed. Students spending time with a transformed teacher will be impacted.

Teachers do not make transformation happen but rather nurture it by creating conditions conducive to transformation.

Onetime Experience or Process?

As Christians who are educators, we work for the ah-ha moments when students grasp long division, swing a bat to hit a ball, care for a classmate without expecting anything in return, and verbalize an understanding of God's love for them. But ah-ha moments are usually preceded by many incremental steps or exposures that make up the process of change. As teachers, we keep our eyes on Jesus and trust, like the apostle Paul, that He will bring to completion the good work (of transformation) He has begun in the life of the student (Philippians 1:6).

Questions to consider:

1. What are some things you do as a teacher to create environments conducive to transformation?

2. What do you think about this statement: "transformed people are transformational"?

Section 4

What Comes after Belief? Nurturing Passion

In this handbook, you will repeatedly read that the traditional hallmarks of Christian education, worldview instruction and biblical integration, are rarely sufficient for the transformation of lives. Christian education begins by teaching the biblical stories and cultivating a Christian worldview. With this foundation, the worldview is applied to understanding how we should personally and corporately live. Often the story stops there. This beginning is necessary; however, knowledge is not enough. Students may

> Transformational educators usher students into God's presence, nurturing a desire and passion for God and His kingdom.

excel in Bible study and may correctly answer questions about applying the Bible but lack a desire to love and live for Christ. Their knowledge is empty; motivation is absent; no one is transformed. The community of believers has no impact for Christ in the culture. What is needed is a desire for God and His kingdom. Deep love motivates, and deep love is fulfilling. True lovers of God are transformed and, hence, transforming.

The problem is, how do transformational educators disciple the heart? How do you properly form human desire?

This question is central to this entire book. Other chapters will highlight different responses to this question, with this section focusing on ushering the student to personal encounters with God through the development of spiritual disciplines.

The imagery I prefer here is the teacher as an usher or guide taking the student to engage with God directly, not filtered by the teacher. The teacher-usher is a fellow sojourner although someone who possibly walked the way for a longer time. Students engage or encounter God through what we usually refer to as the spiritual disciplines, which are best cultivated in Christian community.

Imagine yourself as an usher escorting the student into the presence of God.

What are some practical ways teachers can usher?

- Talk less; allow students' time to reflect and react.
- Have students journal about their engagement with God, their prayers, their disappointments and hopes.

- Provide contemplative practices, such as silent retreats, walking labyrinths, Lectio Divina, beholding, or a ritual or ceremony unique to your school for God's glory.
- Allow opportunities for you and your students to be transparent with one another about encounters with God.
- Allow time for reflection after students hear scripture, an inspiring story, inspirational music, and so on.
- Create an appropriate means for regularly practicing confession.
- Be wary of public approval or congratulations for acts of devotion or service to God.

  Apply the practice in Matthew 6:2: "So when you give to the needy, do not announce it with trumpets, as the hypocrites do in the synagogues and on the streets, to be honored by others. Truly I tell you, they have received their reward in full."

  Apply the practice in Matthew 6:16–18: "When you fast, do not look somber as the hypocrites do, for they disfigure their faces to show others they are fasting. Truly I tell you, they have received their reward in full. But when you fast, put oil on your head and wash your face, so that it will not be obvious to others that you are fasting, but only to your Father, who is unseen; and your Father, who sees what is done in secret, will reward you."

- Study other ways you can incorporate the spiritual disciplines in your interaction with students and use discernment about how the students are developing their identity as faithful, devoted followers of Christ.

> Worship is the "imagination station" that incubates our loves and longings so that our cultural endeavors are indexed toward God and his kingdom. Worship is about "formation" more than "expression." It is God himself meeting us to shape us into the kind of people who do His will, not just an outpouring of our sincere feelings about Him. (Smith 2013)

Probably echoing Aristotle, "For when there is a question as to whether a man is good, one does not ask what he believes, or what he hopes, but what he loves." James K. A. Smith wrote that "humans are lovers at their core and their loves drive their actions" (Smith 2013).

Section 5

Friends of Transformation

When considering conditions conducive to transformation, priority attention must be given to suffering. Not that we create suffering so that our students will be transformed, but we teach and model some frequently misunderstood or ignored truths about God and suffering.

First Peter 5:9–10 says, "Resist him, standing firm in the faith, because you know that the family of believers throughout the world is undergoing the same kind of sufferings. And the God of all grace, who called you to his eternal glory in Christ, after you have suffered a little while, will himself restore you and make you strong, firm, and steadfast."

Although transformation is presented as a desired outcome for us and our students, that does not mean it is easy or fun. In fact, I suggest that most transformation is painful and, if left to choose, would be avoided. Who in their right mind would opt for grief, confusion, insecurity, or sadness? Our impulse is to protect ourselves and our students from experiences that may provoke transformation.

> Transformational educators know that God often changes and grows people through suffering, transitions, confusion, novel experiences, and overwhelming blessing. Instead of insulating students from all of these type experiences, the transformational educator helps the student benefit as much as possible from their acquaintance with these friends of transformation.

To love a student is to work on behalf of their growth and their journey toward being transformed by the Holy Spirit. As teachers, we need the courage to allow consequences, practice tough love, be honest about harsh realities, and take unpopular stands when necessary.

Of course, some friends of transformation are positive and welcomed. Many novel experiences are energizing and exciting while also being transformational. My first trip to another country was exhilarating while also being one of the most transformational experiences of my life.

"Before the truth sets you free, it tends to make you miserable." (Rohr 2011)

Examples of Some Friends of Transformation

Gratitude

For when we truly know our good fortune did not come from our own effort

For experiencing God's love

For immense thankfulness due to an event or special blessing

For the peace that accompanies forgiveness

Loss

Death of a parent

Death of grandparent or other special relatives

Teacher leaving

Breakup with a girlfriend

Best friend moving away

Losing a job or desired position, such as school president or team captain

Pet death

Miscarriage

Divorce

Not achieving your dream, such as not being admitted to desired university

Loss or destruction of material possessions (e.g., house burning down)

Transitions

Moving to a new place where no one knows you

Moving from a parent's home to having to provide for oneself

Going abroad for the first time

Friend moving away

Cognitive Dissonance

Realizing God does exist

Believing for a lifetime that only Christians go to heaven, then confronting that supposition upon forming a strong friendship with someone of another faith

Not knowing the theology or correct answers but surrendering one's allegiance to Jesus

Believing your country's government is moral, then seeing firsthand some immoral activities

Succumbing to the understanding that the pursuit of happiness is like chasing a receding rainbow

Aesop's fable *The Fox and the Grapes* (the fox couldn't reach the grapes so decided he did not want them after all because they were probably sour)

Wrestling deeply with hard dilemmas posed by literature, science, or history

Novel Experience

Mission trip to a very different culture

Spending an entire grading period assigned to a cooperate group of students from different friend groups or perspectives

Playing on a sports team with a coach who maximizes deep relationships among players from different backgrounds and values

Dormitory life

During a transformative experience, students may benefit immensely from the presence of a safe, trusted adult with whom to process the changes. Being a listening and unshockable confidant provides the student who is walking through an impenetrable fog with hope that shape and substance will yet emerge. Later, in chapter 5, the crucial skills of communication and listening are examined, but in this context, it should be stated that the teacher as listener-confidant is using very intentional ways of ensuring students know they have been heard. This does not mean agreement with the student's thinking or behavior; it means respect and care for what he or she is processing. Chances are the

> Listening does not mean agreement with the student's thinking or behavior, it means respect and care for what he or she is processing. Chances are the student already knows your beliefs.

student already knows your beliefs. What they may be seeking is a person safe enough to go with them through novel, sometimes scary, territory.

The friends of transformation are not always treated as friends. In fact, they can be received in ways that lead to unresolved bitterness, anger, depression, and denial. Sometimes these reactions are directed toward God. Selective reading of scripture and the belief that God is a kind of cosmic sugar daddy can distort a believer's embrace of the pain and suffering that can transform. Instead, the students may choose a destructive reaction to suffering.

Teachers must know their ethical and legal responsibility to act on the privileged information shared by a student if self-harm is communicated. A student will often share with a trusted teacher using subtle hints that he or she is contemplating self-harm. The following are examples of such statements: "I won't be needing that anymore," "You will be better off without me," "I just want to be done," "I am so tired," "I just want to be alone." A teacher should also be on the lookout for behaviors that may warn of potential suicide, such as:

- persistent sadness, anger, or moodiness
- hopelessness
- sleep difficulties
- dangerous or self-harmful behavior
- recent losses or trauma
- sudden calmness
- changes in personality and/or appearance
- making preparations, such as giving away items personally valued or making a will

If a student raises concerns for you, it is imperative to further assess their thinking and seek protection for them. No need to be alarmist; just probe the student's well-being. You may ask, "Have you had thoughts of hurting yourself?" To assess a student's potential self-harm, use the suicide screening instrument that follows or similar questions. Ethically and legally, a student at significant risk for self-harm must be committed to professional care.

Questions to consider:

1. What would you add to the list of friends of transformation?

2. Are you prepared to identify, assess, and get help for a student who is considering self-harm?

3. Is there something in addition to selective scripture reading and a misunderstanding of God's character that may lead to a believer reacting negatively to friends of transformation?

Resources:

National Suicide Prevention Lifeline	1-800-273-8255

Colombia-Suicide Severity Rating Scale

		Past month	
Ask questions that are bolded and <u>underlined</u>.		YES	NO
Ask Questions 1 and 2			
1) ***Have you wished you were dead or wished you could go to sleep and not wake up?***			
2) ***Have you actually had any thoughts of killing yourself?***			
If YES to 2, ask questions 3, 4, 5, and 6. If NO to 2, go directly to question 6.			
3) ***Have you been thinking about how you might do this?*** E.g. *"I thought about taking an overdose but I never made a specific plan as to when where or how I would actually do it....and I would never go through with it."*			

	Past month	
Ask questions that are bolded and <u>underlined</u>.	**YES**	**NO**
4) *__Have you had these thoughts and had some intention of acting on them?__* As opposed to *"I have the thoughts but I definitely will not do anything about them."*		
5) *__Have you started to work out or worked out the details of how to kill yourself? Do you intend to carry out this plan?__*		

	YES	NO
6) *__Have you ever done anything, started to do anything, or prepared to do anything to end your life?__* Examples: Collected pills, obtained a gun, gave away valuables, wrote a will or suicide note, took out pills but didn't swallow any, held a gun but changed your mind or it was grabbed from your hand, went to the roof but didn't jump; or actually took pills, tried to shoot yourself, cut yourself, tried to hang yourself, etc. **If YES, ask:** *__Was this within the past three months?__*		

☐ Low Risk

▨ Moderate Risk

■ High Risk

For inquiries and training information contact: Kelly Posner, Ph.D.
New York State Psychiatric Institute, 1051 Riverside Drive, New York, New York, 10032; posnerk@nyspi.columbia.edu
© 2008 The Research Foundation for Mental Hygiene, Inc.

CLOSING PRAYER

Thank You for loving us enough to not let us remain as we are.

We ask You to transform us and the students we teach. Make us faithful pray-ers.

Reveal to us the conditions that nurture transformation and
make us into yielded colaborers with the Spirit.

Show us how to respond to those who react to the
friends of transformation in harmful ways.

We pray this in the strong name of Jesus.

Amen.

CHAPTER 3

CORAM DEO OR FRAGMENTATION

No single piece of our mental world is to be hermetically (airtight) sealed off from the rest, and there is not a square inch in the whole domain of our human existence over which Christ, who is Sovereign overall, does not cry: "Mine!"

—Abraham Kuyper (Bratt 1998, 461)

Coram Deo is Latin meaning "before the face of God." Living life before the face of God acknowledges His love, His authority, His unity, and His involvement over all of life and is not limited to what is considered the religious aspects of life. Life is not fragmented or separated into some areas that belong to God and some areas that do not. The transformational educator presents a unified worldview helping students *live out* that God is involved in every aspect of life. There is no sacred/secular split, no spiritual and unspiritual separation, no dualism. This chapter explores what it would look like to ditch dualism and teach from a Christian worldview that reveals all of life before the face of God.

> Earth's crammed with heaven,
> And every common bush afire with God,
> But only he who sees takes off his shoes;
> The rest sit round and pluck blackberries. (Browning 2008)

Topics included in this chapter:

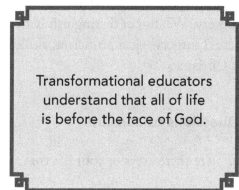

Section 1

Scripture Speaks That All of Life Is Before the Face of God

God's living presence permeates all things, at all times, in all places. Knowing God's creation of and involvement in every aspect of life will change how we go about our daily lives. Our classrooms and kitchens, our grocery stores and cathedrals, our sports fields and baptismal fonts are all holy ground.

> Transformational educators understand that all of life is before the face of God.

Activity #3-1

Meditate on the following scriptures, asking God how to know Him through His creation; how to obey because of His established natural order; how to glorify Him through His works.

> The earth is the LORD's, and everything in it, the world, and all who live in it. (Psalm 24:1)

> For in him we live and move and have our being. (Acts 17:28)

> Do not conform to the pattern of this world but be transformed by the renewing of your mind. Then you will be able to test and approve what God's will is—his good, pleasing and perfect will. (Romans 12:2)

> So whether you eat or drink or whatever you do, do it all for the glory of God. (1 Corinthians 10:31)

> Whatever you do, work at it with all your heart, as working for the Lord, not for human masters, since you know that you will receive an inheritance from the Lord as a reward. It is the Lord Christ you are serving. (Colossians 3:23–24)

> And this is my prayer: that your love may abound more and more in knowledge and depth of insight, so that you may be able to discern what is best and may be pure and blameless for the day of Christ. (Philippians 1:9–10)

> We demolish arguments and every pretension that sets itself up against the knowledge of God, and we take captive every thought to make it obedient to Christ. (2 Corinthians 10:5)

When I read these scriptures, I understand that my work as a teacher is to be done as unto God whether I am teaching in a Christian school or not. Of course, a Christian school would allow more overt Christian expressions, but it does not change who I am as a teacher or as a Christian. I can serve God by teaching the academic content promised to the students or parents and do it as an agent of transformation. A Christian surgeon must still practice skilled surgery just as the non-Christian surgeon. Although she may pray and may interact with the patient and the attending staff in a different way, she is still a surgeon performing surgery. We do not distinguish between Christian and non-Christian when it comes to the actual surgery—just proficient, skilled medicine please. This, because it was done for Christ, is Christian.

Questions to consider:

1. Are there areas of your life that are less submitted to God than others?

2. Looking at Philippians 1:9–10, how do you explain the connection between love and insight and knowledge?

3. How does one "eat to the glory of God"?

Resources for further exploration:

The Bible

Total Truth by Nancy Pearcey

Section 2

The Sacred/Secular Split

Before reading further, give this exercise a try:

Activity #3-2

Find two other people to join you in doing this activity or, of course, do it by yourself. Divide the words into two groups based on how they are alike or different in some way. After you have created the two groups, give a descriptive name for each group.

> Transformational educators recognize the error of designating some things as spiritual and others as nonspiritual. They teach in a way that helps students recognize this dualism and develop a unified view of all of life.

heart	private	secular
morality	religion	scripture memory
mind	opinion	feelings	personal
pastor	values	subjective	freedom
facts	public	sacred	mind
tolerance	objective	
engineer	multiplication facts	science

Does your list look similar to the one below? What descriptive title would you give to the two groups into which you divided the words?

List 1	*List 2*
morality	tolerance
pastor	science
personal	freedom
sacred	mind
scripture memory	facts
subjective	engineer
religion	public
pastor	objective
opinion	multiplication facts

private   secular

feelings

values

heart

Consider the lists above. What do you think about the way words were grouped? Did you make list 1 as being *sacred* words and list 2 as *secular* words? The point of this exercise is to help discover how easy it is to use language that assumes a divide between what is spiritual and what isn't. This division is as old as Greek influence in Christianity itself yet remains in Christian practice today. It continues to distort how God designed the world. This distortion is so pervasive that we rarely think about it. When things come up in life, we decide which compartment, sacred or secular, is relevant to the issue. Some of us think this compartmentalization explains why Christianity does not have a stronger impact on the current culture. We buy into the idea that there are arenas in life where our faith and Christian worldview are not applicable. In many parts of the world, Christianity is acceptable if it stays in its place as a preference or private conviction shared by like-minded people. However, not acceptable is the Christian having a public influence. Examples follow: A Christian may prefer tighter gun laws but should never suggest the whole country should seek these. A Christian may choose not to abort a baby but should never prevent anyone else from doing so. There is a public demand that research be used as a basis for policy unless the research affirms a biblical belief. A blatant example of this is the refusal to address the well-established research on the outcomes associated with married and unmarried parenting. Public policy does not translate the research into statements promoting marriage for parenting. If one's views are influenced by anything except Christianity, then they are neutral and acceptable, but if one's views are influenced by Christian faith, they are often considered biased and unacceptable. Tolerance and pluralism are not the same thing.

Compartmentalization leads to errors such as the following:

1. The church excitedly rallies around the decision of a young adult to pursue a career in missions but does not recognize the decision of another Christian youth who is planning to be a cosmetologist or salesperson.

2. A man shares his opposition to a law allowing abortion up until birth. His viewpoint is automatically labelled as religious and therefore does not warrant consideration. Other viewpoints are considered neutral and worthy of consideration.

3. A Christian school has a system for honoring students based on their memorization of scripture but does not recognize memorization of multiplication tables as significant in God's scheme of life.

4. Science is determined as the only way to know what is true, and everything else is up for grabs. Things like the claims of Jesus cannot be proven scientifically so remain outside the realm of truth or meaning and value.

5. Students are not nurtured to understand how their vocation is to be in service to God and His kingdom; they are led to believe ministry careers are more spiritual or of more service to God.

6. A business owner is honored for donating large amounts of money to a Christian ministry but has a reputation for low wages and poor treatment of employees.

What is a Christian pie?

The pie plate has John 3:16 inscribed, and the crust is embossed with a cross.

Or ...

- The pie is made from excellent apples from a well-tended orchard.
- The orchard has fair practice among the growers and pickers.
- Pricing is fair for the purchasing of ingredients and the selling of the pies.
- The pie baker uses creativity and experimentation to develop a tasty recipe.
- The baker is grateful for all the ingredients and the ability to cook pies well.

> "Rather than trying to teach biblical truths alongside so called 'neutral truths,' we are called to re-story, to take what we are teaching out of an explanatory story that says there is no God and placing them firmly within God's story" (Beech 2015, 125).

Questions to consider:

1. What recognitions and rewards does your educational setting give to students? Is a sacred/secular divide promoted by what is honored?

2. What have you observed in how the sacred/secular divide plays out in textbook selection?

3. Is there a secular and a sacred way to teach students?

Resource for further exploration:

Total Truth by Nancy Pearcey

Section 3

The Bible's Impact on Culture

The flipside of the sacred/secular dualism is failing to realize how much Christianity, rooted in the Bible, has permeated culture in extremely positive ways through the centuries. The worship of God has bled into culture by contributing truth, beauty, and goodness, often beyond our recognition. Bringing these contributions to students' attention may be fodder for transformation. These cultural transformations demonstrate that God's Word is alive, it penetrates and judges, and it has the power to change the human heart (excerpts from Hebrews 4:12).

> Transformational educators learn and teach about the Bible's impact on culture as a way of understanding the potential transformational power of the gospel historically, presently, and for the future.

Here's a quick nod to a few examples before we move on to the Christian educator's use of the Bible as a friend of transformation—that is, as an agent the Holy Spirit uses to bring the student into truth that will enlighten and transform an individual.

The Bible and Art

While living in Budapest, Hungary, I frequently attended a course at Hungary's premier Museum of Fine Arts. The course was taught by Jane Stevens, a volunteer docent at the museum, as an extension of her love of art, love of Jesus, and love of people. The course was titled "The Bible Illuminates Art." We began each session in one of the museum's classrooms with Bibles in hand and read the actual scriptural accounts about our biblical theme for the day, such as the creation, the miracles, Jesus's birth, the parables, or the flood. After hearing from the Bible, we toured the museum's paintings on the theme of the session. Jane included background information about the artist, the period in which the artist painted, the techniques the painter used, and reflection on the Bible story. People from all over the world participated in the course. Their motivation? They couldn't understand a large majority of the museum's art because they did not know the Bible stories that inspired the paintings.

Jane explaining art

The creation of art to magnify the stories of God and His beauty is just one example of how Christianity has impacted the culture. Literature, government, medicine, law, education, commerce, music, language, theatre—virtually all aspects of culture carry the same biblical impact. They have been immensely inspired by the principles, stories, and language of the Bible. A person cannot be thoroughly educated without a fundamental literacy in the Bible. And our world would be less healthy, less peaceful, and less knowledgeable without the transformation wrought by centuries of Christian influence. Knowing this will inspire students to live out their calling for God's kingdom to come and His will to be done on earth.

Questions to consider:

1. What benefit would identifying Christianity's impact on culture have for your students?

2. Are your students acquainted with the negative impact that a distorted understanding of Christianity has had on our culture? If so, what can you do to help them differentiate when scripture is being wisely or wrongly applied to cultural issues?

Resources for further exploration:

What If Jesus Had Never Been Born? by D. James Kennedy and Jerry Newcombe

What's So Great about Christianity by Dinesh D'Souza

The Reason for God by Timothy Keller

Section 4

Is Biblical Integration Really the Term We Want to Use?

The previous two sections have asserted that all of life is unified before God and that the common separation made between that which is secular and that which is sacred is a false dichotomy. God created and sustains the universe and has given His children great responsibility in caring for the creation and restoring it. This would be a difficult task if we were all preachers. Who would grow the food, find cures for diseases, build the houses, and cultivate our God-given affinity for music? Educators have the task of

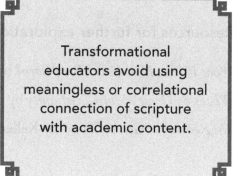

Transformational educators avoid using meaningless or correlational connection of scripture with academic content.

leading students into an understanding of God's design for their life and their contribution to caring for and building God's kingdom. Transformational educators equip students in finding and developing their God-given purposes. This could mean providing a strong academic foundation in chemistry, coupled with grand curiosity of what could be done with this knowledge or exploring with awe God's brilliance in chemical design. This kind of teaching, transformational teaching, is not prescriptive, formulaic, or easy to capture in a curriculum guide. Efforts to train Christian teachers have led to something called biblical integration. Biblical integration is defined generally as connecting an instructional objective to scripture. Curricula defined as Christian usually have a section titled "Biblical Integration" that highlights the way the lesson objective connects to scripture.

Is *biblical integration* really the term we mean to use? I think not.

I recommend removing the term *biblical integration* from the language of transformational education. Before getting pelted with copies of *The Encyclopedia of Biblical Truth*, let me explain the concern. First, the term itself, *biblical integration*, inadvertently succumbs to this error of dualism by implying there is something that stands alone to which the Bible is integrated. To integrate means to combine one thing with another so they become a whole. It implies adding the Bible on to an existing curriculum or that Christianity can be reduced to symbols or sayings we add on to something else. Yet the Bible already tells us that the earth is the Lord's and the fullness thereof. Biblical integration is a poor term because it implies that knowledge is somehow secular or neutral and that Christian educators add (integrate) the Bible into the academic subjects. Often the scripture is selected *to go with* a unit of study and serves as little more than a correlation of a word found in scripture with a word studied in a lesson. Some teachers try to Christianize a lesson by adding a Bible verse to the worksheet, using a Bible verse to teach diagramming a sentence, or adding biblical stories or illustrations that only connect tangentially to the lesson. The message given is that a superficial addition of something Christian matters.

The idea of integrating the Bible into the curriculum is unfortunately what does happen. The Bible is an add-on, at worst a match between a Bible verse and a supposedly neutral topic. There are numerous terrible but amusing examples of where this has gone awry.

- a math lesson on the concept of inverse proportions biblically integrated with the words of John 3:30: "He must increase, but I must decrease."
- a lesson on math fact *families* integrated by talking about God's family
- a lesson on ratio drafting made biblical by using the measurements of Noah's ark or Ezekiel's instructions for the temple
- repeatedly saying, to the point it becomes weird, that math is orderly just like God is a God of order
- Jesus being the light of the world (John 8:12) added to a lesson on light rays

Using the Bible this way inadvertently teaches students to misread the biblical text. Jesus being the light of the world is a profound verse, but it is a metaphor and not about light rays that were unknown at the time of this biblical writing.

Besides not really advancing a student's understanding of the gospel message or challenging them to live for Christ, I fear this methodology will foster cynicism and mockery among students, to say nothing of unbelief.

The alternative to biblical integration is to teach from a biblical worldview. Transformational educators are acutely aware that everything they teach is ultimately about God and God's creation. The academic content is presented in a way that helps students view a subject within God's design and see how this understanding impacts them personally, as well as society at large. This is not Sunday school lessons about the Bible; it is not some correlation between verses and a topic; it is not injecting students with a belief system alone but rather teaching out of the Christian way of thinking.

> I suggest that our responsibility as Christian teachers is to find the courage and the insight needed to live not as those who add devotional decorations to otherwise unmodified teaching processes, but as those who design teaching out of a vision of learners that combines theological depth and spiritual engagement. (D. I. Smith, On Viewing Learners as Spiritual Beings: Implications for Language Educators 2009)

Questions to consider:

1. Suggest a better word to use in place of *biblical integration*.

2. Briefly describe the difference between biblical integration and teaching from a biblical worldview.

Resources for further exploration:

Richard Riesen's *Piety and Philosophy*

Section 5

Teaching from a Christian Worldview

What is a worldview?

A worldview is a set of beliefs and assumptions that a person uses when interpreting the world around them.

Instead of using scripture as a superficial add-on, transformational teachers employ academic pursuits to uncover God's truth, to call out worship by observing the magnificence of God's creation, to cause lament at how humanity has distorted God's intentions, to unveil God's purposes for His creatures, to expose error in our assumptions, to bring us into cheerful submission, and to employ similar objectives to glorify God and foster a worldview that is thoroughly Christo-centric.

> Transformational educators use their lessons to uncover God's design of and manifestation throughout all creation. They teach from a Christian worldview.

- It explains who I am, giving meaning and value to my individual life.
- It explains who God is and how I am in relation to Him.
- It explains nature and beauty.
- It accounts for sin, death, catastrophe, illness, natural disaster, and all forms of brokenness.
- It explains who Jesus is, what He did for us, and why we need Him.
- It outlines our purpose in life.

So what exactly is a Christian worldview? Is there one agreed-upon Christian worldview?

Much has been written to explain worldview. To begin with, the scriptures indicate that God Himself wrote fundamental aspects of the worldview into human DNA so that we would be able to know Him, know what is, and know what really works in the universe He created. (Ecclesiastes 3:11). It has been described as the glasses through which we see and understand the world, an all-encompassing perspective on all which exists, an ideology, a harmony of all beliefs about reality. Undoubtedly, there are a variety of perceptions of a Christian worldview just as there are a variety of beliefs about the Bible and Christianity. In the Christian understanding of these things, all worldviews are derivatives of one that we all have the capacity to understand and live by, once transformed.

One way to understand a Christian worldview is the biblical metanarrative. A metanarrative is an overarching story that pulls together and connects all the small stories within that larger story. Other common names for the biblical metanarrative are the four-story gospel and the grand story arc of the Bible. Although biblical scholars have opinions on the contours of the biblical metanarrative, it has been historically expressed in ancient creedal statements as the creation, fall, redemption, and restoration. Trevin Wax (Wax 2011), in his book *Counterfeit Gospels*, describes the four cornerstones of the biblical metanarrative:

Creation: One Hebrew word sums up the picture of Genesis 1 and 2: *shalom*. Peace. Earth was full of God's shalom, the kind of peace in which everything works according to God's intention. The world was made for human flourishing, where we could live in joy in the presence of our Maker, worshiping God by loving Him and one another forever."

Application: We will truly know that it is God who made us and not we ourselves; we are His creatures and He alone in the omnipotent Creator We will love God and worship His excellence with all our hearts, minds, and being. We will create and be creative. We will value beauty and create beauty.

Fall: Adam and Eve rejected God's rule over them. We refer to their rebellious choice as "the fall," and because they represented all of humanity, their action affects us too. We have, through our attitudes and actions, declared ourselves to be God's enemies. This rebellion results in physical and spiritual death."

Application: We will understand the depths of our fallenness and sin. We will grieve our own brokenness and be repentant. We will grieve the brokenness of our fellow humankind and of all creation. We will be forever humbled.

Redemption: Thankfully the loving Creator who rightly shows Himself to be wrathful toward our sin is determined to turn evil and suffering we have caused into good that will be to His ultimate glory. So the next movement shows God implementing a master plan for redeeming His world and rescuing fallen sinners. In the Person of Jesus Christ, God Himself comes to renew the world and restore His people.

Application: We will embrace the redeeming work of Jesus Christ by giving our entire lives for Him and His kingdom. We will be the like Christ and reflect His character. We were redeemed to glorify God and enjoy Him forever. It is true that when the race fell into sin, it lost the capacity to read the creation correctly, so God provided Christ. *Redemption includes the whole of reality as well as our individual souls.* The Bible explains it as embracing the restoration of the creation to what God originally intended it to be.

Restoration: The story doesn't end with redemption. God has promised to renew the whole world. As His children our purpose is to be agents of this restoration."

Application: We will be His agents of restoring the creation to what God originally intended. We will introduce to the unredeemed the Lordship of Christ. We will seek the full gamut of peace -from interpersonal to world peace. We will feed the hungry, clothe the naked, house the indigent, heal the sick, educate the uneducated, love the unlovely, serve the handicapped, care for the elderly and infirmed, train the unemployable, create jobs for the jobless and whatever His will is on earth as it is in heaven. We were saved to co-labor with Christ in His creation.

As we seek God in this endeavour to be transformational educators, the biblical meta-narrative of creation, fall, redemption, and restoration can be helpful. Not only does this big picture of God's story give us pegs on which to hang our understanding and actions, but it also avoids many of the controversial questions associated with denominational differences. (Wax 2011)

Harold Klassen developed a tool for understanding Christian worldview called *The Visual Valet*. He describes it as a visual organizer that can act as a personal assistant for teachers and students. It helps organize biblical truths, guides in making connections to all of life and learning, and suggests critical questions that need to be answered. Find out more about this tool at https://transformingteachers.org/en/about-us/faqs/26-what-is-the-visual-valet.

Activity #3-3

Try drawing a poster (a pictogram) of the four stories in the metanarrative (to aid in committing to memory) and give examples of how something you teach would lend itself to explanation from a Christian worldview.

Two warnings:

1. Christianity does not belong to any one culture; the gospel of Jesus Christ transcends any culture and any time. A prodigious challenge of any transformational educator is to identify the insidious ways in which one's culture masquerades as Christian. Honest conversations with Christ followers from different cultures are one of the best ways to shed false narratives about Christianity. Learning from historical and linguistical scholars can shed light on scriptural texts that may even alter our habitually culture-infused ways of understanding scripture.
2. The transformational educator is aware that simply telling students about varying worldviews or verbally connecting scripture to educational content does not necessarily transform lives. Even the devil knew scripture, and how many philosophically astute students have lives void of God's love? Christianity does have answers for the philosophical questions of life, but it is so much more. Worldview and apologetics

classes are important but incomplete in and of themselves. Herein lies our challenge to ask God for transformation and not reformation alone. Transformational educators will not only disseminate knowledge about a Christian worldview but will *embody the metanarrative*. The teacher's life is a "letter from Christ, the result of our ministry, written not in ink but with the Spirit of the living God, not on tablets of stone but on tablets of human hearts" (2 Corinthians 3:3).

Essential Questions

Christian worldview is often summarized as answers to essential questions. The questions vary from one expert to another, but all tap into the human quest for meaning and purpose of life. See a variety of questions from scholars.

1. Harold Klassen in *The Visual Valet* (Klassen 2005)

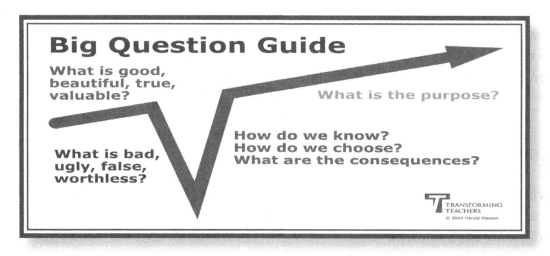

Joel Settecase organized the following sets of worldview questions (Settecase 2019):

2. RAVI ZACHARIAS

1. origin – Where do the universe and human beings come from?
2. meaning – What is the meaning or purpose of life?
3. morality – How do we know what is right and what is wrong?
4. destiny – What happens to us after we die?

3. ALBERT MOHLER

1. Where do we come from?
2. What's wrong with us?
3. Is there any hope?
4. Where are we going?

4. **JAMES SIRE** (Sire 2009)

What is prime reality?

1. What is the nature of external reality, that is, the world around us?
2. What is a human being?
3. What happens to a person at death?
4. Why is it possible to know anything at all?
5. How do we know what is right and wrong?
6. What is the meaning of human history?

5. **BARRY A. WARREN the creator of the <u>Perspective Cards</u>**

1. The nature of God?
2. The meaning and purpose of life?
3. Human nature?
4. Jesus is?
5. Source of spiritual truth?

6. **Worldviews address these three questions** (Worldview? n.d.)

1. Where did we come from? (and why are we here?)
2. What is wrong with the world?
3. How can we fix it?

7. **Questions for Worldviews** (Settecase 2019)

1. What is real?
   What is the nature of prime reality?
   What is ultimately real?
   What is God like?
2. What is good?
   What is good and how do we know?
   What does it mean to sin or contravene the standard of goodness?
   What is beauty?
3. What is true?
   What is truth and how do we come to know it?
   Is truth universal or subjective?
4. What is man?
   What does it mean to be human?
   What's wrong with humanity?
   How do we fix what's wrong with us?

5. What is the meaning?

   Is there a point to all this?

   Does God have a purpose and how do we discover it?
6. What is our destiny?

   Where are all things headed?

   Will justice finally prevail?

   Is history more like a Greek comedy or a tragedy?
7. Who is Jesus?

   Is Jesus merely a man, a created, divine being, or God?

   What did Jesus claim about himself and are those claims true? (Settecase 2019)

Take a challenge: prepare your responses to the questions above and "be prepared to give an answer for the hope which lies within you" (1 Peter 3:15).

At the heart of transformational teaching is Abraham Kuyper's (Henderson 2008, 12-14) declaration that "there is not a square inch in the whole domain of our human existence over which Christ, who is Sovereign overall, does not cry, Mine!" As already noted, the Bible refutes the idea of a sacred and a secular life. The subject content, the methods for teaching, the instructional milieu, and the teacher-learner relationships should all reflect our belief that God is the creator, redeemer, sustainer, and Lord of all creation. Our classrooms are holy spaces where God becomes known, loved, obeyed, worshipped, and enjoyed.

Questions to consider:

1. Which set of worldview questions do you prefer?

2. How much confidence do you have in how to respond to these worldview questions?

3. What, in addition to a worldview, comprises Christian faith?

Resources for further exploration:

Harold Klassen, *The Visual Valet*

Works by the writers of the essential questions mentioned above

James Sire, *The Universe Next Door*

Christians as Teachers, What Might It Look Like? by Geoff Beech

Section 6

The Cultivation of Christian Learners

Ushering our students before the Lord is the main task of a transformational educator. Students must develop a deep desire to love God with all their hearts, minds, and souls.

> Tell me the story of Jesus,
> Write on my heart every word;
> Tell me the story most precious,
> Sweetest that ever was heard.
> (Frances J. Crosby)

How do teachers nurture students in developing this loving intimacy? Teachers pray for the Holy Spirit to draw the student to Christ. Teachers also help students develop habits that allow the Spirit's work. Many of these habits are described as the spiritual disciplines, which include prayer, worship, Bible study, fasting, worship, and so on. The focus should be on the student interacting with Christ personally. Silence, meditating on the scriptures, the arts, observing God's creation, participating in the Eucharist, and others can be experiences designed to bring the student to a personal encounter with the love of God that transforms.

One time during a teacher training seminar, I washed a participant's feet while the other participants listened to the scripture reading of Jesus washing the disciples' feet. The participants got very quiet, and most had tears streaming down their faces. They later reported an intimate encounter with their Lord during this remembrance of Jesus's love in action.

During a teacher retreat, I was surprisingly impacted by God's forgiveness. The teachers were instructed to go to different stations as part of the devotions of the retreat. One station had a wooden cross implanted in the dirt, a bench for participants to sit upon, and a side table with a Bible, paper, a hammer, and nails. The participants were to read scriptures about God's

> Transformational educators begin by teaching the stories of Jesus and the importance of applying His teachings to how we live. The stories and applications may be modelled by the teacher or directly taught. They serve as an important foundation for a transformed life—either leading up to transformation or following it. Most significant, though, is the student developing authentic love for Christ—a love so deep that the student's life is given over to Christ. The student is *in Christ*, and their life overflows with the love and deeds of Christ. It is not a belief system held by the student, and it is not a code of behavior; it is a love relationship fully given over to the object of that love—Jesus Christ.

forgiveness, then write about their own sin. Once their writing was finished, they were to fold it and nail it to the cross. When I went to this station, there was a participant bowed and weeping. Her contrition shocked me at first, then overwhelmed me. I wondered when the last time was that I wept over my sin. With tears, I asked forgiveness for my casual relationship with sin and asked God to deepen my hate of sin and increase my gratitude for his forgiveness.

Ushering our students before the Lord—I think this is the main task of a transformational educator. What can we say and do to place students in a personal encounter with Christ? We present them to Christ, then get out of the way so that the relationship grows between the two of them. We nurture their relationship by praying for them and by offering opportunities that allow the student to engage directly with Christ.

Teaching for Transformation (teachingfortransformation.org) has developed the Throughlines listed below as a framework for developing learning experiences which I believe usher students into engaging directly with Christ. **Teaching for TransformationThroughlines**

GOD WORSHIPER Students will understand that worshiping God is about celebrating who God is, what God has done and is doing, and what God has created.

IMAGE REFLECTOR Students bear the image of God in their daily lives. Being an image bearer isn't something we DO. Image bearer is who we ARE.

JUSTICE SEEKER Students will act as agents of restoration.

EARTH KEEPER Students will respond to God's call to be stewards of all of creation.

SERVANT WORKER Students will work actively to heal brokenness and bring joy to individuals and to culture.

IDOLATRY DISCERNER Students need to learn to "read" a worldview by asking questions about what is being portrayed in regard to culture, values, and belief systems.

CREATION ENJOYER Students will celebrate God's beautiful handiwork and give testimony to the presence of God in creation.

BEAUTY CREATOR Students will create beauty that praises God and enriches our world.

COMMUNITY BUILDER Students will be active pursuers and builders of community in their classrooms, in their neighborhoods, and in the global village.

ORDER DISCOVERER Students see God's masterful planning and His fingerprints all over creation. (Teaching for Transformation n.d.)

In Closing

As much as many of us love black-and-white check-off lists and objective measures, an understanding of transformational education simply does not lend itself to such. YouTube should never have a video on "How to Transform Students" or "Transformational Education for Dummies." Once again, we are attempting to master that which should master us. We are colaborers, at best, with the Holy Spirit who transforms lives. For those of us who like control, this is one area over which we do not have control. However, for some reason, God has indeed given us a role in the transformation of His creation.

Protagoras: "Man is the measure of all things" (Farlex Dictionary of Idioms. © 2015 Farlex, Inc, 2015)

versus

Proverbs 8:4: "Who is man that you are mindful of him."

PRAYER

Holy God,

All praise to You, Holy God, for the cohesive, unified universe You created. Help us to live in the truth that You are Lord of all.

Help us as educators to avoid the pitfalls of a sacred/secular split and help us to see all of life unified in You.

Grow in us a deeper and deeper love relationship with You.

And help us know how to usher students into Your loving presence.

We pray in the strong name of Jesus.

CHAPTER 4

SWEET AROMA OF CHRIST OR BUG SPRAY

For we are to God the pleasing aroma of Christ among those who are being saved and those who are perishing. To the one we are an aroma that brings death; to the other, an aroma that brings life. And who is equal to such a task?

—2 Corinthians (2:15–16)

We read about the sweet aroma of Christ in 2 Corinthians. Paul compared the sweet aroma of Christ to a Roman victory celebration. After defeating an enemy, the commander, officers, and troops made a triumphal entry into the city and paraded around in celebration for the citizens. At the end of the parade were chained prisoners of war who were destined to be killed by wild animals in the arena. During this victory parade, censers released the aroma of incense everywhere. To the citizens, this aroma became associated with victory, and to the captives, it became associated with death.

Paul told us to be the sweet aroma of Christ to one another, celebrating the victory of Jesus over death. The task of effectively applying God's Word within one's cultural context may make this challenging. In some learning environments, both North American and globally, the teacher is to be feared. All teachers need to find a way to communicate respect and Christlike love for students, whether they come from a high-power distance culture (a culture where the teacher is accepted as having much power over the student) or low-power distance educational environments. This does not imply casualness, niceness, permissiveness, or buddy-buddy relationships, but it does rule out indifference, manipulation, and domination through fear. Whether the teacher's relational style is formal or casual, students can sense when the teacher is *for them*. Clearly, as Christians, we are to be the sweet aroma of Christ as we respect, correct, encourage, and genuinely love our students.

> The transformational teacher's life emanates the sweet aroma of Christ. The biblical Christ is winsome, gentle, beloved, and a friend of sinners. It seems the prophetic voice of Jesus was primarily to address the religious leadership of the day. So why then are we Christians often known to the masses for what we are against more than what we are for? Do we exude the sweet aroma of Christ in our classrooms or some type of the bug spray disguised as Christian piety?

Topics included in this chapter:

Section 1: The Hospitality of a Teacher

Section 2: The Necessary Practice of the Spiritual Disciplines

Section 3: Forming Loving Relationships

Section 4: Communication

Section 5: Rage Is the Rage

Section 6: Enjoying God

Section 1

The Hospitality of a Teacher

When you did it to the least of these you have done it to me. (Matthew 25:40)

Do not forget to show hospitality to strangers, for by so doing some people have shown hospitality to angels without knowing it. (Hebrews 13:2)

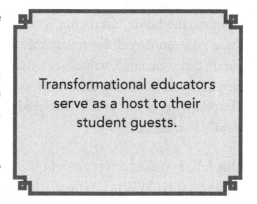

Transformational educators serve as a host to their student guests.

What is your favorite metaphor for a teacher? coach? babysitter? drill sergeant, sage, orchestra conductor?

For the classroom of a transformational educator, how about the metaphor of the *teacher as host* and the *student as guest*? Jesus repeatedly taught about and acted as a host. Hospitality is deeply rooted in Christianity.

The Porter

In Benedictine monasteries, the porter was the first person to greet and welcome strangers coming to the monastery for food, lodging, fellowship, and care. He essentially was the face of the monastery. The porter's room was near the front of the monastery so he could be on the lookout to welcome weary sojourners. Once a traveler was spotted, the porter would notify the other monks who assembled in the entrance hall to greet the visitor. The monks would bow to their guest and say, "We are in the presence of Jesus." The visitor was their honored guest and seated at the head of their dining table for the shared meal (Roska 2021).

Hospitality is often thought of as good manners or entertaining. For many people, it means cleaning the house, arranging special table settings, and preparing food. The hospitality of the classroom may differ from other settings but includes anything that makes the student-guests feel welcomed, valued, cared for, and comfortable. Parker Palmer describes a teacher's hospitality as "receiving each other, our struggles, our new-born ideas, and openness with care. Hospitality is not an end. It is offered for the sake of what it can allow, permit, encourage and yield" (Palmer 2017, 7).

One fall, I worked a recruitment fair on the campus of a university that had a strong culture of hospitality. When I arrived, there was very clear signage on where to park, and a staff member met me in the parking lot with a rolling cart for my display and an escort to where I was to set up. I was treated to a welcome lunch, a gift bag, and all-day hospitality drink and snack area. Staff and faculty members made their way to my spot to thank our organization for being represented and personally greet me, while the students could not have been more polite and interested in the positions for which we were recruiting. After the fair, staff members helped me get my materials back to my car. But, by far, the general friendliness and kindness demonstrated to me when students and faculty did not know I was with the recruiting fair impressed me the most. They had a strong culture of hospitality that truly blessed me.

Activity #4-1

Conduct a personal assessment by considering questions that follow the description of a host's behavior. How do you as a teacher welcome, introduce, provide for, and serve the students? Note these questions apply to a classroom teacher, but you can adapt them to your own educational setting.

1) A host welcomes.

How does the teacher welcome students to class? One of the biggest fears reported by students at the beginning of a new class is not knowing where the class is located. Welcoming on the first day of class involves helping students know they are in the correct location. The teacher welcomes students by being stationed at the entranceway to offer personalized greetings (handshakes, personal questions, smiles). This is a good time for the teacher-host to assess the current needs or emotional state of their student-guests. Name tags at the students' seats with a welcome sign on them or on the board is also a way of welcome. What other ways welcome students?

Instructional: Teacher-hosts are also in the position of welcoming students to a new sphere of learning, new ideas, and challenging tasks. Providing an atmosphere of acceptance and intellectual freedom allows the student-guests to learn and explore with a trusted teacher-host by their side.

2) A host introduces.

Who in your class already knows you or the other classmates? How do you plan to introduce yourself to the students and the students to one another? What teaching techniques, such as cooperative learning groups (see chapter 6), can you use to introduce and facilitate new relationships among the students? Some teachers train students to be a host or friend for new students. This student-host tells the new student what they need to know, helps the new student navigate the campus, and sits with them at lunch or snack time. The host-student also further acquaints the new student with classmates.

Are there other people you should introduce to the students? At the school I led, the kindergarten teachers always gave the students a tour of the campus with introductions to me and other administrative staff on the first day.

Instructional: Perhaps you are introducing your guests to a new subject, a new idea, a new author, or a new concept.

3) A host provides.

What do your students need to be responsible learners? Are their physical needs met, such as food, drink, adequate lighting, and temperature? How about the physical needs of correct desk and chair sizes, well-ventilated air, time to move and exercise after sitting or standing awhile? Are appropriate hygienic practices in place to prevent illness? Do they have the supplies and materials they need for class? One idea is to have a selection of school supplies from which students may borrow when they forget their own. This is also a great way to encourage students to contribute to the stockpile as members of a learning community who are looking out for one another. Teachers may keep snacks or other food items for students who forgot theirs or who may be feeling sick. Teacher-hosts often meet these needs by calling them to the attention of the parents or other school officials to address.

Instructional: How well are the students' academic needs being addressed? Has thought been given to advanced students who need greater challenges? Weaker students who need support? Does the teacher offer excellent classroom management so the student-guests have a safe and predictable place to learn?

4) A host serves.

Servant leadership is a concept and practice well known to transformational educators. Jesus taught this by washing His disciples' feet and by demonstrating a lowly stance throughout

His life. The leader is to be one who serves, not glorifies himself. What are some ways that a teacher relinquishes privilege for the sake of serving their students in class? Research has demonstrated that observing someone being kind, unselfish or serving others inspires similar behaviors from those who observe (Haidt 2005).

Instructional: What ways are students allowed or encouraged to serve the teacher or classmates on academic tasks? Are peer tutors allowed or cooperative learning tasks utilized? Does the teacher promote the sharing of encouraging and celebratory words by classmates to other classmates regarding academic tasks? Teacher may have a bulletin board devoted to posting students' best work.

Creating a Physically Hospitable Environment

Another responsibility of a host is to create a hospitable environment. The setting of a classroom speaks volumes of a teacher's hospitality. What are some ways to demonstrate hospitality by the physical space of your classroom? How can you humanize the classroom space? The following list has some ideas.

In the Classroom

- The door into the classroom has signage clearly stating the room number and teacher's name or class name to help students and guests know they are in the correct place.
- The door has words of welcome or invitation.
- The door may have attractive decorations, such as the season, the historical period being studied, or the personalities of the students.
- Students are recognized and honored. Examples are bulletin boards introducing the students, graphs of the teeth lost per student (grade 1) or obtaining their driver's license during the year (grade 10), and samples of students' work.
- Students' desks and chairs fit the size of the students.
- Comfortable places for students to read or do cooperative work (mats, cushions, sofa, loft) are available.
- No visible clutter or disorganization exists.
- Aesthetically pleasing walls, ceiling hangings, bulletin board, and display table are visible.
- The classroom has a pleasant scent.
- Classroom procedures exist for having students monitoring the cleanliness of their space and entire class.
- There is a refreshment area where students can go get water or possibly coffee and tea.
- The lighting is controlled for the benefit of the students. Lamps may be added.
- The desks are arranged to accommodate the type of instruction taking place.

Staff Introduction Hospitality

I never counted the number of times, but the number was notable that visitors expressed something intangible and positive about our Christian school's atmosphere when they entered the doors. We all knew it was the sweet aroma of Christ. It was as if the teachers' beings, not just their words, emanated the Christ in them.

Idea: Use the reception area or other high-visibility area of the learning environment to introduce the staff. Place a photograph of the staff member followed by a few facts about them, such as marital status, children, school from which they graduated and what they majored in, favorite topics to teach, awards, hobbies, name of their church, favorite sports team, favorite music.

On-the-Campus Hospitality

Is hospitality demonstrated by designating convenient parking spaces for new-to-the-school visitors?

Does the school have signage that informs new-to-the-school visitors of where to enter the building?

Does signage around the school use welcoming words or only make demands of the visitor, such as "do not" "no____"?

Whether a multimillion-dollar complex or a mud hut, is the school clean, well kept, and with some beautification such as flowers?

Does a guard or receptionist warmly welcome or kindly acknowledge visitors?

Is there an effort to offer something to drink, toilets, or seating to visitors?

Questions to consider:

1. What aspects of the teacher/student dynamic are missed by this metaphor of teacher as host and student as guest? For example, what does a host do about guests who break rules or do not complete assignments or show disrespect?

2. How would hospitality look in a classroom where the authority and power of the teacher is a strong feature of the student/teacher dynamic? In other words, what does teacher hospitality look like in a high-power distance culture?

3. What would be different about your teaching if you imagined yourself as a *host* and your students as your guests?

Resources:

Dane Ortland, *Gentle and Lowly*

Parker Palmer, *The Courage to Teach*

George Jacobs, Gan Siowck Lee, Jessica Ball, *Learning Cooperative Learning Via Cooperative Learning* (1997)

Section 2

The Necessary Practice of Spiritual Disciplines

The practice of spiritual disciplines nurtures the sweet aroma of a transformed person.

How do teachers become the sweet aroma of Christ to their students? In other words, how does the Holy Spirit transform us? Although we cannot make this happen on our own, we can create conditions conducive for the Spirit's work in our lives (see chapter 1). The practice of the spiritual disciplines, confession, worship, service, gratitude, and obedience open us to God's presence in our lives. By spiritual disciplines, I am referring to both the private and shared practices listed below by Richard Foster (Foster 2001), page 151:

Internal disciplines

- Meditation
- Prayer
- Fasting
- Study

External Disciplines

- Service
- Simplicity
- Stewardship
- Solitude
- Submission

Corporate Disciplines

- Celebration
- Confession
- Seeking Guidance
- Worship
- Fellowship

Taking the time to practice the spiritual disciplines invariably leaves me wondering why I do not practice them more often, more thoroughly, and with more devotion. I love the outcome. However, as long as we keep longing for more of God, He promises to keep meeting us. Through a day-by-day process, God frequently does His transforming work. Sometimes an instantaneous burst of divine presence instigates immediate transformation like the Damascus

Road experience, Moses with the burning bush, or memorable events in our own lives. However, transformation is likely a gradual, incremental movement. As transformational educators, we'd be wise to spur one another on in the practice of the spiritual disciplines.

Warning! The practice of spiritual disciplines can be tricky. They can become idols when the focus becomes the practice of the discipline rather than the communion with God. The length of a person's quiet time, the days of a fast, and the amount of scripture memorized can be pursued as a kind of self-salvation (God owes me for being so righteous). The practice must always be appreciated only for its benefit in bringing us into deeper fellowship with God. The disciplines bring us to where the change can occur.

Questions to consider:

1. Looking at the list of the spiritual disciplines, which ones do you consider private and which ones as shared disciplines? Are many of them both private and shared?

2. Which one or one(s) do you want to practice more faithfully?

3. Would you add or delete any of the listed disciplines? Why?

4. Does your church nurture the habit of spiritual disciplines in a way that invites transformed lives?

Resources:

Any of Richard Foster's books:

Celebration of Discipline

Prayer: Finding the Heart's True Home

Freedom of Simplicity

> We have real difficulty here because everyone thinks of changing the world, but where, oh where, are those who think of changing themselves? People may genuinely want to be good, but seldom are they prepared to do what it takes to produce the inward life of goodness that can form the soul. Personal formation into the likeness of Christ is arduous and lifelong. (Lund 2018)

"Love God and do whatever you want," credited to Augustine, may be paraphrasing from 1 John 4:4–12, which says, "Live according to your new life in the Holy spirit, and you won't be doing what your sinful nature craves."

Section 3

Forming Loving Relationships

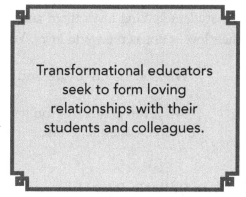

Transformational educators exude the sweet aroma of Christ, God's love. Far more than friendliness or social skills, this love reflects the characteristics described in 1 Corinthians 13:4–8a: "Love is patient, love is kind. It does not envy, it does not boast, it is not proud. It does not dishonor others, it is not self-seeking, it is not easily angered, it keeps no record of wrongs. Love does not delight in evil but rejoices with the truth. It always protects, always trusts, always hopes, always perseveres. Love never fails."

> Transformational educators seek to form loving relationships with their students and colleagues.

Different types and locations of educational environments have vastly different norms for student-to-teacher, teacher-to-teacher, and teacher-to-supervisor behavior. Yet within each of these relationships, we seek to love as God loves, expressed convincingly within the cultural context.

Love Our Students

Too bad the English language does not have better categories for the word *love*. The type of love that teachers are to have for students is one that attempts to see students the way God sees them. Out of love, the teacher seeks to know the way God created the student, then draw out of the student his or her God-created design. Each life is meaningful and purposeful. Individual differences are observed and celebrated. This is more than acceptance of a student's unique design; the teacher has a fundamental curiosity. It involves asking the question of how God made this student so the teacher can nurture and equip him or her to fulfill their place in God's world. All students have God-designed contributions to make.

Views of the Student

Behavior to be managed?
A customer/consumer?
Intellects to be moved forward?
Forces to be controlled?
Empty vessels to fill?

Or ...

Images of God called to faithful living and called to love of God, neighbor, and creation?

To love students does not imply being chummy friends with them. Teachers are in a place of authority, delegated to them by the student's parents/caregiver or adult learners who willingly submit to a teacher's expertise.

Authority need not be controlling or distant to be able to effectively serve and lead students. Love is expressed as honor, respect, care, and attention. Because the teacher is seeking to love the student as God loves them and to equip the student to fulfill their God-given nature, their love is not as the world loves. We are not talking about just being friendly to students.

"Whoever claims to love God yet hates a brother or sister is a liar" (1 John 4:20).

"Whoever spares the rod hates their children, but the one who loves their children is careful to discipline them" (Proverbs 13:24).

Lync's Bulletin Board

Lync Myers served several years as the beloved Bible teacher at an international Christian school. It was common to see students huddled around him, discussing serious theological ideas, or shooting the breeze with him outside of class time. Each year, Lync had a bulletin board in his classroom to introduce himself as a person and not simply as their teacher. The board included photos of his family and hobbies, his history, and his loves. He clearly wanted to be known by students, which is the basis of relationship building.

Like all aspects of being a transformational teacher, the Holy Spirit is the source and substance of how we serve as agents of transformation in our schools. The sweet aroma of Christ in a school or classroom cannot be achieved by a to-do list. However, it is worth examining some of the advice that educators hear that may hold back the Spirit's work.

Questions to consider:

1. Discuss some of the ways teachers should and should not share themselves with their students.

2. Discuss some of the ways a teacher should / should not interact personally with their students.

3. Could bad habits or misinformation be keeping a transformed teacher from exuding the sweet aroma of Christ? Should you …

   • not smile until Christmas?
   • not reveal any personal information in the name of professionalism?
   • not admit your errors to students so they will have confidence in you?
   • disregard extenuating circumstances for the sake of always treating every student the same way?

4. How can the development of a personal relationship between the student and the teacher facilitate transformation?

Scripture to encourage loving relationships:

> "My command is this: Love each other as I have loved you." (John 15:12)

> Be devoted to one another in love. Honor one another above yourselves. (Romans 12:10)

> Live in harmony with one another. Do not be proud but be willing to associate with people of low position. Do not be conceited. (Romans 12:16)

> Do nothing from rivalry or conceit, but in humility count others more significant than yourselves. (Philippians 2:3)

Love Our Colleagues

For me, learning the history of how Christianity expanded through the centuries is at once challenging and inspirational because the growth seems often to have occurred as Christians lived out their faith as *holy* people—that is, literally separated, called-out people. They lived in the culture but were not subsumed by it. While this attracted new people to the community, it often resulted in opposition. In a sense, martyrdom has been the most successful missionary method across the centuries. Only people able to see a different, lasting reality can face lions in a coliseum or plague infested neighborhoods and not flee for safety. Eric Liddle and the Ten Boom sisters illustrate the enduring, attractive legacy of those who have sacrificed even life itself. Even during the turbulence of 2020's natural disasters and COVID-19 pandemic, in almost every corner of the world, faithful Christians were volunteering to aid the poor, fight fires, respond to hurricanes, and clean up the most challenging of messes in damaged areas. One of the untold stories in the modern world is the high percentage of sincere Christians who comprise the volunteer teams that sacrificially love people in need. Nevertheless, the truth cannot be suppressed, and the church grows because of the grace and love of Christians serving as called-out followers of Christ who taught us how to love in this way.

My family and I had the opportunity to serve in the Sichuan, China, region after the 2008 earthquake that left five million people homeless. Other people, both Chinese and international groups, were also serving alongside us. After one week of getting to know one another by working side by side, a Chinese volunteer (self-avowed atheist) asked me if all volunteers in America were Christian. Even the Chinese American volunteers were Christians, so her question made sense. We observed a similar situation in Hampstead, North Carolina, which was ravaged by post hurricane flooding. Many volunteer groups were on-site, all wearing T-shirts indicating a Christian affiliation. The homeowner of the house I was working on declared she would be in church Sunday if this was what church was about. This is a true statement, and I praised God for what she was seeing.

As you know, teachers are in a highly visible role. Christian love is not just evident in the great crises of life; it is a daily reality. Our expression of love in times of unusual challenge is a Spirit-empowered, supernatural outworking of the daily love He brings to our transforming hearts. For us as teachers, this shows up in the way in which we genuinely respect and honor our colleagues. Our students know when a colleague is being rude, self-seeking, or unjust. They will see something attractive and different in our turning the other cheek or refusing the kind of competition rooted in making ourselves standout as superior to our colleagues. They will see something attractive and different when we give the place of honor to our coworkers, genuinely praise them, work for their success, and sacrificially demonstrate personal care for them and their families. Our students are blessed and changed by the difference that an authentic community of faith demonstrates. These communities are not built by just being nice and friendly people, but rather through the hard work of prayer, humility, and seeking of God's power to love even those we feel are unlovable.

What can teachers do:

- Pray for yourself and your colleagues to build a genuine community of faith.
- Carve out time to know and be known within your learning community.
- Guard your tongue, speaking things that will build up those who are difficult coworkers.
- Focus attention on getting to know your colleagues, especially those who are difficult, so that you can honor them genuinely.
- Quickly settle accounts, not giving room for negative feelings to fester.

Questions to consider:

1. Think of the colleagues in your career who have affirmed and honored you above themselves. Why do you think they did that?

2. How do you honor and respect your colleagues besides just being nice?

3. Ask someone you respect—or if you are in a group, discuss—how to get along with difficult people.

> God did not make others as I would have made them. God did not give them to me so I could dominate and control them, but so that I might find the Creator by means of them. Now other people, in the freedom with which they were created, become an occasion for me to rejoice, whereas before they were only a nuisance and a trouble for me. God does not want me to mold others into the image that seems good to me, that is, into my own image. Instead, in their freedom from me, God made other people in God's own image. (Dietrich Bonhoeffer 1963)

Transformational educators develop healthy relationships and teach their students to do likewise.

Research

Researcher and expert on relationships, John Gottman, identified four markers of relationship failure: criticism, defensiveness, contempt, and stonewalling. By using these markers, Gottman's research predicted a couple's divorce with 93 percent accuracy. This highly predictable research deserves attention because of the insights that may transfer to a community setting like a school. Gottman points out that contrary to our common assumption, it is not conflict itself that indicates a failed relationship. Conflict can be productive in helping people in a relationship negotiate what works for them. The problem is how people in relationship deal with conflict. Persistent criticism, defensiveness, contempt, and stonewalling are counterproductive behaviors that negatively affect a relationship.

Gottman's research defines the predictive behaviors between couples. Think about how these characteristics may lend themselves to predicting relationship failures within a school.

Criticism: It is the first behavior that is typically used by couples in conflict. Criticism refers to attacking one's character or personality, rather than the behavior itself. "You are so lazy" is an example of criticism. Instead, using "I" statements such as: "It frustrates me when you don't help out around the house," targets your partner's problem behavior without the use of criticism.

Defensiveness: Becoming defensive is an easy behavior to engage in when in conflict. The problem with defensiveness is that once you engage in it, you naturally tune out what your partner is trying to say to you and begin making excuses, blaming your partner, and not taking responsibility for your part in the conflict.

Contempt: You know you are contemptuous when you show blatant disrespect for your partner by doing things like sneering, rolling your eyes, or using "humor" to down your partner. Try to be aware of your behaviors and understand what it is that you are really upset about and target that rather than using passive-aggressive ways to tell your partner how you feel. This can sometimes be hard to do, but it pays off!

Stonewalling: Couples who regularly engage in this behavior are more likely to get divorced. Research shows that this is the most damaging behavior to engage in. Simply put, stonewalling is when you become nonresponsive. (Lund 2018)

Activity # 4-3: Gottman's markers of failed relationship

Apply the four characteristics to school relationships between a teacher and students / other teachers / administrators or parents by giving examples. I offered an example in italics. Give your own examples.

1. Example of criticism: *"You are so rude."*

   Example of an "I statement": *"I would like to hear what other students have to say, so please raise your hand and wait until I call on you."*

2. Example of defensiveness: *"I had a hundred and forty papers to grade. What did you expect?"*

   Example of taking responsibility: *"I will spread out my test dates so in the future I can get the graded papers back to you in a timely manner."*

3. Example of a sarcastic statement posing as humor but is actually contempt: *"Oh how nice you finally showed up on time to class."*

   Example of identifying the root of contempt and expressing it directly: *"Thank you for being on time for class. Not having to repeat what you missed saves time for the rest of the class."*

4. Example of how a teacher can stonewall a student: *"You'll find out when you need to know."*

   Example of how a student can stonewall a teacher: *The student gives no eye contact and no verbal responses.*

Questions to consider:

1. What can you do if you observe any of the four characteristics in your classroom or school?

2. Do you see any of these behavioral patterns in yourself?

3. Would you agree that scripture teaches against these behavioral patterns in relationships? Does the research shed light on biblical teaching? How?

When Things Go Wrong: Peacemaking

The sweet aroma of Christ also is demonstrated in how Christians handle relational problems. When there is offense within a relationship or community, Christians are compelled to restore it. "For if you forgive other people when they sin against you, your heavenly Father will also forgive you. But if you do not forgive others their sins, your Father will not forgive your sins" (Matthew 6:14–15).

From my experience, forgiveness and restoration are problematic for Christian schools and Christian teams of workers. We often fail at it. The recourse is usually to sever relationships rather than restore them. "Out of sight, out of mind" can be a momentary relief from damaged relationships, but it is not God's solution for His children. The principles from scripture are practical and true.

Activity #4-4

You will need something to write with, such as a computer or paper and pen. Follow the instructions below.

1. Read Proverbs 18 silently and a make a list of principles relevant to settling disputes, using one word or a short phrase to identity them. (Example: For verse 15, "listen to all sides" or "give due diligence to settling disputes.")

2. Read Matthew 18:15–17 silently and list steps for addressing grievances. What have you observed as the outcome when the offended person talks to everyone except the person who offended him or her?

3. Develop your own standard (steps you will do) for personally addressing offenses. Write it down to retrieve for implementation when you get offended. Compare your plan for addressing offense to your school's or team's policy. Adjust your own steps for reconciliation or recommend adjustments to your school's or team's grievance policy.

Resources abound on how to handle offense and grievance. Some refer to it as peacemaking that combines restoration (restoring the broken relationship) and reparation (how to make things right with the offended person). *Mediation* and *arbitration* are also terms one may find when researching a plan. Both terms involve three members, the two sides of the dispute and an impartial third person, who come together in a structured discussion to negotiate the dispute or offense. In mediation, the impartial third party (called a mediator) assists disputing parties in resolving conflict through and in arbitration. The impartial third party (called an arbitrator) does not actively participate in the discussion and makes a final resolution much like a judge would do. Professional mediators and arbitrators are trained to use specialized communication and negotiation techniques.

Read more: https://www.whatchristianswanttoknow.com/5-biblical-steps-for-restoring-broken-relationships/#ixzz6Xe8oi87x.

Richard Rohr (Rohr, A Healing Process 2020) describes a relationship-healing procedure the Navajos use, which can be helpfully adapted to a school setting as follows:

1. **Prayer** A traditional prayer puts people in the right frame of mind for the talking out of differences.

2. **Venting or expressing feelings** After prayer, everyone has a say about what happened. They also express how *they feel* about what happened. In peacemaking, you must know how I feel, and I must know how you feel. That is part of making or restoring a healthy relationship.

3. **The Lecture** When the prayers have been said, when emotions have been expressed, and when people have told their stories, it is time for guidance from the naat'aanii [peacemaker or elder]. The peacemaker does some teaching. By offering guidance from Navajo stories, traditions, and ceremonies, and applying them to the situation, the peacemakers teach the law.

4. **Discussion** Who participates in the peacemaking? The parties themselves (who are the "judges"), a leader, a planner, and relatives. The discussion phase also gets at the *causes* of problems.

5. **Reconciliation** If you operate a "winner take all system of justice, expect ongoing problems. If you have a system that works toward reconciliation, you may resolve the conflicts that underlie ongoing problems. Navajo justice is restorative justice.

6. **Consensus** Finally, based upon the prayer, venting, discussion, and knowledge of the traditional way of doing things, the people themselves usually reach a consensus about what to do. Planning is a central Navajo justice concept, and the people plan a very practical resolution to the problem. Today, it is put in writing, and the parties sign it. Consensus is what makes the Navajo justice and harmony ceremony—peacemaking—a healing process.

Questions to consider:

1. Discuss some of the appropriate and inappropriate ways that teachers may share with students about themselves.

2. What about being known by students could contribute to transformation?

3. Do you plan to change anything about settling grievances or peacemaking? If so, what will you change?

Section 4

Communication

Make no mistake, communication may be a trendy topic, but its importance resonates throughout the Bible. Sharpening our communication skills is one way we can be the sweet aroma of Christ. Peruse the scripture below as just a reminder of the wisdom about communication sealed through the centuries in the Bible.

Avoid godless chatter, because those who indulge in it will become more and more ungodly. (2 Timothy 2:16)

Let your conversation be always full of grace, seasoned with salt, so that you may know how to answer everyone. (Colossians 4:6)

But now you must also rid yourselves of all such things as these: anger, rage, malice, slander, and filthy language from your lips. (Colossians 3:8)

My dear brothers and sisters, take note of this: Everyone should be quick to listen, slow to speak and slow to become angry. (James 1:19)

Do not let any unwholesome talk come out of your mouths, but only what is helpful for building others up according to their needs, that it may benefit those who listen. (Ephesians 4:29)

Sin is not ended by multiplying words, but the prudent hold their tongues. (Proverbs 10:19)

The words of the reckless pierce like swords, but the tongue of the wise brings healing. (Proverbs 12:18)

To answer before listening—that is folly and shame. (Proverbs 18:13)

Fools find no pleasure in understanding but delight in airing their own opinions. (Proverbs 18:2)

Like an earring of gold or an ornament of fine gold is the rebuke of a wise judge to a listening ear. (Proverbs 25:12)

Gracious words are a honeycomb, sweet to the soul and healing to the bones. (Proverbs 16:24)

A good man brings good things out of the good stored up in his heart, and an evil man brings evil things out of the evil stored up in his heart. For the mouth speaks what the heart is full of. (Luke 6:45)

Likewise, the tongue is a small part of the body, but it makes great boasts. Consider what a great forest is set on fire by a small spark. (James 3:5)

Do not rebuke an older man harshly but exhort him as if he were your father. Treat younger men as brothers, older women as mothers, and younger women as sisters, with absolute purity. (1 Timothy 5:1–2)

It's humbling to read these verses, isn't it?

As teachers, how do we dispense the sweet aroma of Christ to our students in ways other than by what we say? What do we communicate to our students through body language? Do our students believe we care by the way we listen? Are our students being taught how to communicate with others in authentic, meaningful, and caring ways? Teachers know that communication is important, so hopefully this chapter is a call for intentionality in the kinds of communication that foster the Holy Spirit's transformative work.

A. Verbal Communication

Words of Praise and Affirmation

For starters, transformational educators use words of praise and affirmation of their students. There are some things to consider about praise to make it more effective. Teachers may feel they are being positive by saying "well done" or "good job" often, but could their praise be even more effective by making some changes? The research, suggestions, and examples that follow come out of Peabody College of Vanderbilt University and can be found at www.iris.Peabody.

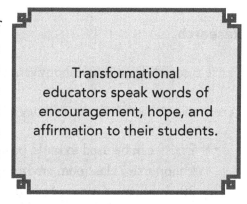

Transformational educators speak words of encouragement, hope, and affirmation to their students.

Effective praise can be verbal or written and must be received as positive by the student. Keep in mind that some ages, middle schoolers for example, may be embarrassed by being singled out by the teacher for positive behavior.

Research

Praise research from iris.peabody.vanderbilt.edu

Peruse these research summaries regarding research on the use of praise.

- Praise can be used to build positive relationships with students and assist in creating a supportive classroom environment (Brophy, 1998; Emmer, Evertson, & Worsham, 2003; Shores, Gunter, & Jack, 1993).
- Powerful, appropriate praise is: non-judgmental; specific and descriptive; contingent and immediate; and sincere (Brophy, 1998; Duncan, Kemple & Smith, 200; Weinstein, 2003).
- A variety of types of praise should be used to avoid overuse and satiation (Brophy, 1998). In some cases praise should be used in conjunction with other types of reinforcements or rewards (Duncan et al., 2000; Kerr & Nelson, 2002).
- All students need to experience success. Ensure that each student receives some form of sincere and accurate praise or recognition (Evertson, Emmer, & Worsham., 2003).
- Some students, particularly adolescents, do not find public praise reinforcing or pleasant (Emmer et al., 2003; Maag, 2001; Weinstein, 2003).

- Teachers must adjust their use of praise and how it is delivered for individual students. Some students have long histories of obtaining attention through misbehavior rather than appropriate conduct. For these students, combining praise with other forms of reinforcement and behavior strategies may be needed. (Piazza et al., 1999).
- The effectiveness of the praise depends on the "richness" of the reinforcement currently available in the student's environment (Sulzer-Azaroff & Mayer, 1991).

Tips for Implementation...

a. Be non-judgmental. Praise the student's accomplishment or behavior, not his or her achievement when compared with that of others.

Example: "Doug, you really did a great job of being prepared for class today by bringing your pencils and notebook."

Non-example: "Doug, I'm glad you brought your supplies today like everyone else."

b. Avoid global positive statements.

Example: "Wow, Keesha! You used several vivid terms in your paragraph to describe the story setting. Your use of adjectives has really increased."

Non-example. "Wow, Keesha! Great writing today!"

c. Use statements that underscore the student's actual efforts and accomplishments. Make sure your voice and body language match the content of your message.

Example: "Hector, you set up the multiplication problem correctly, placing all numbers in the appropriate columns. You are ready now to work on the next part of the problem."

Non-example: "Hector, you really did a great job solving your multiplication problems today."

d. Deliver immediate praise near the student for whom the praise is intended. Move around the classroom frequently so you note praiseworthy behaviors.
e. Utilize a variety of verbal and written praise.
f. Offer praise to several students at the same time. Or provide praise privately to avoid the embarrassment some students feel when being singled out in public.
g. Evaluate and Adjust Praise

   – Is the praise effective? Do the students seem to like the attention?
   – Do students maintain or improve the praised behavior?

- Do I offer each student some form of praise every day?
- Do I maintain a positive balance of positive and negative statements in my classroom?
- Do I include variety in my use of praise?

h. Change the type, the way, or how often the praise is given based upon individual student responses or needs.
i. Use frequent praise when new behavior and skills are taught. As the skill is mastered, this frequency should be gradually reduced to a more intermittent schedule.

Activity#4-5: Practice for yourself

Below, read the student behavior and the less-effective praise statements the teacher makes regarding the behavior. Then rewrite the praise statements to make them more effective using the guidelines above. Notice the first one is an example to show you what to do.

Example:

1. Jane scored an A on a math test.

Ineffective: You're smart Jane.

More effective: Jane, the extra time you put into studying resulted in an excellent grade.

2. Jack shows you his artwork.

Ineffective: What a pretty picture, Jack!

More effective:

_____

_____

3. Lupe helps you hand out papers to the class.

Ineffective: You are so good, Lupe.

More effective:

_____

_____

4. After months of losing privileges due to not turning in homework, Mary turns in homework on time every day for a week.

Ineffective: At last, Mary, you are getting your work in on time.

More effective:

_____

_____

5. Sayeed scored two goals during the game.

Ineffective: You are a great player.

More effective:

_____

_____

Be wary of setting up opportunities where selfless service is overshadowed by the student anticipating a reward or being praised as their goal!

Other Ways of Honoring Students

God made our students in His image with unique strengths and weaknesses. We should expect differences among our students while not valuing some students more than others just because their strengths fall into whatever we happen to be teaching. An excellent musician may not be excelling in our language school, and an achieving swimmer may find math confusing. How are we treating students with less measurable strengths, such as consistent kindness and strong perseverance? Most learning environments have systems to honor the best and brightest in the field of study. Such systems offer tremendous recognition for 10 percent of the learning population and *zero* recognition for the other 90 percent. Consider developing ways to recognize all students for their contributions to the school and community as a way of helping all students understand the concept of God making us with varied strengths and weaknesses. Note that this also implies helping students understand that there are areas in which they will have weaknesses.

Add your own good ideas to the ones listed for celebrating the various wonderful ways God has created people.

1. *Write the name in the heart (for the young student).* Reward students who are improving by having a heart shape on a wall where you can write the student's name in the heart. Call the student to your side and explain to the class why you are honoring the student in this way. Students who are struggling in certain areas need as much

positive recognition as they can get to keep them motivated to continue their efforts. It is important to make time to let them know you noticed a difference.

2. *Wall of fame.* A wall of fame recognizes student contributions or achievements in out-of-school-time activities. Give students, parents, teachers, and community organizations an opportunity to post photos, news articles, and so forth on an electronic board or a bulletin board showing all of the different contributions your students make to their community. It is nice if the students' peers are the ones to keep the wall of fame current as they learn to celebrate others' accomplishments.

3. *Student of the week.* Through random drawings or a class rotation, highlight one student, or a student at each grade level, each week. This can be done on a class level or school level. Create an electronic or bulletin board with information the student brings to school, including photos of their hobbies, activities, and family. Give the student some extra privileges like being first in line at lunch or a free homework pass. The principal can interview the student over the morning announcements. Ask teachers, family, and friends to share why they think the student is special and share that information with the student and the school. This can also be adapted for adult students in a way that contributes to being known and knowing others.

4. *High fives.* Create a wall in the school where students and staff can recognize others for doing something special, challenging, generous, or kind by writing the name and recognition on a notecard and pinning it to the board.

5. *Look book.* Several elementary schools have a look book in each classroom. When students deserve affirmation for something unique to them, teachers ask the student to sign the look book. How nice it is when this simple affirmation of the student's behavior is all that is done to encourage him or her—no tangible rewards or community praise added.

6. *I Noticed cards.* Create preprinted notecards (or Post-it Notes) with a sentence starter recognizing something special that an adult might notice about a student. School staff (any staff) then can tear off a card, write a quick note, and hand it to the student.

7. *God made us all.* Create something like a look book (#5) in which a student can write one of their weaknesses and point out a classmate who has it as one of their strengths.

8. Your ideas?

How do these activities and approaches enhance the transformative nature of the environment? The cumulative effect of many teacher actions helps nurture the student in understanding God's unique design for their life, promotes an other-mindedness among the students, and offers encouragement and hope to students needing it.

> Transformational educators speak words of correction, warning, and potentially unwelcomed truth to their students.

As you read the scripture below, you will note that scripture clearly endorses the idea of correction. Correction is a form of caring, a gift, a source of wisdom, and a duty we have as Christians. This contradicts some approaches that avoid correction of students and simply suggest redirecting a misbehaving student to a more acceptable behavior. Research suggests five positive statements of praise for every one statement of correction or rebuke.

> Because the LORD disciplines those he loves, as a father the son he delights in. (Proverbs 3:12)

> Whoever heeds life-giving correction will be at home among the wise. (Proverbs 15:31)

> It is better to heed the rebuke of a wise person than to listen to the song of fools. (Ecclesiastes 7:5)

> A wise son heeds his father's instruction, but a mocker does not respond to rebukes. (Proverbs 13:1)

> Whoever rebukes a person will in the end gain favor, rather than one who has a flattering tongue. (Proverbs 28:23)

> And the Lord's servant must not be quarrelsome but must be kind to everyone, able to teach, not resentful. Opponents must be gently instructed, in the hope that God will grant them repentance leading them to a knowledge of the truth. (2 Timothy 2:24–25)

> Wounds from a friend can be trusted, but an enemy multiplies kisses. (Proverbs 27:6)

> Preach the word; be prepared in season and out of season; correct, rebuke and encourage—with great patience and careful instruction. (2 Timothy 4:2)

> But those elders who are sinning you are to reprove before everyone, so that the others may take warning. (1 Timothy 5:20)

> Brothers and sisters, if someone is caught in a sin, you who live by the Spirit should restore that person gently. But watch yourselves, or you also may be tempted. (Galatians 6:1)

Classroom Discipline

All teachers and most students know there are nonverbal ways of correcting students. The presenter of a classroom-management seminar had my attention the minute she gave credence to *the teacher look*. By far, the most common form of correction, the teacher look, usually takes care of the problem without interrupting instruction or making the student defensive. Carol Evertson developed a hierarchy of intervention that outlines a least intrusive to most intrusive progression of teacher responses to student misbehavior.

Hierarchy of Intervention (Evertson 2013)

Notice the line indicating when interventions interrupt instruction

Ignore
Make eye contact
Increase physical proximity
Touch or gesture
Involve student in an academic response

_____

Remind student of the rule/expectation
Request/demand appropriate behavior
Question student in private about the behavior
Issue negative consequence

Avoid doing the following:

1. *Intimidate the student:* The teacher can always "win" or control students even if it means expelling the student from class. The goal is not to win. The minimum goal is to illicit a behavior change in the student and plant seeds for a positive relationship. Even when they comply, a bullied student will hold onto resentment and work against a positive relationship with the teacher.

2. *Nag:* Under the auspices of teaching the student a lesson, a teacher can simply be nagging the student by going on about why the behavior is wrong, what would Jesus think, and so on. The student may benefit by taking some time to reflect on their own or with the teacher in private, but a public nagging is unhelpful because it produces resentment.

3. *Let it go:* Not attempting to correct the student communicates one of two things: that you fear what the student may do if corrected, or it communicates that you think the student is not worth the trouble, that he or she is hopeless. What a message to give to a student, even a student heavily fortified by a defiant stance! One exception is if the infraction is minor, and the student does not know you observed it. Sometimes it is better to ignore it and keep the instruction moving.

As always, relationship is at the root of effectively correcting student behavior. Loving, firm, grace-filled discipline is a way of setting the student up for success in school and work for the rest of life. The student must sense the teacher is for them. The teacher emanates the sweet aroma of Christ while firmly responding to the student's misbehavior.

B. Nonverbal Communication

> "A good man brings good things out of the good stored up in his heart, and an evil man brings evil things out of the evil stored up in his heart" (Luke 6:45).

The ways in which teachers and students communicate with each other without using words is nonverbal communication. Transformational educators practice effective non-verbal communication. The following are examples of nonverbal communication:

Eye Contact

Teachers must be aware of the cultural norms of the students they are teaching. In some cultures, eye contact is considered disrespectful. In Western culture, too little eye contact may represent little value of the student, and too much eye contact may be intimidating. Teachers must work for just the right amount of eye contact to create interest and engagement with their students. The teacher look is frequently used as an effective means of correcting student behavior.

Posture

When considering posture, think not only of the shoulders being straight or slumped but also of how the arms are held (folded in front of the torso, placed on the hips, etc.), the tilt of the head, and how the legs are placed. Intentional listening is communicated well by facing the speaker squarely and leaning a little forward.

Facial Expression

Changes in the forehead, eyebrows, eyelids, nose, lips, and the chin are examples of facial expressions that reveal what an individual is feeling internally. Even subtle facial expressions communicate messages to the student.

Smiling

Are we really suggesting that smiling at students is important enough to include in a repertoire of transformational educators' practices? Well, it depends on the cultural expectation of the student. Pro-smiling cultures such as the United States tend to see smiling as a sign of acceptance, respect, and congeniality. In Japan's culture, there tends to be less smiling. Less smiling indicates humility, which is highly valued. Russians tend to only smile when genuinely expressing a good mood or personal regard for an acquaintance. Otherwise, smiling is considered insincere. Other cultures associate various meanings to smiles, especially when the two people are of different genders. But in the US and many Western cultures, research reports that smiling goes a long way in promoting acceptance, respect, and goodwill. Smiling benefits the smiler as well as the recipient of the smile. The effect of receiving a smile in known to be passed on.

Research concludes that smiling has the following positive effects:

- initiates a contagious reaction
- activates the release of neuropeptides that work toward fighting off *stress*
- makes us appear more attractive to others
- lifts our mood, as well as the moods of those around us
- lengthens our lives
- relaxes our body and can also lower our heart rate and blood pressure
- serves as an anti-depressant/mood lifter (Hatfield vol.14)

Distance

The distance between the teacher and the students impacts the classroom climate. Being close together promotes intimacy and social interaction. Teachers may also move to a student's space to nonverbally correct their behavior or to solicit more engagement from the student.

Touch

Teachers must learn the legal and cultural appropriateness of touching related to the age group and social norms of their teaching location. It's worth the research to find out if touching is acceptable because in some situations it is very helpful. Research done at Kansas State University notes, "for children in the lower primary grades, touch plays an important developmental role. It can communicate a sense of belonging, security, and understanding to the child. Conversely, when a teacher withholds touch, a child may feel isolated and rejected, which can lead to the acquisition of negative attitudes towards school" (n.d. 2003).

Gesture

Gestures are small hand or finger movements, head movement, or large arm movements that add to what the teacher is saying. As observed for decades in the game Simon Says, people often follow the gesture rather than the spoken command.

C. Listening-Verbal Signs of Attentive Listening

Active listening is about focusing fully on the person talking while also actively showing verbal and nonverbal signs of listening. Active listening is different from hearing. Hearing is involuntary and automatic as opposed to active listening, which is intentional and focused. In a world fraught with distraction and indifference, being listened to well is an effective way to care for and value another person. Transformational educators will endeavor to become active listeners as a way of valuing their students. Just like the previous section on effective praise, there are skills to improve listening well that may benefit teachers and their students.

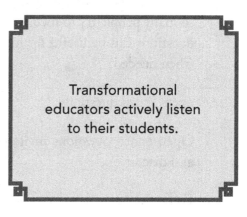

Transformational educators actively listen to their students.

Verbal Signs of Attentive Listening:

Verbal Utterances

Occasionally making verbal utterances such as "uh huh," "yes," "of course," "sure" can be a strong signal of being listened to and provide positive reinforcement for the person speaking to continue. Verbal cues of active listening should be used sparingly as they can be disrupting and sometimes irritating.

Questioning

The listener can demonstrate that they have been paying attention by asking relevant questions and/or making statements that build on or help to clarify what the speaker has said. By asking relevant questions, the listener also helps to reinforce that they have an interest in what the speaker has been saying. There are two main types of questions:

- closed questions

  Closed questions tend to seek only a one- or two-word answer (often simply yes or no). They therefore limit the scope of the response. Two examples of closed questions are:

  "Are you David's only sibling?" and

  "Did you eat at the pub last night?"

These types of questions allow the questioner to remain in control of the communication. This is often not the desired outcome when trying to encourage verbal communication, so many people try to focus on using open questions more often. Nevertheless, closed questions can be useful for focusing discussion and obtaining clear, concise answers when needed.

- open-ended questions

Open-ended questions invite elaboration, hence broadening the scope for response and discussion.

Example:

"What was being the only female sibling like?"

"How did you prepare for the race?"

Open-ended questions may require more time to process before an answer is given. They invite self-expression from the responder and encourage involvement in the conversation.

Reflection

Reflecting is giving feedback to the speaker by closely repeating or paraphrasing what the speaker has said to demonstrate understanding or show comprehension. It is a manner of the listener demonstrating understanding.

Reflecting often involves paraphrasing the message the student communicated. The teacher needs to capture the essence of the student's facts and expressed feelings in his or her response and communicate understanding back to the speaker. It is a useful skill because:

- It provides a way for the listener to confirm he or she has heard the message correctly.
- The student gets feedback about how the message has been received and can then adjust as needed.
- It shows interest in and respect for the student's viewpoint.
- It demonstrates that the listener is considering the other person's viewpoint.

Mentioning a similar situation. This involves sharing a personal anecdote that is similar to what the student just said and indicates understanding by making the connection.

Brief verbal affirmation. Tell the student you appreciate his or her sharing what he or she said.

Clarification

Clarifying involves asking questions of the speaker to ensure that the correct message has been received. Clarification usually involves the use of open questions, which enables the speaker to expand on certain points as necessary.

Summarization

Summarizing what has been said back to the speaker is a technique used by the listener to repeat what has been said in their own words. Summarizing involves taking the main points of the received message and reiterating them in a logical and clear way, giving the student a chance to correct or clarify as needed.

Examples:

- Utterances: "Uh huh," "oh no," "absolutely," "sure," "of course."
- Questioning: "How many absences did you have last year? What are some of the reasons you think this happened?"
- Reflection: "So you wish we would do math first thing, then do music later in the day?"
- Mentioning similar situations: "I experienced those same problems when using that formula."
- Clarification: "So you are saying the real reason he did not come was …?"
- Brief verbal affirmation: "I appreciate the time you've taken to speak to me".
- Asking open-ended questions: "I understand you aren't happy with your class schedule. What changes can we make to it?"
- Summarize group conversations: a teacher summarizing what has been said by the class and asking them if the summary is correct.

Next time you are in a conversation, make a mental note of what active listening skills you use and what skills are used by the other person in your conversation.

D. Listening-Nonverbal Signs of Attentive Listening

People who are listening are more likely to display some of these signs listed below. However, these signs may not be appropriate in all situations and across all cultures. For example, eye contact is a required means of showing respect in some cultures and considered disrespectful in others.

Smile

Combined with nods of the head, smiles can be powerful in affirming that messages are being listened to and understood. Small smiles can be a way of agreeing or being happy about the messages being received.

Eye Contact

It is normal and usually encouraging for the listener to look at the speaker. Eye contact can, however, be intimidating, especially for more shy speakers. Gauge how much eye contact is appropriate for any given situation. Combine eye contact with smiles and other nonverbal messages to encourage the speaker.

Posture

Posture can tell a lot about the sender and receiver in interpersonal interactions. The attentive listener tends to lean slightly forward or sideways while sitting. Other signs of active listening may include a slight slant of the head or resting the head on one hand.

Mirroring

Automatic reflection/mirroring of any facial expressions used by the speaker can be a sign of attentive listening. These reflective expressions can help to show sympathy and empathy in more emotional situations. Attempting to consciously mimic facial expressions (i.e., not automatic reflection of expressions) can be a sign of inattention.

E. Simultaneous Use of Verbal and Nonverbal Attentive Listening

Reinforcement

Reinforcement is the use of encouraging words alongside nonverbal gestures, such as head nods, a warm facial expression, and maintaining eye contact. This helps to build rapport and is more likely to reinforce openness in others.

The use of encouragement and positive reinforcement can:

- encourage others to participate in discussion (particularly in group work)
- show interest in what other people have to say
- pave the way for development and/or maintenance of a relationship
- allay fears and give reassurance

- show warmth and openness
- reduce shyness or nervousness in ourselves

Literally Showing Kindness

> Harmel (1999) summarizes research by Zygouris-Coe who studied fourth graders for 5 ½ months by observing the classroom environment at least twice a week and giving the students written response questions during the class 'journal' time. The questions were open-ended statements such as, 'My teacher thinks that I am …," and the students were encouraged to write several paragraphs to explain their answers."

Zygouris-Coe found that students often interpret things such as their teachers' body language, the order in which they are called on, and the intensity with which they are listened to as signs of their teachers' feelings toward them. Many students even cast a skeptical eye on teachers' compliments, she said.

- Positive nonverbal feedback from teachers—in the form of making eye contact, paying attention when students speak, and letting them know that you understand their strengths and weaknesses—can make all the difference in the world in removing barriers to the learning process.
- "I hope that this will make teachers a bit more aware of how children interpret what happens in the classroom," Zygouris-Coe said. "I definitely recommend to teachers to give very specific feedback to children, not necessarily about every aspect of their behavior, but to make frequent attempts to let children know what they think about their progress, their behavior and other specific elements of their lives" (Harmel 1999).

The value of a smile: "It costs nothing but creates much. It enriches those who receive it, without impoverishing those who give it. It happens in a flash, and the memory of it sometimes lasts forever. None are so rich that they can get along without it, and none so poor but are richer for its benefits. It creates happiness in the home, fosters good will in business, and is the countersign of friends. It is rest to the weary, daylight to the discouraged, sunshine to the sad, and nature's best antidote for trouble. Yet it cannot be bought, begged, borrowed, or stolen, for it is no earthly good until it is given away." (Anonymous)

Transformational educators monitor their hearts, knowing their nonverbal communication may communicate what their words do not.

We have considered verbal, nonverbal, and a combination of verbal and nonverbal listening skills, which are all important elements in the learning environment because each has the compacity to enhance the transformative potential. Like a midwife, they don't create the delivery, but they provide many supportive strategies for assisting the mother through her birth experience.

The first task of a transformational educator is to sincerely ask God for personal transformation. It is impossible to fake it. We can try to monitor our behavior and tongue, but eventually people will see or feel our truth. What we harbor in our heart will become visible. Yes, until our hearts are changed, we should guard our tongues, but students and colleagues will eventually see past our controlled words and actions. Nonverbal communication will shout out the truth. Hence, we should monitor our hearts, asking God for transformation.

Actions speak louder than words.

Preach the Gospel at all times. Use words if necessary.

A picture is worth a thousand words.

Do as I say, not as I do.

Resources:

https://www.skillsyouneed.com/ips/verbal-communication.html

Section 5

Rage Is the Rage

In the past few decades, the world seems to have become meaner, less tolerant, and angrier. Much of this has played out on the digital stage. Anonymity, distance versus face-to-face interchange, and the one-sided nature (versus conversation) of internet posts create a perfect storm for rude and provocative comments. Where did civility and manners go? Pundits on culture are using titles such as "Rage Is All the Rage" and "The Age of Outrage." Our students may not remember a kinder, gentler time

> Transformational educators teach and model integrity, engagement, and peaceful living in our diverse world while rebuking one-sided, prejudiced thought and actions.

when a person respectfully disagreed. No doubt the intolerance, anger, and dislike were as present then as now but just not unleashed so readily. As followers of Christ, we are called to a higher standard based on love. The way we treat nonbelievers may be one of the best ways we co-labor with the Holy Spirit in demonstrating that God loves them.

So how can educators foster a transformation of our vitriolic culture? In the scriptures, we find the best advice; see the following sampling of verses:

> If your enemy "is hungry, feed him; if he is thirsty, give him something to drink. In doing this, you will heap burning coals on his head." Do not be overcome by evil but overcome evil with good. (Romans 12:20–21)

> But I say to you that listen, love your enemies, do good to those who hate you. (Luke 6:27)

> Blessed are the peacemakers, for they will be called the children of God. (Matthew 5:9)

> Get rid of all bitterness, rage and anger, brawling and slander, along with every form of malice. Be kind and compassionate to one another, forgiving each other, just as in Christ God forgave you. (Ephesians 4:31–32)

> My dear brothers and sisters, take note of this: Everyone should be quick to listen, slow to speak and slow to become angry. (James 1:19)

> With the tongue we praise our LORD and Father, and with it we curse human beings, who have been made in God's likeness. Out of the same mouth come praise and cursing. My brothers and sisters, this should not be. (James 3:9–10)

Research

Researcher Jonathan Haidt uses the term *elevation* for his finding that just witnessing someone doing acts of kindness can uplift and inspire the observer. "Across cultures, human beings are moved and inspired when they see others acting with courage or compassion, and this elevation makes them more likely to want to help others and become better people" (Haidt 2005).

What can teachers do:

1. Avoid giving rewards for kindness.

    Doing acts of kindness inherently rewards the person by giving them uplifted, satisfied, and positive feelings. The reward is inherent from the act. Conversely, giving rewards for doing acts of kindness can diminish elevation and decrease the occurrence of doing acts of kindness.

2. Promote doing kindness.

    Tell stories about acts of kindness, do acts of kindness to your students and colleagues, and even share the research about the broad positive effects of being kind. Apparently, people are emotionally responsive to being kind and observing kindness.

3. Express gratitude.

    When we express gratitude, it requires us to see how we've been blessed by other people. This strengthens the relationships.

Questions to consider:

1. What do you think about the research that concludes that doing acts of kindness is intrinsically rewarding?

2. Are there ways that your school rewards kindness versus promoting it and thanking people for their kindness?

3. Do you have personal experience with the benefit of overcoming evil with good?

Resources for further exploration:

1. "Three Ways for Schools to Help Kids Cultivate Kindness" by Vicki Zakrzewski, July 1, 2014, in *Greater Good Magazine: Science Based Insights for a Meaningful Life*

2. William J. Bennett's *The Book of Virtues: A Treasury of Great Moral Stories*

Section 6

Enjoying God

Transformational educators enjoy God. The root of their praises of God comes from a delight in the God who planted profound joy through their identity in Him. God liberates the soul through forgiveness, through value, through purpose, through belonging, and through being the object of God's immeasurable love. This liberation transforms His follower from one who is duty bound, guilty, alone, uncertain, and joyless to one with a deep security and understanding that they are a precious child and heir of the one, true God almighty.

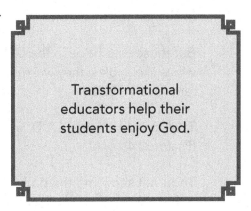

Transformational educators help their students enjoy God.

Things They Don't Teach You in Seminary That You Really Need to Know by Kathy Escobar :

October 17, 2018

> **The difference between "To", "For", and "With."** These <u>three prepositions matter</u>; most everything in the world is built upon "To" and "For" relationships, where we do things *to* people (which is patriarchal and creates oppression) or *for* people (which is matriarchal and creates codependence). *With* relationships, where no one is above or below another, is incarnational and creates true transformation. It seems overly simple but it's difficult to do, especially in a world that primarily teaches us to be over or under others.

The first question and answer of the Westminster Shorter Catechism is as follows: "What is the chief end of man? Man's chief end is to glorify God, and to enjoy him forever." Because of my religious tradition, I never made acquaintance with a catechism until well into adulthood. Upon my first exposure, I was taken back by the first question. Our chief end is to glorify God (no surprise) and to enjoy Him forever (what?). I had not been acquainted with the importance of enjoying God. In fact, I never thought about enjoying God. Now I think enjoying God is one of the marks of transformed person.

> This is how we know what love is: Jesus Christ laid down his life for us. (1 John 3:16)

> There is no fear in love. But perfect love drives out fear, because fear has to do with punishment. The one who fears is not made perfect in love. We love because he first loved us. (John 4:18–19)

Moreover, when God gives someone wealth and possessions, and the ability to enjoy them, to accept their lot and be happy in their toil-this is a gift of God. (Ecclesiastes 5:19)

I know that there is nothing better for people than to be happy and to do good while they live. That each of them may eat and drink and find satisfaction in all their toil-this is the gift of God. (Ecclesiastes 3:12–13)

But those who hope in the LORD will renew their strength. They will soar on wings like eagles; they will run and not grow weary; they will walk and not be faint. (Isaiah 40:31)

Take delight in the LORD, and he will give you the desires of your heart. (Psalm 37:4)

Thou wilt show me the path of life: in thy presence [is] fulness of joy; at thy right hand [there are] pleasures for evermore. (Psalms 16:11)

"Come to me, all you who are weary and burdened, and I will give you rest. Take my yoke upon you and learn from me, for I am gentle and humble in heart, and you will find rest for your souls." (Matthew 11:28–29)

"These things I have spoken unto you, that in me ye might have peace. In the world ye shall have tribulation: but be of good cheer; I have overcome the world." (John 16:33)

"These things I have spoken to you so that My joy may be in you, and that your joy may be made full." (John 15:11)

You make known to me the path of life; you will fill me with joy in your presence, with eternal pleasures at your right hand. (Psalm 16:11)

May the God of hope fill you with all joy and peace as you trust in him, so that you may overflow with hope by the power of the Holy Spirit. (Romans 15:13)

"I am coming to you now, but I say these things while I am still in the world, so that they may have the full measure of my joy within them." (John 17:13)

The natural world exhibits God's artistic nature. He insists that the exquisite lily from His own hand is still more beautiful than the greatest artistic manifestation from Solomon's time (Luke 12:27). Rejoicing over the beauty of the created world brims with praise for the Creator and His creation.

Paul instructs believers from different cultures that it is important to evaluate and discriminate between worthy and less worthy aspects of aesthetic expression. A believer is not floundering in a miasma of personal choices and standards with no absolutes to guide. "The gospel is no cosmetic facelift," writes Calvin Johansson, "but a matter of life-changing orientation running deep and swift in its cleansing, shaping, and loving power. It shows to man the fallacy of phoniness and of being concerned for the effect without concern for the cause. The gospel of Jesus Christ stands for the integrity, wholeness, and creativity. Genuine newness is the result of an inward dynamic at work—a creativity that breaks new ground with imagination and integrity. ... The gospel requires the highest standard of living." (Johansson 1988, 43-44)

Resource for further exploration:

Gentle and Lowly, The Heart of Christ for Sinners and Sufferers by Dane Ortlund (2020)

Commensality

Transformational educators will tap into the biblical theme of breaking bread together with students for the purpose of enjoying God in community.

Commensality is a new word introduced to me by Kendall Vanderslice's book titled *We Will Feast* (Vanderslice 2019). Commensality means the practice of eating together at the same table, implying fellowship by a shared meal. The connection being made here is probably obvious to those among you who love to eat and fellowship around a table. Maybe not so recognized is the noteworthy emphasis that commensality had in Jesus's ministry and why we should be imitators of this aspect of His ministry.

Vanderslice says the Bible is a story of meals and notes that Jesus commanded His followers to eat together. Although commonly done in a sanctuary and called communion or the Eucharist, Vanderslice says that 'worship at the communion table is much more than a taste of bread and wine" p. 2 and that 'something powerful happens at the table

The Bible is a story of meals:

> The Bible begins in a garden and ends with a banquet/feast
> Jesus told parables about food
> Jeus told his disciples to eat and feed others
> Jesus said to set the table not only for people like you but also for the cripple lame and blind
> Jesus revealed his risen self over a meal on the road to Emmaus
> Jesus gave forgiveness to Peter with the offer of fresh fish
> re-member and heal the divisions of the broken body made one in Christ"

The coming kingdom is an eternal banquet in the presence of God and an end to death, pain, and evil.

Experiencing the Eucharist

In the church tradition I experienced growing up, the Lord's Supper involved silently passing a plate of thumb-size crackers and thimble-size juice glasses. Living abroad as an adult cast me into new church traditions and forms of partaking in communion. Whether it be the delight of something new or simply a better practice, I experienced an entirely new appreciation for celebrating communion in a liturgical worship setting.

In my new church setting, the following delighted me:

- I had to initiate getting out of my seat to go to the altar versus passively waiting for a tray to impersonally be handed to me.
- I kneeled before God.
- There was movement of people all around as they were also kneeling, walking to and from the altar, or going for prayer. I did this as an individual *and* in a community.
- The bread and wine were given to me by a fellow believer who often said my name before saying, "The body of Christ broken for you" or "The blood of Christ spilled for you." It was deeply personal.
- I had to wait while many people made their way to the altar. I took in the flickering candles, the emotive music, the church's beauty. There was plenty of time to be still and know He is God.

Put it altogether, and I experienced deep joy in the Eucharist; I enjoyed God.

I also enjoy God when I belly laugh with friends or eat food with family, frequently pausing between smiles and bites of delicious food to thank God for such rich relationships and good times. This is the overlap of enjoying God and gratitude to God. In Acts and Tertullian, the early Christians were known for defying the accustomed social stratification and having everyone eat together, sharing the resources so the poor had plenty, and the rich had sufficiency.

Two important themes come together here, celebrating the Eucharist (remembering Christ) and enjoying food and fellowship. How could this be part of a transformational classroom?

CLOSING PRAYER

Source of my being:

Stretch me beyond the demand for personal advantages.

Increase my capacity for silence. Diminish my negative reactivity.

Teach me the balanced way of holding life-tensions with hope.

Expand my tolerance for ambiguity and acceptance of others just where they are, reducing my addiction to making others wrong.

Cultivate in me a skillfulness to love, using every situation and life experience as a means for growth toward your likeness.

Amen. (Peter Traben 2003)

CHAPTER 5

FIRE INSURANCE OR GOD'S KINGDOM PLAN

Your kingdom come, your will be done, on earth as it is in heaven.

—Matthew 6:10

Section 1: What Is a Christian?

Section 2: Avoiding Hell and Seeking the Kingdom of God

Section 3: Grace and Counterfeits

Section 4: Cheap Grace versus Costly Discipleship

Section 5: Parable of the Sower

Section 6: What Makes a School a Christian School?

Transformational educators follow God's lead in sharing the good news and trust God with the process of transforming lives.

As educators, our purpose is not to ensure that all students get saved so they can avoid hell (fire insurance) but to be faithful to God in seeking for His will to be done on earth as it is in heaven. Scripture tells us that much more is involved in following Christ than claiming our security in eternal life. He designed and purposed us for His kingdom work on earth.

Section 1

What Is a Christian?

A Christian is:

> Someone who has been saved? What does *saved* actually mean?

> A follower of the teachings of Jesus? Someone who does good deeds?

> A person who has said the sinner's prayer or who has been baptized?

> A good person who attends church?

> Someone who has repented of their sins?

In the New Testament, the word *Christian* is used rarely and probably as an insult (see Acts 11:26). People who were Christians referred to themselves as *brethren* (Acts 15:1; 1 Corinthians 16:20 NAS), *disciples* (Acts 11:26; 14:24 NKJV), and *saints* (Acts 9:13; 2 Corinthians 13:13 ESV). Before his conversion, Paul referred to those "who belonged to the Way" (Acts 9:2). In the book of Acts, we see the unbelieving Jews referring to Christians as those "of the Nazarene sect" (Acts 24:5).Depending on the resource used, the word Christian is used only a handful of times in the New Testament, yet, the words "in Christ" appear abundantly more (some sources say 130 times).

So if the term Christian is rarely used and "in Christ" or "in Him" is used often, it makes sense to understand the meaning of "in Christ".

Activity #5-1

Write your definition of "in Christ" based on the sampling of scripture below.

> Therefore, if anyone is in Christ, the new creation has come: The old has gone, the new is here! (2 Corinthians 5:17)

> And all are justified freely by his grace through the redemption that came by Christ Jesus. (Romans 3:24)

> He has saved us and called us to a holy life-not because of anything we have done but because of his own purpose and grace. This grace was given us in Christ Jesus before the beginning of time. (2 Timothy 1:9)

For he chose us in him before the creation of the world to be holy and blameless in his sight. (Ephesians 1:4)

For I am convinced that neither death nor life, neither angels nor demons, neither the present nor the future, nor any powers, neither height nor depth, nor anything else in all creation, will be able to separate us from the love of God that is in Christ Jesus our Lord. (Romans 8:38–39)

In him we have redemption through his blood, the forgiveness of sins, in accordance with the riches of God's grace. (Ephesians 1:7)

Activity #5-2

Try filling in the following job description template for a job called "Christian."

Job Description for a Christian

Job title:

Effective date:

Location:

Position summary:

Answers to:

Supervises:

Relates to:

Qualifications:

Responsibilities:

Questions to consider:

1. How does your understanding of "in Christ" mesh with your understanding of "Christian"?

2. What sections of the job description were difficult to fill out? Does being a Christian even lend itself to a job description? Why or why not?

3. What word do you prefer to describe yourself? A Christian? Follower of Jesus? A follower of the way? Something else?

> Christianity is not a religion that gives some people a ticket to heaven and makes them judgmental of others. Rather, it's a call to a relationship which changes all our other relationships. … Christian conversion involves more than just a destiny of the soul it involves the way we live in the world. (Wallace 2013, 4)

> For many, God is seen—and used—as a partner in our private evacuation plan more than any Love Encounter that transforms mind or liberates heart. (Rohr, Just This 2017, 17)

> Woe to you, teachers of the law and Pharisees, you hypocrites! You clean the outside of the cup and dish, but inside they are full of greed and self-indulgence. Blind Pharisee! First clean the inside of the cup and dish, and then the outside also will be clean. (Matthew 23:25, 26)

The Deadly Eight

Heather Pace was a Bible school graduate, aspiring missionary, and committed evangelist only to later believe she had missed the point; she was not a Christian. In her article titled "Don't Trust in Your Christianity" (Pace 2019), she identified eight practices listed here, which she believes may distort an understanding of the transforming relationship in Christ:

1. I said the 'sinner's prayer.

We all know a rote prayer doesn't save a soul, yet a particular prayer is often pointed to as the primary evidence of one's salvation. Prayer *is* often associated with the moment of conversion, but no matter how memorable a prayer is, salvation only occurs when wholehearted repentance and faith (Acts 20:21) is a reality in a person's heart.

2. I'm convicted when I sin.

Whether Christian or non-Christian, God's law is written on our hearts, and therefore we should feel guilty when we sin (Rom. 2:15). Even unrighteous Esau cried over the consequences of his sin (Heb. 12:17). Non-Christians often feel bad about their sin, but what we do with our conviction—that is, whether we repent and obey God—is most telling (2 Cor. 7:10).

3. I feel close with God.

Feelings are one of the most common deceivers in this day and age. What we feel is quickly elevated to the status of truth. But the truth is, we can feel a whole host of things that may or may not align with reality.

4. I'm becoming godly.
This was my most prevalent flaw: I was convinced I was saved because I was far more Christlike (and humble!) than most other people. The pre-converted apostle Paul probably felt the same way. In Philippians 3, he says if anyone had reason to trust in his own righteousness, he had more! In fact, when it came to "righteousness under the law," he was "blameless" (Phil. 3:6). As a young man, Paul would've been "godly" by today's standards—and he wasn't yet converted.

5. I pray, read the Bible, and go to church.

Prayer, Scripture reading, and church attendance are central habits for the Christian life. Yet some people who attend our churches are not saved (Matt. 13:24–30). Some taste the goodness of God's Word and have no relationship with God (Heb. 6:4–9). And non-Christians everywhere pray for any number of reasons (Matt.6:5).

6. God is blessing my life.

God kindly gives sunshine and rain to Christians and non-Christians alike (Matt. 5:45), along with a multitude of other daily blessings (James 1:17). His common grace fills our lives. Though we're right to credit God for his kindness, we can't assume his gifts imply his saving grace.

7. I've made a difference for Jesus.

Matthew 7:22–23 is abundantly clear that some who think they've done great works for the cause of Christ will be denied access into heaven. No amount of leading small groups, helping with service projects, or going on mission trips can ensure salvation. Many with such résumés will hear the Savior's chilling words: "Depart from me, I never knew you" (Matt. 7:23).

8. I know Jesus died and rose again.
This one is, by far, the most deceiving of what might be considered spiritual fruit. Agreeing with the facts of the gospel isn't equivalent to saving faith. Just think, the demons have far deeper theological understanding than do any of us, yet not one is saved (James 2:19)." (Pace 2019)

The natural result of being reconciled to God is to share this good news with others, and this experience, by its nature itself, makes us want others to know and follow Him. Call it evangelism, giving testimony to, being a witness, or whatever else; we desire for others to know and love Jesus, who has radically changed our own lives for good. We want to pass it on.

In our zeal to pass along the love of God, we can lose sight of the fact that *only the Holy Spirit can spark a soul to Christ.* As much as we desire to see students come to a relationship with Christ, this is not something we can make happen. Even upon hearing the good news from Jesus, God incarnate, some people did not receive it. In the story of the four kinds of soil (Mark 4, Matthew 13, Luke 8) Jesus told us *to expect* a variety of responses to the good news. If Jesus had people refusing His message, we should certainly expect the same when we share.

Jesus also experienced the sadness we experience when others refused him. Luke 19:41–42 tells of Jesus's lament: "As he approached Jerusalem and saw the city, he wept over it and said, 'If you, even you, had only known on this day what would bring you peace-but now it is hidden from your eyes.'"

We also know how Jesus reacted when people chose to deny Him. He let them walk away. He did not chase them, demean them, shame them, manipulate them, or scare them. From the perfect example of Jesus, not everyone will receive Him when hearing the good news, and one should not attempt to make that happen through our own means. As teachers, we realize that not all our students may respond to God through Jesus. We continue to pray and love the student without attempting to elicit salvation based on human manipulation.

What does such manipulation look like?

- *External appearance*: Insist that students follow a Christian moral code without much concern for the spiritual condition of their heart.
- *Fear*: "What happens if you die tonight? God sees and knows every thought and action you do."
- *Shame*: "How could you deny Him after all He has done for you?"
- *Chasing:* Being insensitively persistent. Not really loving the person but seeing them as an evangelistic project to be won.
- *Demean:* Loathing a specific type of sin over more acceptable sin, name-calling.
- *Lying:* Saying things as if they are in the Bible when they are not (not acknowledging common grace and God's love for all people).
- *Guilt:* "What would your grandmother think about you not being saved?"
- *Substitute "religion" for "the gospel":* This is the most challenging counterfeit and probably the most common in schools. (Section 3 explores this idea more.)

The kind of Jesus we believe in will determine the kind of Christianity we practice. (Wallace 2013, 13)

Questions to consider:

1. What do you do with your disappointment in not seeing students or colleagues commit to Christ?

2. Do any of the manipulations or distortions in sharing the gospel sound familiar?

3. Do you feel you are being more faithful in service to God if the people with whom you share the gospel receive it?

Resources to explore further:

Sermons by Tim Keller about self-salvation, https://gospelinlife.com, and Keller's book, *The Reason for God*

Christians as Teachers, What Might It Look Like? by Geoff Beech

Section 2

Avoiding Hell and Seeking the Kingdom of God

Originating in the early centuries, most likely from Greco-Roman influence, one idea of heaven and hell were adopted into Christian theology. Heaven was in the celestial realm where God and angels lived. When a person died, if he or she were truly Christian, they could knock on St. Peter's gate and be admitted into heaven. On the other hand, if they were not Christian, they would go down to a place called hell, where they would burn and suffer for eternity. A person's task in life was to secure a place in heaven and avoid hell. In other words, the goal was to obtain fire insurance against going to hell. The act of saying the sinner's prayer, being baptized, being moral, or going to church were perceived as guarantors of fire insurance.

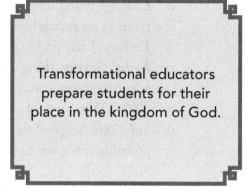

> Transformational educators prepare students for their place in the kingdom of God.

Preachers, teachers, writers, and theologians have expounded on what heaven and hell mean, and they are not in agreement. Although exploring the varying positions on heaven and hell is beyond the scope of this chapter, the *point is that transformational educators do not present the gospel as fire insurance.* Transformation is not so much what one has been saved from (hell or fire) but what one is saved for (the kingdom of God on earth and heaven).

The Kingdom of God

Jesus's numerous references to the kingdom of God or the kingdom of heaven certainly imply the foundational importance He places on this teaching. We better take note. What is the kingdom of God and what significance does it have in our lives and the lives of our students?

> "For I tell you that unless your righteousness surpasses that of the Pharisees and the teachers of the law, you will certainly not enter the kingdom of heaven." (Matthew 5:20)

> "Not everyone who says to me, 'LORD, LORD,' will enter the kingdom of heaven, but only the one who does the will of my Father who is in heaven." (Matthew 7:21)

And he said: "Truly I tell you, unless you change and become like little children, you will never enter the kingdom of heaven." (Matthew 18:3)

Then Jesus said to his disciples, "Truly I tell you; it is hard for someone who is rich to enter the kingdom of heaven." (Matthew 19:23)

Jesus replied, "Very truly I tell you, no one can see the kingdom of God unless they are born again." (John 3:3)

Jesus answered, "Very truly I tell you, no one can enter the kingdom of God unless they are born of water and the Spirit." (John 3:5)

Jesus said, "My kingdom is not of this world. If it were, my servants would fight to prevent my arrest by the Jewish leaders. But now my kingdom is from another place." (John 18:36)

From that time on Jesus began to preach, "Repent, for the kingdom of heaven has come near." (Matthew 4:17)

The kingdom of God is often mistaken to be a synonym for heaven, as in the heaven away from earth where Christians go when they are dead. (Matthew used the phrase "kingdom of heaven" because he was writing to Jews who never use the word for "God," hence substituting "heaven.") However, that is inconsistent with how Jesus referred to the kingdom of God. Jesus Himself specifically contradicts it when He says, "The kingdom of heaven is *within* you" (that is, here) and "at hand" (that is, now). It's not limited to later, such as after death.

Jesus also said His kingdom is not of this world, so it not an earthly utopia alone.

The kingdom of God is not so much a geographic place but is where God reigns. The people in God's kingdom submit to Him as King. People enter His kingdom when they become Christians. As subjects to King Jesus, our service begins during our time on earth. Our service is to pray and work toward His will on earth as it is in heaven.

Preparing Students for Their Place in the Kingdom of God

1. A significant way that teachers prepare students for their place in the kingdom of God is helping them realize that their lives are purposeful for their role in ushering in God's kingdom on earth. When we offer them a quality education, we are equipping them with skills and wisdom they will need in assuming their roles. Sanitation workers help remove unpleasant and disease-producing waste, the grocery checkout helps meet our need for food, medical personnel help heal the sick, and the creation mandate expressed in Genesis 1:28 becomes our service in God's kingdom on earth.

2. Teachers prepare their students for their roles in the kingdom of God by nurturing them as justice seekers. "The Spirit of the LORD is on me, because he has anointed me to proclaim good news to the poor. He has sent me to proclaim freedom for the prisoners and recovery of sight for the blind, to set the oppressed free" (Luke 4:18).

3. Our kingdom work is to destroy the evil one's work. Teachers inspire students toward righteous living by what they say, model, and correct in their students. They uphold this ideal of righteousness with a clear communication that it can only be obtained through Christ—not by trying to be good. "The reason the Son of God appeared was to destroy the devil's work" (1 John 3:8).

Compare the following:

Atonement-only gospel	Kingdom-of-God gospel
Profession of faith	Practice of faith
Gospel for the hereafter	Gospel for the here and now
Comfortable saved Christians	Matthew 25 Christians
You die into it	You awaken into it

Questions to consider:

1. What are ways you prepare students for their place in God's kingdom?

2. How do you differentiate a doing-good-works type of gospel from taking-your-place-in-the-work-of-the-kingdom-of-God type gospel?

Section 3

Grace and Counterfeits

> The Gospel is like a caged lion. It does not need to be
> defended; it just needs to be let out of its cage.
>
> —Charles H. Spurgeon (Pearcey 2008)

How do you react when someone says, "I try to be a Christian"? What do you think when someone answers the question, "Are you a Christian?" by saying, "Yes, I go to church." Both responses worry me in thinking the respondent may be confusing religion and the gospel. Tim Keller (Keller, Prodigal God: Belief in an Age of Skepticism 2008) talks about substituting religion for the gospel by explaining three ways that people live:

1. You follow Jesus, do His will, repent of your sins and your self-righteousness
2. You reject Jesus and do your own thing; you never repent.
3. You try to earn your own salvation by following all the rules. Your own moral behavior is your self-salvation. God is important but not as Savior. You never repent of sins or your self-righteousness. Your religion attempts to control God by good behavior and has no sense of a broken, contrite heart receiving His grace.

We are familiar with the dichotomy of #1 and #2 of Tim Keller's explanation of ways people respond, but less familiar with #3, which he refers to as "self-salvation." Do we, as Christian teachers, subtlety support the idea of self-salvation? Do we allow our students to approach God with an idea that their good deeds warrant salvation? Keller says, "That is why the Christian is in a different position from other people who are trying to be good. They hope by being good, to please God if there is one; or-if they think there is not-at least they hope to deserve approval from good men. But the Christian thinks any good he does comes from the Christ-life inside him. He does not think God will love us because we are good, but that God will make us good because he loves us ...?" (Keller 2008)

> But the Christian thinks any good he does comes from the Christ-life inside him. He does not think God will love us because we are good, but that God will make us good because he loves us ...?" (Keller 2008)

But the Christian thinks any good he does comes from the Christ-life inside him. He does not think God will love us because we are good, but that God will make us good because he loves us ...?" (Keller 2008)

As transformational educators, how do we dispel the error of self-salvation?

1. Do we inadvertently try to "socialize" students in Christian schools by using praise and correction for their behaviors without calling into question the heart attitude behind their behavior? The Holy Spirit changes people from the inside out with a heart change, manifesting in changed outward action.

2. Do we help students examine their motives? Are they serving another student just to be recognized for their good deed? Are they compliant behaviorally so they can consider themselves superior to everyone else in the class?

Self-Salvation

The prodigal son, a Bible story found in Luke 15, gives a picture of what self-salvation looks like. Read the story if you are not familiar with it. The elder brother is furious that his devotion has never led his father to honor him with a big party and fatted calf. The elder brother thought his compliance earned him a feast and resented his younger brother receiving an "undeserved" feast. In the hopes of internal, godly transformation, teachers must be willing to lovingly help the compliant or self-righteous student evaluate his or her motives.

When I served as a head of school, a teacher named Lorrie came up to me one morning after our opening assembly to apologize for being late (I had not noticed and certainly did not need an apology). Her follow-up statement grabbed my attention though. She said, "There goes my on-time self-righteousness." Lorrie indeed was always early or on time but never appeared to flaunt it. Being on time is a good quality, so her comment about being self-righteous made me pause and do some self-evaluating. For what good habits or disciplines in my life was I self-righteous? Who was I kidding with thinking my little attempts at being good carried weight before Goodness Himself?

Socialization for Classroom Management

How does the transformational educator encourage students with praise or offer consequences without conditioning students to perform for the praise or rewards?

The praise and consequences question is tricky because as teachers we definitely need to develop a classroom atmosphere where learning can take place. We liberally use consequences, praise, and a variety of classroom-management techniques to help students be respectful members of the class community. The challenge is how to do this without students mistaking "compliance because Mr. Doe needs to teach the class" with compliance because "God will withdraw His approval of me if I do not make Him love me by my good actions."

For example, the school board at a school I directed wanted to implement some rules regarding student appearance. They were targeting things such as hair color and styles, body piercings, and clothing coverage, all of which are culturally contextualized. Our school board wanted to make a statement about the message given off by certain outward appearances (in 1999 in our community, lots of body piercings, blue colored hair, tattoos, etc. tended toward antiestablishment, rebellious messages). We committed to making the rules serve as statements about conventional norms in our respective community while ensuring our students did not think blue hair was against a specific biblical mandate. It was important for our students to understand the difference between rules for convention and rules we believe follow God's design for humankind.

Most people with a high view of scripture separate the *principles* of outward appearance mentioned in the Bible (such as the need for modesty, not showing off wealth) from the culture-specific rules (such as women wearing a head covering and men not cutting their sideburns). We apply the principles in a thoughtful way, while not always viewing scripture as a manual for specific behavior in all cultures.

To make sure our students understood the difference between conventional rules and biblical principles, we had a speaker address the topic in an assembly. The speaker was the mom of a former student, a student known as a follower of Christ and a good guy. He had chosen to wear a radical hairstyle (radical for that specific time in our city) and added some body piercings. The mom shared how he was turned down for his desired job because of his look. Her son had not disobeyed God, but rather he disobeyed or did not acknowledge a convention for his community. We wanted our students to understand this difference, especially as it related to the rules we were implementing at the school.

Several times I have heard about the response of evangelist Billy Graham's wife, Ruth Graham, to the ear piercings of her grandson, Tullian Tchividjian. Tchividjian lived his teenage years in cultural rebellion. However, Mrs. Graham insightfully differentiated between his cultural rebellion, male earrings, and spiritual rebellion, which is an offense against God. In his day and culture, males wearing earrings was countercultural and a visible symbol of nonconformity. Not to be unnerved by her grandson's fashion statement, Grandmother Ruth Graham brought him a gift of new earrings when she saw him. On holidays, she selected themed ones and always searched for clever earrings that she thought he would enjoy. He knew she was not mocking him but demonstrating her love for him just as he was. Decades later, he cited this as one of the contributors to his spiritual transformation.

To extend this further, teachers should help students understand that rules or procedures, such as raising a hand before speaking, putting homework in a certain location, and being in the assigned seat when the bell rings, are not God's laws but rather norms that communities use to make life work. God *does* speak about principles such as respecting authority, honoring our parents, loving our neighbors, being modest in our appearance and behavior—but how these are accomplished varies from community to community and over time.

Questions to consider:

1. Is there a possibility that students think their classroom or school behavior has anything to do with God's love for them or their salvation?

2. Do your students understand the difference in God's law and cultural conventions?

3. How do you help your compliant or "good" students evaluate their motives and *heart* behind their good deeds?

Section 4

Cheap Grace versus Costly Discipleship

Transformational educators challenge students with both the blessing and cost of following Jesus.

Some years ago in the American Bible Belt, some Christians schools marketed themselves by promoting how many *decisions* the school could claim for a particular academic year. "Decisions" represented the hallmark of Christian schooling—the number of students praying a prayer, or often repeating a prayer that someone else dictated. Verbalizing the prayer signified that the person had been saved, and it was the minimum requirement to ensure a passage to heaven. Don't get me wrong. As a Christian myself, I believe in prayer of repentance, thanksgiving for the sacrifice of Christ, and commitment to follow Jesus. Nothing is better than students' embrace of Jesus! However, this practice of schools accumulating decisions as the premier goal of Christian education is short-sighted at best.

> Transformational teachers ensure students know that following Jesus is a costly, lifelong, live-giving commitment. Although a one-time decision or baptism is simple, the Christian journey demands everything we are and have—a demand joyfully pursued.

Why? For an assortment of reasons listed below.

1. Any focus on decisions alone promotes a very individualistic and self-centered gospel, one missing the bigger picture of *what we were saved for*. Was Christ's work on the cross just to provide us with our own earthly evacuation plan or fire insurance? Is salvation just for one's personal benefit, or is there more?

2. What is a one-minute prayer of decision? Is it a lifetime commitment to follow Christ? A quick way to appease eager teachers and parents? An impulsive response during an emotionally charged gathering? Only God really knows the substance of a decision. As we know, many students want to please the adult authority figures in their lives— maybe even making decisions and saying prayers that they know will get approval from their authorities. Could a teacher's enthusiasm and praise be the unintentional but actual reason for a student saying a prayer of decision? What we don't want to discover is that once the praise and the approval is removed, there is nothing left. Could this, as well as other practices of Christian schooling, be acts of socializing students to Christianese?

3. A one-time prayer or baptism does not ask anything in terms of real ongoing change in us.

Dietrich Bonhoeffer's classic book, *The Cost of Discipleship* (Bonhoeffer 1963), stimulates thinking about cheap grace and costly discipleship. How does one fuse the teachings about Jesus freely securing salvation for us while also applying the scripture about what being a follower of Christ demands of our lives? Bonhoeffer demonstrated with his life the truth of the words he professed. On April 9, 1945, just days before American troops liberated the POWs, the Nazis hung Bonhoeffer in Flossenburg prison.

> Cheap grace is the grace we bestow on ourselves. Cheap grace is the preaching of forgiveness without requiring repentance, baptism without church discipline, Communion without confession … Cheap grace is grace without discipleship, grace without the cross, grace without Jesus Christ, living and incarnation. (Bonhoeffer 1963)

Activity #5-3

In Luke 14, Jesus explained this idea of counting the cost of following Him. Read the scriptural passage in Luke 14 and then compare the two viewpoints presented by John Stott and "the shovel" regarding the verses in Luke. Are the two interpretations compatible? How would you explain the cost of discipleship to students?

> Large crowds were traveling with Jesus and turning to them he said: "If anyone comes to me and does not hate father and mother, wife and children, brothers and sisters—yes, even their own life—such a person cannot be my disciple. And whoever does not carry their cross and follow me cannot be my disciple.
>
> Suppose one of you wants to build a tower. Won't you first sit down and estimate the cost to see if you have enough money to complete it? For if you lay the foundation and are not able to finish it, everyone who sees it will ridicule you, saying, "This person began to build and wasn't able to finish."
>
> Or suppose a king is about to go to war against another king. Won't he first sit down and consider whether he is able with ten thousand men to oppose the one coming against him with twenty thousand? If he is not able, he will send a delegation while the other is still a long way off and will ask for terms of peace. In the same way, those of you who do not give up everything you have cannot be my disciples.
>
> Salt is good, but if it loses its saltiness, how can it be made salty again? It is fit neither for the soil nor for the manure pile; it is thrown out. (Luke 14:25–35)

John Stott wrote:

> Jesus never concealed the fact that his religion included a demand as well as an offer. Indeed, the demand was as total as the offer was free. If he offered men

his salvation, he also demanded their submission. He gave no encouragement whatever to thoughtless applicants for discipleship. He brought no pressure to bear on any inquirer. He sent irresponsible enthusiasts away empty. Luke tells of three men who either volunteered, or were invited, to follow Jesus; but no one passed the Lord's test. The rich young ruler, too, moral, earnest and attractive, who wanted eternal life on his own terms, went away sorrowful, with his riches intact but with neither life nor Christ as his possession ... The Christian landscape is strewn with the wreckage of derelict, half-built towers—the ruins of those who began to build and were unable to finish. For thousands of people still ignore Christ's warning and undertake to follow him without first pausing to reflect on the cost of doing so. The result is the great scandal of Christendom today, so called "nominal Christianity." In countries to which Christian civilization has spread, large numbers of people have covered themselves with a decent, but thin, veneer of Christianity. They have allowed themselves to become somewhat involved, enough to be respectable but not enough to be uncomfortable. Their religion is a great, soft cushion. It protects them from the hard unpleasantness of life, while changing its place and shape to suit their convenience. No wonder the cynics speak of hypocrites in the church and dismiss religion as escapism ... The message of Jesus was very different. He never lowered his standards or modified his conditions to make his call more readily acceptable. He asked his first disciples, and he has asked every disciple since, to give him their thoughtful and total commitment. (Stott 2012)

Now read the excerpt from "the shovel" ("The Great Cost to Follow Jesus" 2000):

> The whole push to "count the cost" comes from fleshly motivations because of the lack of resting in God's sufficiency. I've heard Luke 14:28 (KJV) used many times in "following Jesus" sermons.

> "For which of you, intending to build a tower, sitteth not down first, and counteth the cost, whether he have sufficient to finish it?" Luke 14:28

The amazing thing is that we overlook the obvious point that if they were to sit down and calculate the cost, they would realize that they didn't have enough to complete it! Look at the full passage and you'll see that Jesus preceded the "following Me" with taking up a cross, which would have been seen as telling them that following Him would lead to the death of those condemned by both man and God. His message to man was simple: you don't have what it takes to follow Me. This only highlights the amazing reality of God's grace toward us in making us the righteousness of God and giving us His Spirit. It is no surprise that you now want to follow Jesus!

The great cost to follow Jesus.

The comparison of John Stott and "the shovel" might elicit, "So which approach is right?" Thinking people may see a difference in these two interpretations about the cost of discipleship, sensing that both could be supported by scripture. How about the other perspectives mentioned in scripture about spiritual formation and discipleship? Some of us may be stuck in a one-size-fits-all, which really does not make sense when considering all the diversity that otherwise exists in the body of Christ. Help for this question can be found in Ken Boa's book *Conformed to His Image* (Boa 2001). The Annotated Contents identifies and gives examples of twelve biblical approaches to spiritual formation. While identifying the variation, Ken Boa challenges readers to see how all the approaches contribute to a whole picture of discipleship and to consider using approaches different from one's own tradition or comfort level. I found his identification of differing ways to pursue God found in the Bible to be clarifying and liberating. In quick summary, the twelve approaches are outlined below:

1. *Relational spirituality.* As a communion of three persons, God is a relational being. He is the originator of a personal relationship with us. And our high and holy calling is to respond to his loving initiatives. By loving God completely, we discover who and whose we are as we come to see ourselves as God sees us. In this way, we become more secure to become others-centered, and this enables us to become givers rather than grabbers.

2. *Paradigm spirituality.* This approach to spirituality centers on the radical contrasts between the temporal and eternal value systems and emphasizes the need for a paradigm shift from a cultural to a biblical way of seeing life. Experiencing our mortality can help us transfer our hope from the seen to the unseen and realize the preciousness of present opportunities. Our presuppositions shape our perspective, our perspective shapes our priorities, and our priorities shape our practice.

3. *Disciplined spirituality.* There has been a resurgence of interest in the classical disciplines of the spiritual life, and this approach stresses the benefits of these varied disciplines. At the same time, it recognizes the needed balance between radical dependence on God and personal discipline as an expression of obedience and application.

4. *Exchanged life spirituality.* The twentieth century saw the growth of an experiential approach to the spiritual life that is based on the believer's new identity in Christ. Identification with Christ in his crucifixion and resurrection (Romans 6; Galatians 2:20) means that our old life has been exchanged for the life of Christ. This approach to spirituality moves from a works to a grace orientation and from legalism to liberty because it centers on our acknowledgement that Christ's life is our life.

5. *Motivated spirituality.* People are motivated to satisfy their needs for security, significance, and fulfilment, but they turn to the wrong places to have their needs met. This approach emphasizes looking to Christ rather than the world to meet our needs. A study of scripture reveals a number of biblical motivators: fear, love and gratitude, rewards, identity, purpose and hope, and longing for God. Our task is to

be more motivated by the things God declares to be important than by the things the world says are important.

6. *Devotional spirituality.* What are the keys to loving God, and how can we cultivate a growing intimacy with him? This approach explores what it means to enjoy God and a trust in him. We gradually become conformed to what we most love and admire and are most satisfied when we seek God's pleasure above our own.

7. *Holistic spirituality.* There is a general tendency to treat Christianity as a component of life along with other components such as family, work, and finances. This compartmentalization fosters a dichotomy between the secular and the spiritual. The biblical alternative is to understand the implications of Christ's lordship in such a way that even the most mundane components of life can become expressions of the life of Christ in us.

8. *Process spirituality.* In our culture, we increasingly tend to be human doings rather than human beings. The world tells us that what we achieve and accomplish determines who we are, but the scriptures teach that who we are in Christ should be the basis of what we do. The dynamics of growth are inside out rather than outside in. This approach considers what it means to be faithful to the process of life rather than one product to the next. It also focuses an abiding in Christ and practicing his presence.

9. *Spirit-filled spirituality.* Although there are divergent views of spiritual gifts, charismatics and non-charismatics agree that until recently, the role of the Holy Spirit has been somewhat neglected as a central dynamic of the spiritual life. This approach considers how to appropriate the love, wisdom, and power of the Spirit and stresses the biblical implications of the Holy Spirit as a personal presence rather than a mere force.

10. *Warfare spirituality.* Spiritual warfare is not optional for believers in Christ. Scripture teaches and illustrates the realities of this warfare on the three fronts of the world, the flesh, and the devil. The worldly and the demonic systems are external to the believer, but they entice and provide opportunities for the flesh, which is the capacity for sin within the believer. This approach develops a biblical strategy for dealing with each of these barriers to spiritual growth.

11. *Nurturing spirituality.* The believer's highest calling in ministry is to reproduce the life of Christ in others. Reproduction takes the form of evangelism for those who do not know Christ and edification for those who do. It is important to develop a philosophy of discipleship and evangelism and view edification and evangelism as a way of life; lifestyle discipleship and evangelism are the most effective and realistic approaches to unbelievers and believers within our sphere of influence.

12. *Corporate spirituality.* We come to faith as individuals, but we grow in community. A meaningful context of encouragement, accountability, and worship is essential to spiritual maturity since this involves the others-centered use of spiritual gifts for mutual edification. This approach stressed the need for community, challenges and creators of community, the nature and purpose of the church, soul care, servant leadership, accountability, and renewal. (Boa 2001, 11-13)

The challenge for transformational educators is to display the cost of following Christ while showing the joy and privilege it is to serve our Beloved. Devotion to Christ comes willingly from His followers, although it can require self-denial, suffering, loneliness, and loss. When educators acknowledge their own suffering, loneliness, and victories in self-denial for Christ's sake, they may be inspiring their students to do likewise. Although the teacher does not want to be the object of praise, students do need to see what a transformed life looks like. A popular saying today is "you can't be what you can't see."

Another way in which I have been challenged to follow Christ when doing so feels like a hardship is to read biographies (or watch as a movie) of people who have followed Christ at great cost. I find the fortitude of their character resonates in my mind and gives me strength when I am personally challenged.

Embracing the cost of discipleship is a significant concern for the transformational educator in a world where happiness is the ultimate purpose in life. To transform the world as God intended, we as his colaborers must be ready to bear the cost.

Question to consider:

1. How has following Jesus been costly to you?

2. As a teacher, how can you inspire students to count the cost?

3. Does Ken Boa's listing of different emphases of spiritual formation resonate with what you have observed?

4. Which of Boa's descriptions of spiritual formation best fits you now? In your past? What would it take for you to try out some of the others? Which one(s) would you like to sample?

Resources:

Deitrich Bonhoeffer's *The Cost of Discipleship* (1963)

Ken Boa's *Conformed to His Image* (2001)

Section 5

The Parable of the Sower

As much as we want, we cannot transform our students by our own effort. God is blessed by our desire to see students grow in Christlikeness; He has the same desire. He has invited us to colabor, but our efforts alone are insufficient. Scripture informs us that the gospel will not take root and thrive in all who hear it.

> Transformational educators serve all their students by gladly seeking their well-being, knowing not all will come to faith.

The Parable of the Sower

Recall the story of the four types of soil or read Mark 4:1–20 where Jesus describes the seed as the Word of God. The seed is sown on four different types of soil, yielding four different outcomes. Jesus shares four outcomes of hearing the Word:

> Mark 4:15b: seed sown on a path where birds eat it. As soon as they hear the Word, Satan comes and takes away the Word sown in them.

> Mark 4:16: seed sown on rocks. Others hear the Word and immediately receive it with joy, but because they have not grown roots, they last only a short time.

> Mark 4:18: seed sown among thorns. Others hear the Word, but the worries of this world, the deceitfulness of wealth, and the desires for other things come in and choke the Word, making it unfruitful

> Mark 4:20: seed that fell on good soil. Others hear the Word, accept it, and produce a crop.

Not all who hear the good news will take root and thrive.

Don't misunderstand; reformation, not to be confused with salvation through Jesus Christ, can be serving God's world. God uses Christians and non-Christians in accomplishing His purposes. Though always asking God for complete transformation in our students, we are to be about the business of making the world a better place. Why? Two main reasons are:

- Christians serve people all over the world who may never come to faith. Jesus cared deeply about the poor, the sick, the imprisoned, and for anyone fitting the description of "the least of these" (Matthew 25:40). Jesus told us to do likewise by serving the disenfranchised, the brokenhearted, the ill, and those in prison.

- Genesis 1:28 is often referred to as the creation mandate: "God blessed them and said to them, 'Be fruitful and increase in number; fill the earth and subdue it. Rule over the fish in the sea and the birds in the sky and over every living creature that moves on the ground.'"

As transformational educators, we serve not knowing all that God intends to accomplish through us. We educate people who will make the world more like God intended, some of whom will come to faith in Christ.

Questions to consider:

1. Explain how we misappropriate the gospel when education is discounted because it is not considered *church planting*.

2. Must serving "the least of these" always include a gospel presentation?

3. Is there a difference between a not-for-profit agency and a Christian ministry serving the poor? If so, what difference is made by one or the other?

Section 6

What Makes a School a Christian School?

What makes a Christian school? A full list will vary depending on who compiles it, but the following three core characteristics will be on most lists:

- The teachers and staff are professing Christians.
- The curriculum is taught from a biblical worldview.
- Prayer, Bible reading/study, and a chapel service are scheduled.

> While shepherding students to full transformation in Christ, transformational educators create learning environments that prepare students to usher in God's kingdom on earth.

Now, imagine the Christian school classroom described in the paragraph below. The principal verifies that the three characteristics mentioned above are all applicable to this school.

The teacher is not in the classroom when the students enter on a beautiful Monday morning. Before going to their desks, which are all facing the wall around the perimeter of the room, the students drop their large homework packet of worksheets on the teacher's desk. On their desk is a new packet of worksheets for them to start. All students have the exact same packet of worksheets and are to silently work on them unless they raise their hand for the teacher to come address their question or comment. When the teacher arrives, not a word is said. He glances around the room, checking to see if any student has a question or comment, then proceeds to handle the packets on his desk to record who turned in the weekend homework. Once recorded, the homework sheets are stashed in the trash can.

What concerns you about this Christian class? Did you include any of the statements that follow? What can you add? What teacher behaviors or classroom designs do you think may contribute to a false narrative about God's story? Why?

- A late teacher misses the opportunity to greet the students as they begin the class.
- Desks facing the wall around the perimeters signals an independent, nonpersonal relationship with peers and the teacher. Basically, the interaction is only between student and teacher and is focused on academics, not interpersonal.
- Lots of homework due first thing on a Monday may work against a time for Sabbath worship, rest, and service, as well as dictate the available time for a family to interact with one another.
- Worksheets may minimize the capacity for thinking and creativity the students have as image bearers of God.

- The teacher does not exude any personal care for the students or their production of homework.
- The students missed the opportunity to learn from teacher feedback on their homework.
- Large amounts of trashed, not recycled, papers demonstrate a lack of care for the environment and lack of concern for the school budget.

What else did you conclude? Without the teacher uttering a word, what is being communicated?

One premise of transformational education is that *how* we teach, not just *what* we teach, is highly significant. The entire chapter 6 of this book is devoted to this topic.

A theme of transformational education is for students to discover how God made them to fulfill their purpose for His kingdom. This involves His kingdom on earth as well as eternity. A truly Christian school will take seriously the mandate to prepare students for the present and future life for which God will establish His kingdom on earth.

Questions to consider:

1. What would you add to the three characteristics of a Christian school listed at the beginning of this section?

2. How do you cultivate in students their purpose in God's will being done and His kingdom coming on earth?

3. Do your students think your excellent teaching is for the purpose of preparing them for their kingdom work on earth? What are some alternative interpretations? For example, to get highest test scores in the county, to get into prestigious universities, to prepare for testing? What else?

4. Does understanding that we are created by God with meaning and purpose affect a student's self-esteem and resiliency during hard times?

CLOSING PRAYER

Creator God,

praise to You God for how wonderfully You made each of Your human creatures. Thank You for valuing each of us. Help us to discern Your design and purpose and help us faithfully seek You in how to nurture each of our students according to your plan.

Amen.

CHAPTER 6

NOT JUST WHAT BUT HOW PEDAGOGY

The challenge of being a Christian who teaches is not just a matter of spotting when to say Christian things, or of being a kind person, but of figuring out what might be the "pattern of this world" to which we are conforming and being transformed.

—David Smith, 2018, 51 (D. I. Smith, On Christian Teaching: practicing faith in the classroom 2018, 51)

Ask any Christian educator about Christian teaching, and you will likely hear about biblical integration, vetted curricula, Christian worldview, and spiritual formation programs. The focus will be on *what* is taught. As David Smith (2018) points out, rarely will the discussion be about *how* the teaching is done. The focus in Christian teaching is almost exclusively on the what, ensuring that the content (the material to learn or subject matter) reflects God's story. Of course, the content is of critical significance, but knowledge alone does not transform. Even Satan had knowledge of the scriptures (Matthew 4:6). The how (pedagogy or instructional methods) should be included in the conversation of teaching Christianly. Sometimes the pedagogy, the how, has a louder voice than the content, leading to a stronger impact than that of the content. This chapter will examine how educators teach in a way that may cultivate transformation.

The transformational educator ensures that *how* they teach, and not just *what* they teach, clearly communicates God's story.

Activity #6-1, Self-Assessment

Take a moment to reflect upon the questions below regarding personal practices as a Christian and as a teacher.

1. Are our Christian beliefs the foundation for how we teach? Do our students clearly know in whom are we placing our faith?
2. Would our students know we are Christians by our love? How is the transformational educator's love for their student demonstrated in ways other than being nice and kind?
3. Is trust a hallmark of our relationship with students? Within this trust, is there a place for doubt and "I don't know" answers to questions about belief and faith?
4. How does our stance as an authority figure and our practice of classroom management reflect biblical relationships?
5. Do our questions and assignments demand that students think critically and creatively like the God whose image our students reflect?
6. Does our pedagogy and classroom management cultivate more of a community of care or individuals in competition?
7. Do we recognize and foster the unique, God-given capacity of each student to achieve their meaning and purpose in life?
8. What do we value in our schools as evidenced by whom and what we honor and award?
9. Do our instructional methods and assessments assume that all students learn and demonstrate learning in the same way, or do we recognize the God-given diversity, aptitude, and calling of each student?
10. What do we have in place to develop and respect our students as being capable and responsible for their own behavior and learning?
11. Are we cultivating passive hearers and information receivers or active doers and explorers?
12. What does our classroom arrangement, where we place ourselves during instruction, student furniture, school walls, or school entrance say about our beliefs and practices?

13. Do our communications with parents, our homework practices, and our personal attitudes respectfully acknowledge parents as responsible for their child's education and our responsibility as one delegated to us by parents?
14. Do our students believe that we treat them and perceive them as capable learners, or do they believe they are in our class as empty vessels to be filled and managed?
15. What does the signage around and inside the school communicate? Hospitality? Control? Invitation? No or don't? Welcome?

Section 1

Jesus as a Transformational Teacher

Not only was Jesus frequently referred to as "teacher," but teaching was His main activity during His ministry years on earth. People were amazed at His teaching because He taught with authority. The power of His teaching was not from the instructional techniques He used, but those methods are indeed worthy of attention because they were used by Him. As we observe how Jesus taught, we must not use scripture to defend our favorite pedagogical methods as if the Bible were a book on pedagogy but rather glean from the Master Teacher.

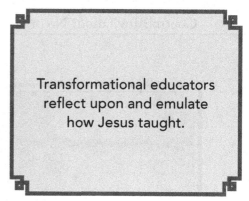

Transformational educators reflect upon and emulate how Jesus taught.

What would it look like to model how we teach after how Jesus taught? (Luke 6:40: "The student is not above the teacher, but everyone who is fully trained will be like their teacher.")

Familiar references: Jesus, the teacher, shared conventional wisdom and used references His hearers would know. He used ordinary settings and circumstances. His metaphors were easily understood. He was relevant to His students' lives.

High-order questioning: Jesus's teaching, laced with higher-order questioning, served to provoke new ways of thinking and living. Martin B. Copenhaver wrote an entire book titled *Jesus Is the Question: The 307 Questions Jesus Asked and the 3 He Answered.*

Object lessons: Jesus used object lessons to visually make a point. A few examples of the types of object lessons are found in Matthew 19, Mark 12, John 4, and John 13.

Doers, not just hearers: Jesus's teaching never ended in a paper and pencil test with knowledge being the ultimate outcome. Jesus engaged His learners in doing what he taught them. One example is in Luke 9:1–6, 10 when Jesus sent out the disciples with instructions on what to do and report back to Him.

Use of contrast and comparison: Often Jesus would use comparison to clarify His teaching, such as in Matthew 13.

Socratic method: Jesus would engage learners by having a dialogue infused with higher-order questioning.

Storytelling: Jesus told stories. Parables and aphorisms were tools He commonly used.

Modelling: Most importantly, Jesus lived what He taught. How He interacted with His learners and the people He encountered is worthy of our attention as teachers. His methods challenged students to see from new perspectives and invited changed living. Jesus was a transformational teacher.

Again, the Bible is not a pedagogical handbook, and Jesus's purpose was not to model instructional techniques. Because His whole life is worthy of emulation, it is worthwhile to notice how Jesus engaged and transformed learners.

Section 2

Content versus Pedagogy

What is the content, the subject, the material, the curriculum.

How is the way it is taught, the pedagogy, the hidden curriculum, the instructional and management strategies.

> Transformational educators search the scriptures, learn how their students learn, and ask God for wisdom in how to teach.

Most of us remember those teachers who inspired, challenged, or ministered to us in significant ways, as well as those who thwarted our spirits and questioned our value. When I was a high school junior, I distinctly remember coming alive with a teacher who made me think. He wasn't particularly nice, nor did he demonstrate a lot of warmth, but nothing could beat being affirmed by him when he thought a comment was astute. It was very exciting; I knew the class was different and loved it. Looking back, I think his method of challenging our minds and assigning us tasks that required creativity respected our God-given nature.

As a teacher, I received a gift and heart-warming message from a Hungarian student who thanked me profusely for allowing her to choose the manner of demonstrating what she learned (as opposed to the normative method of taking a test). She chose to write a book. She poured herself into this project and demonstrated not only a mastery of the material but her blossoming prowess as a writer. Her peers affirmed her, and she beamed with joy. I believe the *how* of this assessment method was transformative in her being affirmed in her God-given gift of writing. As a seventh grader, she was discovering her gifts and affinities. As a teacher, I wish I had offered such assessment options more frequently.

Do these anecdotes have any relevance to transformational education? Maybe. Although pedagogy, the method and practice of teaching, is not an overtly biblical concept (there is not a uniquely Christian way to teach, no linear connection between scripture and classroom methods, no biblical injunctions regarding pedagogy), the Bible does provide an abundance of applicable principles. Thankfully, God gave us good minds and one another to discern how to apply those principles to our teaching. As students of our students, we can learn to be sensitive to what helps our students thrive. Most of all, God gave us His grace—not a technique or self-help regime but His promise to take our lives and consecrate them to living in Christ.

There is no prescription on how to teach transformationally.

No black and white.

No blueprint.

No template.

Examine the scriptures, examine traditions, study the research, pray for discernment, receive input from colleagues, be a student of your students, reflect on your pedagogy, and trust God to direct your teaching. The amount of scripture applicable to how we teach is exhaustive. There is no way to provide the biblical underpinnings for how to teach Christianly without referencing an extremely large amount of the Bible.

Activity #6-2

Read over the few scriptural excerpts below and think about how each one is relevant to the how of your teaching. Discuss with others if possible.

> Do not let any unwholesome talk come out of your mouths, but only what is helpful for building others up according to their needs, that it may benefit those who listen. (Ephesians 4:29)

> Wounds from a friend can be trusted; but an enemy multiplies kisses. (Proverbs 27:6)

> Bear with each other and forgive one another if any of you has a grievance against someone. Forgive as the LORD forgave you. (Colossians 3:13)

> Therefore if you have any encouragement from being united with Christ, if any comfort from his love, if any common sharing in the Spirit, if any tenderness and compassion, then make my joy complete by being like-minded, having the same love, being one spirit and of one mind. Do nothing out of selfish ambition or vain conceit. Rather, in humility value others above yourselves, not looking to your own interests but each of you to the interests of the others. (Philippians 2:1–30)

> Do not merely listen to the word, and so deceive yourselves. Do what it says. (James 1:22)

> Finally, brothers and sisters, whatever is true, whatever is noble, whatever is right, whatever is pure, whatever is lovely, whatever is admirable-if anything is excellent or praiseworthy-think about such things. (Philippians 4:8)

Questions to consider:

1. Can you identify any ways that your methods may be communicating a message you really do not want communicated?

2. What has observing your students taught you about teaching?

3. Did any of the verses from activity #6-2 prompt personal reflection or possibly change in how you teach?

Resources for further exploration:

Teaching Redemptively by Donovan Graham

The First Days of School by Harry Wong

On Christian Teaching; Practicing Faith in the Classroom by David Smith

Section 3

The Hidden Curriculum

The older fish asked the younger fish, "How's the water today?" The younger fish replied, "What's water?" (from Professor David Foster Wallace speech to the graduating class at Kenyon College in 2015)

As teachers, we can become so consumed with the class that we are not cognizant of the *water* in which we teach. Things, like water to the fish, may be hidden in plain sight simply because we lack awareness. We take for granted that our assumptions about the world are, in fact, the reality for everyone. We may communicate *unintended messages* to our students. The term *hidden curriculum* references this tendency.

> Transformational educators seek feedback about and examine ways they may be inadvertently communicating unintended messages by how they teach.

Wikipedia defines hidden curriculum as: "a side effect of an education, '[lessons] which are learned but not openly intended' such as the transmission of norms, values, and beliefs conveyed in the classroom and the social environment."

The term was introduced in the late sixties when there was a national effort to address gender-role stereotyping, to racially integrate classrooms, and to see schools become avenues of eradicating poverty. During the following years, those of us in university teacher-training programs were sensitized to the many ways we implicitly reenforced traditional messages by how long we waited for students to answer questions, how we chose which student to do certain tasks, how we let stereotypes in textbooks go unchallenged, and so on. Possibly more significantly, we noted what was missing and the messages conveyed in the absence of stories with racial minorities in positions of influence, boys being nurturing, poor children as academic achievers, and such. As transformational educators, our task is to use godly discernment to identify our hidden curriculum.

What are the wrong and/or missing messages we inadvertently communicate by how we teach?

Apply this concept of a hidden curriculum to transformational education. For example:

- We teach that humans are created in the image of God but use instructional methods that squelch Godly characteristics, such as creating, thinking, caring.
- We teach that we should be the hands and feet of Jesus yet never do anything about the issues we are studying.
- Our math word problems or foreign language practice dialogues regularly communicate consumerism or tourism, missing opportunities to acquaint students with ideals such as giving, hospitality, justice, or serving.
- Our assessment practices are based on competition among students versus against a known standard or against a student's own record.

For example, what if a student participates for twelve years of Christian schooling in a Bible curriculum, which is taught on information about the Bible, and assessment is done by a paper and pencil test recall of information? The student is not asked to be any more than a "hearer of the word" (James 1:22). Essentially, the Bible is presented as information to learn, then produce on paper. The school staff may believe that they are faithfully instructing the student in the scriptures by offering twelve years of Bible class. However, the outcome of this kind of pedagogy would likely be passive students unchallenged to live out God's Word through all aspects of their lives.

Activity #6-3

Discuss with a colleague or think on your own about the hidden curriculum in response to the list below.

1. When we teach about the evils of other people's sin, but we ignore our own sin, such as gossip, pride, envy, and the idol of appearances.
2. When we consistently ignore certain school rules while demanding that our preferred rules are followed.
3. When we require students to meet deadlines but return graded work whenever we get around to it.
4. When the majority of historical topics we teach are about war and dominion.
5. When students are asked to act differently when someone is observing the class, or we act differently.
6. When we give tokens to students for complying with expectations.
7. When the teacher can have warm coffee or cold water in class but not the student.
8. When learning is centered on "Will it be on the test?"

So how do we uncover our hidden curriculum?

1. Learn about the multiple facets of students by asking, observing, and studying what may be different and what may be similar. I heard an anecdote one time about a missionary teaching the vocabulary of colors to island children. The children were mastering the language of colors until it came to the color blue. The missionary could not understand why the children could not learn this color. Years later, she realized the islanders had multiple words for blue, which, of course, did not translate in the same way to English.
2. Teachers must know themselves and reflect upon their practice in order to get a glimpse of their underlying assumptions. Humility is fundamental for this kind of authentic self-reflection.
3. Asking God to reveal our propagation of false narratives is imperative for transformational teachers. This is done by prayer and willing exposure to how other people understand scripture and live it out.
4. Participation in professional learning communities offers teachers the opportunity to build trust within a small group in a setting where they explore educational practices together.

> Pedagogy is never innocent. It is a medium which carries its own message. (Bruner 1966, 63)

Our pedagogical choices become part of a student's formation. The process of teaching becomes the content. The way we teach has repercussions. How we teach is formational, either for good or bad.

Question to consider:

1. What are some other ways that teachers can discover their hidden curriculum or the false narratives they unknowingly pass on?

2. Do you believe that people generally want to uncover their hidden biases and presuppositions? Is there anything about being a Christ follower that encourages them to do some uncovering?

Resources for further exploration:

Donovan Graham's *Teaching Redemptively*

David Smith's *On Christian Teaching, Practicing Faith in the Classroom*

WhatIfLearning.com

Section 4

Recognizing and Teaching Students as God Made Them to Be

Thankfully, trends in education are increasingly focused on the unique ways students learn and consequently are developing resources and introducing methods to assist teachers in accommodating student differences. This also applies to the unique ways students best demonstrate their learning and apply their gifts for the common good. The *what* or content of what is being taught may be the same, but *how* the student is taught and assessed honors the unique way God made the student.

> Transformational educators teach students according to divine design.

> Train up a child in the way he should go and when he is old, he will not depart from it. (Proverbs 22:6)

Garry K. Brantley (Brantley 1995) offered an interesting way to understand Proverbs 22:6.

"The phrase 'in the way he should go', in Hebrew is: 'according to the mouth of his way.' This enigmatic expression has been the subject of much scholarly discussion. Apparently, however, the phrase is an idiomatic way of referring to a child's specific personality and peculiar traits. The 'way,' therefore, does not refer to the 'straight and narrow path' mapped out by God's Word, but to the singular characteristics of each child. Parents are to inaugurate (from *hanak*, usually translated 'train') their children in the way paved by their unique dispositions."

Transformational educators seek to teach their students in a way that helps all students flourish. They do not demand uniformity in how the student learns or in what the student achieves at any given point along the academic journey. They do not hide behind the "pull yourself up by the bootstraps mentality" or use the excuse about what the student must endure in "the real world." Just as Jesus gave hope, showed mercy, healed, protected, and carried the burdens of others, so does the transformational educator.

"To guarantee fairness, we treat everyone the same. For this test, each of you will be scored on how well you climb the tree. Ready? Go!"

How can you teach students in a way that helps address individual differences and helps them all to flourish?

How is this accomplished? The answer needs to be "with God's help as best as one can." Expecting teachers to meet each learner's unique needs can be overwhelming. Simply managing a one-size-fits-all classroom is challenging enough for most teachers. Awareness, new methods, new technologies, and the will to start somewhere will move teachers toward meeting students where they are. The topics that follow are often presented in teacher-training programs as ways to meet individual student needs. The interested reader can dig through an abundance of blogs, books, sample lessons, and videos for help in implementing these topics. Warning: It is good to stretch one's craft as a teacher but not good to let the overwhelming demands suffocate or shame. Striking a balance is always the toughest part of being a growing teacher.

Use Differentiation

Carol Ann Tomlison coined the word *differentiation* to mean the practice that good teachers have intuitively done for decades, which is responsive teaching rather than one-size-fits-all teaching. It means that a teacher "proactively plans varied approaches to what students need to learn **(content),** how they will learn it **(process),** and/or how they will show what they have learned **(assessment),** in order to increase the likelihood that each student will learn as much as he or she can, as <u>efficiently</u> as possible" (Tomlison 2017). The chart that follows illustrates the variety of ways differentiation may take place. It is easy to see that entire courses could be taught, and lengthy books could be written on how to effectively differentiate instruction.

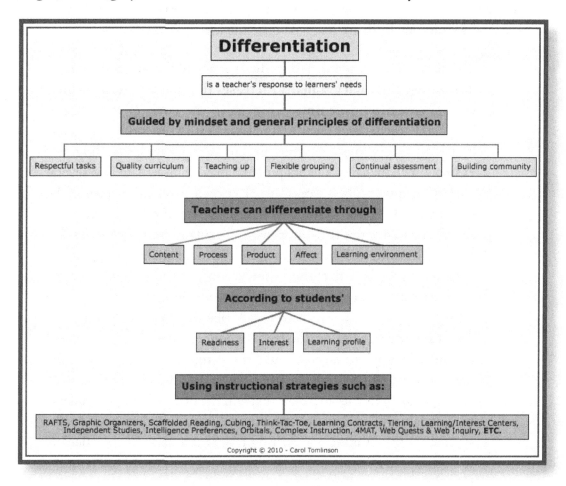

A question that often arises with differentiation is whether all students must ultimately be accountable for the same content, and if not, how does grading or promotion to the next class or graduation indicate such? The answer is as you imagine; different learning environments handle this question in various ways. Happy is the student whose progress can be measured and celebrated within the realm of how God uniquely created him or her.

Use Scaffolding

The Glossary of Education Reform (The Great School partnerships 2015) defines and lists the following examples of scaffolding:

> Scaffolding may be considered as a method of differentiation but is worth mentioning alone. It refers to a variety of instructional techniques used to move students step by step toward mastery. Scaffolding provides supports for the learner as well as breaks down a learning task into manageable tasks which add up to achieving an academic standard. A well-known example of scaffolding is the use of training wheels for learning to ride a bicycle or floatation devices to learning swimming. Both are removed once the learner is confidant.
>
> - **The teacher gives students a simplified version of a lesson, assignment, or reading, and then gradually increases the complexity, difficulty, or sophistication over time.** To achieve the goals of a particular lesson, the teacher may break up the lesson into a series of mini lessons that progressively move students toward stronger understanding. For example, a challenging algebra problem may be broken up into several parts that are taught successively. Between each mini lesson, the teacher checks to see if students have understood the concept, gives them time to practice the equations, and explains how the math skills they are learning will help them solve the more challenging problem (questioning students to check for understanding and giving them time to practice are two common scaffolding strategies). In some cases, the term *guided practice* may be used to describe this general technique
> - **The teacher describes or illustrates a concept, problem, or process in multiple ways to ensure understanding.** A teacher may orally describe a concept to students, use a PowerPoint with visual aids such as images and graphics to further explain the idea, ask several students to illustrate the concept on the SmartBoard, and then provide the students with a reading and writing task that asks them to articulate the concept in their own words. This strategy addresses the multiple ways in which students learn—e.g., visually, orally, kinesthetically, etc.—and increases the likelihood that students will understand the concept being taught.
> - **Students are given an exemplar or model of an assignment they will be asked to complete.** The teacher describes the exemplar assignment's features and why the specific elements represent high-quality work. The model provides students with a concrete example of the learning goals they are expected to achieve or the product they are expected to produce. Similarly, a teacher may also model a process—for example,

a multistep science experiment—so that students can see how it is done before they are asked to do it themselves (teachers may also ask a student to model a process for her classmates).

- **Students are given a vocabulary lesson before they read a difficult text.** The teacher reviews the words most likely to give students trouble, using metaphors, analogies, word-image associations, and other strategies to help students understand the meaning of the most difficult words they will encounter in the text. When the students then read the assignment, they will have greater confidence in their reading ability, be more interested in the content, and be more likely to comprehend and remember what they have read.

- **The teacher clearly describes the purpose of a learning activity, the directions students need to follow, and the learning goals they are expected to achieve.** The teacher may give students a handout with step-by-step instructions they should follow, or provide the scoring guide or **rubric** that will be used to evaluate and grade their work. When students know the reason why they are being asked to complete an assignment, and what they will specifically be graded on, they are more likely to understand its importance and be motivated to achieve the learning goals of the assignment. Similarly, if students clearly understand the process they need to follow, they are less likely to experience frustration or give up because they haven't fully understood what they are expected to do.

- **The teacher explicitly describes how the new lesson builds on the knowledge and skills students were taught in a previous lesson.** By connecting a new lesson to a lesson the students previously completed, the teacher shows students how the concepts and skills they already learned will help them with the new assignment or project (teachers may describe this general strategy as "building on prior knowledge" or "connecting to prior knowledge"). Similarly, the teacher may also make explicit connections between the lesson and the personal interests and experiences of the students as a way to increase understanding or engagement in the learning process. For example, a history teacher may reference a field trip to a museum during which students learned about a particular artifact related to the lesson at hand.

Incorporate Multiple Intelligences

Howard Gardner (2006), professor of education at Harvard University in the 1980s, theorized that intelligence is more than a single ability measured by an IQ test. He proposed several modalities for which people vary in their aptitudes and by which people achieve their potential.

Researchers have built on Gardner's work by adding more modalities and using it as a theory of human cognition influencing curriculum development, instructional methodology, assessment methodology, and even the definition of intelligence. It is beyond the scope of this book to teach about multiple intelligences but rather to refer teachers to the multiple applications of this theory, which can be seen as helping to create a learning environment supportive of the student flourishing we seek.

- **Verbal-Linguistic Intelligence:** Well-developed verbal skills and sensitivity to the sounds, meanings and rhythms of words.
- **Mathematical-Logical Intelligence:** The ability to think conceptually and abstractly, and the capacity to discern logical or numerical patterns.
- **Musical Intelligence:** The ability to produce and appreciate rhythm, pitch and timbre.
- **Visual-Spatial Intelligence:** The capacity to think in images and pictures, to visualize accurately and abstractly.
- **Bodily-Kinesthetic Intelligence:** The ability to control one's body movements and to handle objects skillfully.
- **Interpersonal Intelligence:** The capacity to detect and respond appropriately to the moods, motivations and desires of others.
- **Intrapersonal Intelligence:** The capacity to be self-aware and in tune with inner feelings, values, beliefs and thinking processes.
- **Naturalist Intelligence:** The ability to recognize and categorize plants, animals and other objects in nature.
- **Existential Intelligence:** The sensitivity and capacity to tackle deep questions about human existence, such as the meaning of life, why we die and how we got here. (Armstrong n.d.)

Eve Herndon (Herndon 2018) demonstrates how the multiple intelligence approach can be used:

> For example, if you're teaching or learning about the law of supply and demand in economics, you might read about it (linguistic), study mathematical formulas that express it (logical-mathematical), examine a graphic chart that illustrates the principle (spatial), observe the law in the natural world (naturalist) or in the human world of commerce (interpersonal); examine the law in terms of your own body [e.g. when you supply your body with lots of food, the hunger demand goes down; when there's very little supply, your stomach's demand for food goes way up and you get hungry] (bodily-kinesthetic and intrapersonal); and/or write a song (or find an existing song) that demonstrates the law (perhaps Dylan's "Too Much of Nothing?").

Questions to consider:

1. Explain to someone why differentiation and multiple intelligences should be in a transformational educator's repertoire of teaching skills.

2. How do the different intelligences have significance to the ways people learn about God and how they worship God?

Resources for further exploration:

Carol Tomlison's *How to Differentiate Instruction in Academically Diverse Classrooms*, 3rd edition *(2017)*

Howard Gardner's *Multiple Intelligences: New Horizons in Theory* (2006)

Section 5

Instructional Techniques Conducive to Transformation

There is no technique or method presented here that causes transformation or is the one right way to teach. The Bible offers principles and examples of teaching, but we are remiss if we imply the Bible says more than it does regarding teaching methods. You may think this unbelievable, but a few years ago, I witnessed a phonics versus whole language debate that bordered on becoming a theological debate. To offer practical ideas, the following methods and examples are given to illustrate ways to cultivate relationships and spaces for the Holy Spirit's work. Hopefully these will spark more ideas for readers.

> Transformational educators use instructional techniques that create the relationships and space that nurture transformation.

Use Wait Time

Wait time is the period of silence between the time a question is asked and the time when the student answers. In 1972, the concept of wait time was researched and introduced to the education field by Mary Budd Rowe (Rowe 1987). Essentially, she found that teachers usually allow 1.5 seconds between asking a question and getting a response. If the wait time is increased to three seconds, she found the following outcomes to be true:

- The length and correctness of student responses increases.
- The number of student's "I don't know" and "No answer" responses decrease.
- The number of volunteered, appropriate answers by larger numbers of students greatly increases.
- The scores of students on academic achievement tests tend to increase.

Why is wait time included in a repertoire of transformational pedagogies?

Wait time acknowledges that students are created with different processing times. By allowing a longer window for students to think and then join the ranks of responders to questions, the teacher is essentially honoring individual differences and demonstrating a vote of confidence that the students can respond. Wait time invites student engagement and promotes success. An important part of our work is to equip students academically so they can take their place in caring for our world. Wait time is simple to do yet profound in results.

Use Storytelling

Storytelling is likely the oldest instructional technique and is likely the one most gaining popularity now. Think about how well you remember lessons learned through storytelling and how your attention to lectures and sermons is piqued once a story gets rolling. Research qualifies this. When humans listen to a story, cortisol, dopamine, and oxytocin are released in the brain. "If we are trying to make a point stick, cortisol assists with our formulating memories. Dopamine, which helps regulate our emotional responses, keeps us engaged. When it comes to creating deeper connections with others, oxytocin is associated with empathy, an important element in building, deepening or maintaining good relationships" (Peterson 2017).

Stories allow us to vicariously experience situations and events from which we can learn without having to suffer any consequences ourselves. We gain knowledge quicker and significantly more enduring when we engage with a story. No wonder educators are increasingly seeking to add storytelling to engage their learners.

Mastery storytelling:

1. End with a positive takeaway. In the story, share what wisdom, advice or realization led to a better outcome
2. Get personal. Telling of one's own struggles and victories help the audience connect with the storyteller
3. Keep it simple. Don't try to impress with sophisticated vocabulary or too much detail.
4. Know your audience. Think through how your audience will receive your story, e.g. The president of a major Christian School organization talked about the travails of winterizing his yacht during a time of severe cutbacks in teacher pay.
5. Open with a hook. Begin the story with a "hook" which is an interesting question, problem, or incident to engage your listeners
6. Practice. Practice and get feedback from those who hear your practice
7. Use conflict and tension. Make sure your story has tensions and conflict to resolve
8. Use silence for impact. Silence draws attention to what was just said or what is about to be said (Matter n.d.)

Promote Critical Thinking

> Critical thinking is the intellectually disciplined process of actively and skilfully conceptualizing, applying, analysing, synthesizing, and/or evaluating information gathered from, or generated by, observation, experience, reflection, reasoning, or communication, as a guide to belief and action. (Scriven 1987)

Critical thinking is often the precursor of transformation. A student may have an established, personally comfortable belief (thesis). Then a contradiction to that belief (antithesis) causes confusion, discomfort, and disorientation for the student. Further reflection, experience, or communication may lead to a new or transformed belief (synthesis).

The Bible challenges believers to be critical thinkers in testing the spirit, discerning the will of God, and identifying false teaching.

> "Dear friends, do not believe every spirit, but test the spirits to see whether they are from God, because many false prophets have gone out into the world." (1 John 4:1)

> Do not conform to the pattern of this world but be transformed by the renewing of your mind. Then you will be able to test and approve what God's will is-his good, pleasing and perfect will. (Romans 12:2)

> Then we will no longer be infants, tossed back and forth by the waves, and blown here and there by every wind of teaching and by the cunning and craftiness of people in their deceitful scheming. (Ephesians 4:14)

Apply Bloom's Taxonomy

An excellent tool for ensuring that students engage in higher-level thought is Bloom's taxonomy. In the 1950s, Professor Benjamin Bloom of Harvard University introduced a hierarchy of action verbs that categorizes levels of understanding. Bloom's initial taxonomy has been tweaked over the years, so they all don't look the same. Go to your computer and search for adaptations of Bloom's Taxonomy. Select one for your personal use.

Teach someone an idea, and you help them through one puzzle; teach someone how to think, and you set them up for life. (Unknown source)

Notice that the taxonomy is developmental. Think of how a young child learns by pointing at, then naming things. Early-childhood education draws mostly on lower-level thinking skills. The pattern is similar when we begin to learn a new subject. For example, if a sixty-year-old chooses to learn cello, he or she needs to begin with the low-level skills of naming notes, observing correct handling of the bow, and so on. As those skills are mastered, the cellist then applies the reading of music to playing the cello and may even progress to composing music. The progression follows how people learn:

- Learners must *remember* a concept before *understanding* it.
- Learners must *understand* a concept before *applying* it.
- Learners must *analyse* a concept before *evaluating* it.
- And so on ...

So how can Bloom's taxonomy be used to promote higher-level thinking among students? Teachers can use the action words from whatever level of Bloom's taxonomy to write a lesson objective. The higher levels have action words that build in the critical thinking desired. As you look over the chart, think of how our image-bearing capacities (creating, valuing, discerning, etc.) tend to show up more in higher-level thinking.

Bloom's taxonomy can be used to guide instruction to the use of more high-level thinking. When writing instructional objectives, use the chart to select the levels of thinking desired.

Activity #6-4

By yourself, or if possible, in a group of four, select a movie or book you all know. Create a question about that movie or book from each level of Bloom's taxonomy. Greater familiarity with the action verbs of the taxonomy will lead to greater use of them in your lesson objective writing and in what levels of questions you ask your students. Don't be surprised if you observe more student engagement and more student pleasure in learning once they are asked to engage their minds in higher levels of thinking.

Use Project-Based Learning

> Project-Based Learning (PBL) is a model and framework of teaching and learning where students acquire content knowledge and skills in order to answer a driving question based on an authentic challenge, need, problem or concern. (What is Project Based Learning n.d.)

PBL is done cooperatively among students who direct the inquiry of the project. The teacher monitors both the inquiry and the collaborative workings within the group. The teacher ensures that students reflect upon their collaborative work with others as well as their actual process of inquiry.

Sometime PBL includes a partner from the community. When a community partner is involved, there is often a public presentation of the findings or outcomes of the project. The variety of life and work skills nurtured by PBL is noteworthy.

The research shows that PBL yields positive results in the following areas:

- Increased teacher engagement
- Improved student attendance
- Improved academic performance
- Decreased discipline issues
- Growth in Employability (21st Century) Skills

- Improved community perception and stronger partnerships
- Students discover their value and purpose in the world (What is Project Based Learning n.d.)

Use Cooperative Learning

> Cooperative Learning is an instructional arrangement that allows two to six students the opportunity to work together on a shared task in order to jointly construct their knowledge and understanding of the content. (Jacobs 1997)

Cooperative learning is one of the most researched instructional topics in the field of education. Hundreds of studies have been conducted over a wide range of age groups, a wide range of setting, such as schools, businesses, and community groups, and among various international people groups. The conclusions are consistent across a wide range of age groups and subjects.

The recurrent research results show cooperative learning yields superior results compared to other teaching methods on measures, such as:

1. Achievement
2. Self-esteem
3. Liking of school
4. Intergroup relations
5. Use of higher-lever thinking

Think about placing four students, who do not know one another and who represent the broadest diversity found in your class, in a group that will work together for six weeks. These four students will be required to cooperate for the benefit of the group. They will be seated in a desk quadrant that invites them to socialize with one another between tasks. If necessary, you will work with them on collaborative skills to further promote positive interaction among the group. Imagine how this setup could tear down prejudices, form good relationships, destroy stereotypes, and acquaint students with perspectives different from their own. So much more than academic achievement is fostered through well-managed cooperative groups.

In addition to books, the internet gives many examples of cooperative learning formats. Following is a sampling of the ones I like to use in teaching young people as well as adults.

Cooperative Learning Formats

Three-Step-Interview

Group members assign themselves the letter A, B, C, or D. Person A interviews Person B; Person C interviews Person D. After two minutes they switch so that Person B interviews Person A and Person D interviews Person C. After two minutes, each member takes a turn telling the whole group about the interview he or she conducted.

Example: Students could be assigned an insect or a historical figure to learn about and be interviewed about this insect or figure by others. Students could interview each other on what they observed on a nature walk or in a work of art.

Jigsaw

Step 1: Home Team

> Each member in a home group takes a different letter: A B C D
>
> Each member receives the corresponding reading or handout

Step 2: Form Expert Team

> Each person leaves their home group and forms a group of no more than 4 members with people from other groups who have the same letter. This is their Expert Team. Expert groups read the material, then brainstorm key points and how to present the key learning to members of their home team.

Step 3: Experts Teach Their Home Teams

> People return to their home teams. Beginning with person A, each person has three minutes to teach their piece of the puzzle to other members of their home team. They should be teaching and not reading from the handout.

Example: The teacher divides a textbook chapter into 4 sections and assigns the letter A, B, C, or D to the different sections. I did this one time as an emergency substitute in a class and found that the students enjoyed working together and the time was well spent even though I had no idea what the chapters assigned were about.

One Stay, Two Stray

The groups, each having three members, are given a task or a problem to solve. When all groups are finished, each group will send out two people (the "strayers") to learn what other groups did to accomplish the task or solve the problem. The strayers do not go to the same group. One group member (the "stayer") will remain to explain to strayers from other groups about how his or her group accomplished the task or solved the problem. After six minutes the strayers return to their home group and explain what they learned. The process can repeat with new strayers and stayers selected.

Example:

Groups are asked to create a solution to a problem which has many potential solutions. Use as a method for creative brainstorming. Ask groups to solve a math problem using several different ways of being solved.

Numbered Heads Together

Each group member takes the number 1, 2, 3, or 4. The teacher asks a question which the group discusses among themselves. The teacher calls the number 1, 2, 3, 4, and the group member with the corresponding number answers on paper or a response board on behalf of their group. Groups are motivated to ensure each member knows the correct answer because they do not know which number will be called upon to respond.

Example: reviewing information, peer-tutoring

Inside/Outside Circle

A large area is needed for this cooperative learning activity. Half the group forms a circle and faces outward. Standing directly in front of them is a classmate from the other half of the group, which forms the outside circle. After an exchange between partners, the outside circle rotates to the right so they are facing a new partner.

Example: reviewing facts, brainstorming, learning names or roles in an organization

Talking Chips

Each group member has three chips and must relinquish one chip each time they speak in the group. Once their three chips are gone, they must remain silent and let others carry the discussion.

Example: group problem-solving, brainstorming, small group discussions where reluctant speakers must speak, and overly active talkers must remain silent (Jacobs 1997)

Perform Service Learning

Service learning (like project-based learning) is an experience intentionally designed to require students to apply problem-solving skills with what they are learning in class to address a problem in their community. It is more than simply having students do random volunteer work. Teachers plan for students to conduct research about the community problem, brainstorm and research potential solutions to the problem, take action, and to reflect on and evaluate their work. Research concludes the following positive social and academic outcomes from well-executed service-learning experiences.

- attendance and dropout rates
- academic and civic engagement
- reducing youth risk behaviors
- reducing discipline problems
- school and classroom climate

For transformational educators, the heart of service learning is teaching students to be doers of God's Word and not hearers only. The challenge of service learning is avoiding the do-gooder mentality and leading students to a point of genuinely caring for those they serve. There is a difference, and if it is not clearly articulated, it could leave students with a self-satisfaction about helping someone when we are called to truly care for them. It is important for them to know why they are doing the service and to process what they glean from the experience.

Could it possibly be that Jesus's directive to care for those in need has more to do with our own condition than the condition of the needy? How does a person break out of the sense of self-sufficiency when they have never embraced the lack of control?

Students at William Carey Academy in Bangladesh conducted a large food, clothing, and toy drive for the Rohingya children affected by the attempted genocide in Myanmar. After learning about the crisis in a social studies class, the students considered a variety of responses before agreeing to conduct the drive. Embedded academic lessons included learning about the Rohingya people and their situation in Myanmar. The students learned about the political situation in Myanmar as well as how to appeal to their own government to help the displaced people. The students surveyed how they could communicate the drive and managed all the staging and transportation logistics. Mostly, they experienced the satisfaction of working together for a cause they believed in.

Parker Palmer (Palmer, The Courage to Teach, Exploring the inner landscape of a teacher's life Jossey-Bass Publishers, San Francisco, 1998 (p. 5) 1998, 5) wisely said that "Technique is what teachers use until the real teacher arrives." I think his comment goes together with the assertion that "transformed teachers are transformative." We can and should look at techniques, instructional methods, and educational practices that foster transformation, knowing that the teacher's strong sense of their identity in Christ infusing their work is at the heart of transformative work.

Questions to consider:

1. None of the instructional methods mentioned in this section are considered distinctly Christian, so why would we consider them in a handbook of transformational education?

2. What other instructional methods would you add to this collection for transformational education, and why would you add them?

Resources:

Carol Ann Tomlison, *The Differentiated Classroom, Responding to the Needs of All Learners*

Howard Gardner, any books or articles on multiple intelligences

George Jacobs, Gan Siowck Lee, Jessica Ball, *Learning Cooperative Learning Via Cooperative Learning.*

Harry Wong, *The First Days of School*

Carolyn Evertson, *Classroom Organization and Management Program*

Section 6

Assessing Learning: Doers or Hearers Only

Grading, Evaluating, Reporting, Assessing, Judging, Marking, Appraising, Feedback

Your assessment practices contribute to your students' spiritual formation! Throughout chapters of this book, the emphasis is that we seek transformation as opposed to the transmission of information. What our students experience in the way we conduct assessment speaks volumes about what it means to be an image bearer of God and a recipient of justice and grace. As transformational educators, our goal is always to instruct our students well in the academic disciplines. We measure what we value. For the most part, we cannot *see* learning, so we use assessment to measure if learning is taking place. As transformational educators, we want our students to learn much more than academic content or knowledge. We desire to see students gain in understanding, discernment, wisdom, and responsiveness to God, both now and in the future. Again, our concern in this section is not the *what* of a test or project (there are many good resources on that) but rather the *how* of assessment. Read over van Brummelen's reasons for assessment:

> Transformational educators use methods of assessment that promote learning, fairness, accountability, and action (doers of the word and not hearers only) and offer appropriate encouragement to the student.

Why Assess Learning? Why Grade Students?

- To encourage and improve student learning
- To assess the extent to which the students have met the stated learning outcomes
- To recognize achievements and diagnose learning difficulties so that students learn to build on their strengths and to overcome or cope with their weaknesses.
- To refine instruction and other learning experiences in order to improve both individual and class learning
- To help students practice and develop self-appraisal and self-understanding about their learning
- To help students set meaningful and realistic learning goals and assume responsibility for their own learning

- To communicate meaningful information to students, parents and the school authorities about student learning
- To give realistic and helpful feedback about achievement, capabilities, behavior, attitudes, and dispositions.
- To put teachers, students, and parent/guardians in touch with one another about progress over time
- To provide guidance for educational and vocational choices (Brummelen 2002)

What else would you add?

Further analysis of van Brummelen's list of reason to assess:

Notice that none of these reasons are comparative in nature, intended to motivate, impress parents, or even to equip the student for college or a superior job.

Imagine assessment as an opportunity to encourage students. What would that look like? First Thessalonians 5:11 and numerous other scriptures call on us to encourage one another. "Therefore encourage one another and build one another up, just as you are doing."

Helping students develop their God-given gifts is a major responsibility of a transformational educator. Assessment is a powerful tool in effective teaching, guiding what areas of instruction need more attention and when learners may need additional help. Students may be held accountable for lack of effort in learning on their behalf. The goal is to bring out the best in students, which sometimes means a rebuke.

Several of the listed reasons for assessment refer to helping students and their parents truly understand the aptitude and interests of the learner. The goal is understanding and fulfilling God's intended design of the student. God knows each one of His creations and purposefully made them for their individualized contributions to the kingdom.

Ranking gives the message that assessment is competitive; if others fail, then you succeed.

We read in 1 Corinthians 10:31 that all we do is meant to glorify God. This concept radically changes the value we place on tasks by giving meaning and value to anything done for His glory—a homework assignment, effort in PE, cleaning up after a meal. The value of the task is not determined by external but rather by internal desire to do all to glorify God. As stated by Van Brummelen, "The goal of learning is that students become knowledgeable, discerning, competent, and responsive disciples of Christ" (Brummelen 2002, 143).

Donovan Graham (D. L. Graham 2003, 167) challenges us that competition in grading may:

- inspire only people who think they can win
- discourage people who do not think they can win
- can lead to a breakdown of morality when winning becomes so important that any means of success is acceptable

Fairness

Nowhere does justice come alive as in a classroom when graded assignments are being returned.

Students passionately demand just and fair grading. They will compare their assignments with other students and not hesitate to have the teacher defend the assessment of their work. Demanding justice is good, although wouldn't the world be a better place if our concern was for the justice for all humankind and not just our own? Justice is a biblical principle (Zechariah 7:9, Amos 5:24, Isaiah 28:10, 13, 17, Psalm 106:3). The way a teacher dispenses fairness in assessment is a way to teach about biblical justice.

Harro van Brummelen lists some worthy implications pertinent to fairness in grading practices:

- Our grading procedures are linked to stated learning goals.
- We assess all students based on clearly defined criteria.
- Whenever possible we do not count first efforts for final grades.
- Our test content represents a fair sampling of the important learning outcomes and provides different questions for students with different strengths.
- We are willing to explain why we reached certain conclusions.
- We admit when we have made a mistake.
- Grades are a fair reflection of students' most recent performance.

Questions to consider:

1. In what ways can learning be assessed other than written tests?

2. How does the Bible speak into how we assess learning?

3. Should lower-achieving and higher-achieving students have different assessments according to their aptitudes?

4. Are graded academic tasks the only thing we report in evaluations or should we report on students' effort, other-mindedness, creativity, service to classmates, and so on?

5. How could multiple intelligences, differentiation, and Bloom's taxonomy relate to assessment practices?

Resources for further exploration:

Harro van Brummelen's *Steppingstones to Curriculum*

Donovan Graham's *Teaching Redemptively*

Section 7

Classroom Management

Some Christians rightly say that a teacher should manage a classroom well because God is a God of order, and this should be reflected in the class.

Other Christians rightly say that a teacher should manage a classroom well because the Bible teaches respect and obedience, and this should be reflected in the class.

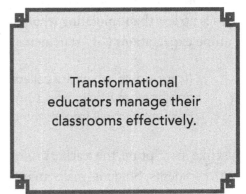

Transformational educators manage their classrooms effectively.

Without negating the above-mentioned reasons, an important reason for a teacher to manage the classroom well is to thoroughly equip students to fulfill their God-ordained roles in the creation mandate, whether it be clothing manufacturers, symphony composers, bridge constructors, food sellers, or theologians. Effective classroom management increases academic learning, so students are better equipped for their God-given work.

So to accomplish any of the above stated reasons to manage a classroom well, it should be noted that educational research consistently documents that classroom management is a major factor governing student learning. Effective classroom management leads to more time on task, which leads to higher academic achievement. *How* the teacher does this is a significant variable governing transformation.

Do not confuse classroom management with classroom discipline. Discipline is what comes after a student chooses to misbehave or not follow a directive. Research documents that effective and ineffective teachers are equally successful in administering discipline. The effectiveness stems from what happens before a student misbehaves in how the teacher manages the classroom.

What is the definition of classroom management? Note the italicized words below.

> Classroom management consists of *teacher* behaviors that produce high levels of *student involvement* in classroom activities, *minimal* amounts of student behavior that *interfere* with the teacher's or other students' work, and *efficient* use of *instructional time*. (C. E. Evertson 2013)

Carol Evertson is an educator whose name is attached to much of the best research on classroom management. She developed an excellent teacher-training program called COMP,

Classroom Organization and Management Program out Peabody College of Vanderbilt University.

Notice that a classroom-management plan is not a discipline plan.

Transformational educators have a plan in place for rules, procedures, and effective consequences. This is no less than emulating what God says in scripture with the "If … then" statements that outline expectations ("if" statements) followed by consequences ("then" statements).

> *If* my people, which are called by my name, shall humble themselves, and pray, and seek my face, and turn from their wicked ways; *then* will I hear from heaven, and will forgive their sin, and will heal their land. (2 Chronicles 7:14)

Just like in scripture, the teacher's rules, procedures, and consequences need to be communicated to the students. Students make an informed decision about whether to comply. With both the teacher and the students knowing the expectations, there will be less arbitrary discipline and more fairness in how the teacher cares for the students. Order and obedience will increase, and students' time will be efficiently used for them to learn. The definitions and examples that follow are from Carol Evertson's work with classroom management.

Goals	Rules	Procedures
• Represent desired direction of student growth • May be class wide or specific to a student	• Govern relationships with other people, time, space, and materials • Are consistent across situations and few in number	• Are the specific how-tos that show students how to follow rules • They help *routinize* everyday tasks

Have a plan in place before you begin teaching.

Teach the plan to your students. Make expectations clear.

Implement the plan with fairness and care.

Goals

We aim to reach goals knowing we may not always achieve them. Teachers give goals to students and invite students to set their own goals. While encouraging students to achieve their goals, students are not given consequences for failure to meet them.

Examples of goals:

- Accept responsibility for your own behavior.
- Honor Christ in all your relationships.
- Always do your best.
- Bring a positive attitude to class.
- Follow all directions correctly the first time.
- Think and make wise decisions.
- Develop skills for lifelong learning.

Procedures

Teachers develop procedures to make their classes run smoothly. They help organize the learning environment; hence adding efficiency to the learning process. Teachers may have many procedures and may change them, ensuring the students are taught the new procedures. When procedures are not followed, the teacher should reteach and practice the procedure with the class. For example, a school courtesy required students to be silent in the hallway to not disturb classes with the door open. When the students became chatty in the hallway, I turned them around to go back to the class, where we discussed the procedure of walking silently in the hallway. We then practiced doing it correctly. Sometimes practicing doing procedures correctly got monotonous, but practice made perfect.

Examples of topics needing procedures:

- student desk and storage cubbies/lockers
- pencil sharpener / waste basket
- shared class set of textbooks, equipment
- signal used to get the whole class attention
- how and when students may address questions and responses
- how should students behave when you or someone else is presenting information
- what students are to do when assigned work is finished
- ending the school day tasks/preparation

Rules

Rules should be taught to students and posted where they can be referred to as needed. Consequences are given when rules are not followed. The number of rules should be limited in number and should remain consistent.

Examples of elementary school rules:

- Show respect to all people.
- Respect other people's property.
- Talk at the appropriate time in the appropriate voice.
- Keep hands, feet, and objects to yourself.
- Obey all school rules.
- Come prepared for class.

Examples of secondary rules:

- Bring all needed materials to class.
- Be in your seat and ready to begin when the bell rings.
- Demonstrate respect to other people and yourself.
- Obey all school rules.
- Respect the property of others and the school.
- Speak at the appropriate times with appropriate recognition. (C. E. Evertson 2013)

Consequences

It is imperative that teachers have a plan for what happens when students choose to break a rule. The consequence should be easy for the teacher to implement (so that it is not also a punishment for the teacher) and should disrupt actual instruction as little as possible. Evertson (2013) developed a Hierarchy of Intervention Scale to guide teachers. Notice the space indicating when instruction is stopped due to the teacher intervening.

Hierarchy of Intervention by Carol Evertson

- Ignore
- Make eye contact
- Increase physical proximity
- Touch or gesture
- Involve student in an academic response

- Remind student of the rule/expectation
- Request/demand appropriate behavior
- Question student in private about the behavior
- Issue negative consequence

This handbook is giving a cursory look at classroom management, yet the importance of managing a classroom well is of utmost importance. Teachers are encouraged to read, ask for help, and observe until they feel very comfortable with how their classrooms run. Harry and Harry and Rosemary Wong's book, *The First Days of School*, Michael Linsin's work on classroom management, and anything by Carol Evertson on classroom management are highly encouraged.

These elements of a classroom management plan are necessary but not sufficient in cultivating a transformational classroom. Why? Because teachers still have the risk of eliciting outward conformity to biblical standards and validating students on their good behavior when the student's behavior is not transformed by the gospel but by the transaction of sufficient pats on the back or words of praise.

The benefits of a well-run classroom are more academic achievement, more peace and calm, more predictability, and better relationships.

One last thing that some teachers taught me:

Name in the Heart

Most praise goes to the student who achieves the highest or best based on some preset standard, such as number of correct answers on a test, or number of basketball rebounds, or compliance with classroom rules. But what if the standard is not a preset standard for the entire class or team but rather a personal achievement toward a student's unique goal? How can teachers honor those students? One effective way for younger students is to draw a heart shape on the board and write their name in the heart. Call attention to the student and explain to the class what the student achieved and why it is important. The other students can join in the celebration of this student's achievement.

In addition to honoring the student who may never receive praise for meeting standards, it implicitly teaches that each student has personal goals to work on based on their individual strengths and weaknesses.

Questions to consider:

1. Is there a difference between managing a class and caring for a class? If so, explain the difference.

2. How is giving consequences different from shaming a student?

3. Should discipline be different for a repentant student?

4. How could you apply the *name in the heart* to an older or adult group of students?

Resources for further exploration:

Any of Carol Evertson's work

CLOSING PRAYER

Most Holy God,

thank You for our privilege to teach and thank You
for the students entrusted to our care.

Your ways are way above our ways, so we come to You, the
perfect Teacher, asking for help in how we teach.

May our interactions and methods be used by Your
Spirit in drawing all students to You.

Transform us to become more transformational as educators.

We pray in the strong name of Jesus.

Amen.

CHAPTER 7

THE STUDENT: IMAGE BEARER OR MASS OF TISSUE

"Fear not, for I have redeemed you; I have
summoned you by name, you are mine."

—Isaiah 43:1

Objects to be manipulated. Little adults? *Tabla rasa*? Pavlov's dogs? Image bearers of God?

> You can't teach without assuming some vision of what a person is. And it matters what vision you assume, because your learners learn what they are as learners by the ways that you teach them. That is the mystery and responsibility of being a teacher. I suggest that our responsibility as Christian teachers is to find the courage and the insight needed to live not as those who add devotional decorations to otherwise unmodified teaching processes, but as those who design teaching out of a vision of learners that combines theological depth and spiritual engagement. (David Smith 2009)

In the quote above, David Smith challenges transformational educators to have a biblically informed vision of who students are so that the way we teach affirms who God designed them to be. In his book *Teaching Redemptively*, Donovan Graham says that the process of teaching often becomes the content. How we teach becomes a message to the student (D. Graham 2003).

What are the ramifications of viewing the child as:

- an empty mind that is filled up by the parent or teacher correctly socializing the child?
- someone who is both a sinner and a beloved person created in the image of God, therefore benefitting from both the nurture and discipline of a teacher?
- a blank slate upon which the student's environment writes the script of what they become?
- someone who is born evil with their parents' job being to save their soul?
- someone who responds to stimuli and should be conditioned to give the right responses?
- someone who is perfect in their natural state, so adults simply need to get out of the way and let the student's innate goodness blossom?
- someone who constructs meaning of their world as they actively engage it?

A biblical view of the children holds that they are born with a sinful nature but still are image bearers of God, albeit marred image bearers. They tend to do evil but also have a capacity to accept correction, repent, and reflect God's character. This view applies to all people throughout life, not just children. Both the transformational educator's view of personhood and their understanding of the responsibility of teaching serve as a conduit for transformation.

Topics in the chapter include:

Section 1: God's Beloved Children

Section 2: Made in the Image of God

Section 3: Children Are Born with a Sinful Nature

Section 4: Repentance and Reconciliation

Section 5: Unlocking Who the Student Is Made to Be

Section 6: Teaching with the Student's Age in Mind

Section 1

God's Beloved Children

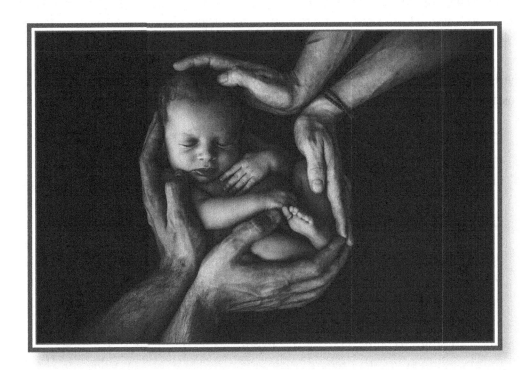

"See what kind of love the Father has given to us, that we should be called children of God; and so we are." (1 John 3:1)

But God put his love on the line for us by offering his Son in sacrificial death while we were of no use whatever to him. (Romans 5:8)

But now, this is what the Lord says—he who created you, O Jacob, he who formed you, O Israel: "Fear not, for I have redeemed you; I have summoned you by name, you are mine." (Isaiah 43:1)

Do this: Write out Isaiah 43:1, replacing "O Jacob" and "O Israel" with your name. How does your understanding of this verse change when you imagine God is talking directly to you?

Psychologists and researchers reveal what students of the Bible have known all along. The well-known psychologist Carl Rogers contributed the theory of unconditional positive regard to the field of counseling. Essentially this theory states that people must receive

> Transformational educators give testimony to the fact they and their students are beloved children of God.

what they construe as unconditional positive regard from their therapist or significant people in their life in order to develop normally. This sounds familiar, does it not? God introduced unconditional positive regard through the sacrifice of His Son. "But God demonstrates His own love toward us, in that while we were yet sinners, Christ died for us" (Romans 5:8). The Bible tells us that when the Spirit of God enters someone, their spirit cries out, "Abba Father." A person born of God loves God. Transformational educators imitate Christ by demonstrating unconditional positive regard to their students.

Dr. Sharie Stines (Stines 2015) explains the subtlety of unconditional positive regard by comparing two positive interactions: unconditional positive regard and conditional positive regard:

> Conditional positive regard leads to contingent interaction. For instance, statements like the following show contingent interactions: "Wow, you got an A on your paper, I'm really proud of you!" or, "You did a great job painting that wall." Think about how statements like this feel to you. They are positive and probably feel really good to hear, but they are based on performance.

> Now, here are some examples of non-contingent interactions: "How is your mother doing?" Or, "What do you do for fun?" How do these questions make you feel? Which types of interactions do you think will increase the level of connection within your relationships? Contingent interactions are performance based and lead to conditional positive regard. Non-contingent interactions lead to unconditional positive regard because you are showing you value someone just because. They don't have to earn it. This helps people feel good around you because they know they are emotionally safe and that you care about them whether or not they perform. (Stines 2015)

Both types of interactions have a place in the instructional setting. God gave commandments, and teachers have rules. In scripture, God clearly says what pleases Him, and teachers affirm students based on their academic and behavioral performance. Contingent positive regard has a significant role in the formation of student lives. But the point of unconditional positive regard is that the root of our love and care for a student is not their performance. We may discipline and correct a student but not in a way that distracts from the unconditional acceptance and care of the student. Scripture asserts that God disciplines those He loves (Hebrews 12:6). Transformational educators ensure that God's unconditional positive regard is the foundation of their relationship with students.

Dr. Stine offers some ideas for developing unconditional positive regard with the students you teach:

- Develop a sense of humor
- Encourage the other person to talk

- Show interest
- Be available
- Know their names
- Know their interests
- Share yourself authentically (self-disclosure)
- Pay attention
- Make space for emotional safety
- Make eye contact
- Listen
- Slow down
- Use authentic praise

To this list by Dr. Stine, I would add confronting students honestly when their work or behavior is subpar. This communicates a respect for the student and expectations regarding the quality of work or behavior of which they are capable.

Questions to consider:

1. Name ways that you help students know they are beloved children of God.

2. Have you ever felt the difference of someone showing you unconditional positive regard versus conditional positive regard?

Resources for further exploration:

You Are Mine by Max Lucado (an illustrated children's book but applicable for all ages)

Section 2

Students Are Made in the Image of God

So *God created man in his own image*, in the image of God he created him; male and female he created them. (Genesis 1:27)

Whoever sheds the blood of man, by man shall his blood be shed, for *God made man in his own image*. (Genesis 9:6)

And to put on the new self, *created after the likeness of God* in true righteousness and holiness. (Ephesians 4:24)

But no human being can tame the tongue. It is a restless evil, full of deadly poison. With it we bless our Lord and Father, and with it we curse *people who are made in the likeness of God*. (James 3:8–10)

Made in the image of God? What does this mean?

Most importantly, what does it have to do with how we teach?

One of the principle tenets of the Judeo-Christian worldview is that God created human beings in His image. This foundational doctrine is embedded in the creation story found in the first chapter of Genesis. Unique in this regard among all of God's creation,

> Transformational educators recognize and treat students as people made in the image of God.

they were endowed with dignity, worth, moral capacity, and responsibility. God declared His image bearers to be "very good," and it was a designation humans had until the sins of pride and disobedience entered the created order. Human history is the history of God's redemption of His marred image bearers. How does this central teaching impact education and learning? The Bible indicates there are many ways including the following:

- We are *personal* beings. We are created as unique beings by a personal God. While humanity has common characteristics, no two people are alike. Since everyone is stamped with the image of God, each human life has significance before God.
- We are *creative* beings. God is the Creator and made us with the capacity to also create (Exodus 35:31–32). Our work is for His glory and pleasure.
- We are *spiritual* beings, created with an awareness of God. We are created to represent and worship our God who is Spirit. We are a living soul and relate to God as a spiritual being, even if it is to deny Him. As spiritual beings, we never die but live forever.

- We are *moral* beings. God is holy and created us with a moral compass. Our conscience may be deadened by sin, but it remains hardwired in people. Our moral capacity makes us accountable to God for our thoughts and actions.
- We are *relational* beings. God created us with the capacity to relate both to God and to others. Humans were not made to live in isolated individualism. The image of God is involved in how we relate to God and to one another.
- We are *rational* beings. God created us with the capacity to think, to know, and to learn, just as He does. Christianity is not a mindless faith. The intellectual aspect of *imago Dei* means that our minds are a vital part of how we are to love God (Matthew 22:37), that we are to cultivate our minds (Ephesians 4:23), and that we are to renew our minds for transformation (Romans 12:2).
- We are *emotional* beings. We are made in the likeness of God, who Himself is love. It is the emotive facet of our makeup that allows us to experience intimacy with those close to us, to feel compassion for others, and to know the deep awe of God that causes us to delight and find soul satisfaction in Him.
- We are *creative* beings. God is the Creator. His glory is displayed in His creation. We have an insatiable desire to create, although our creativity is different from God's, who made everything from nothing.

Activity #7-1

Directions: Match one of the following practices of a transformational educator to one of the ways humans are like God mentioned above

1. Transformational educators create spaces to worship, reflect, repent, and be in awe of God.

2. The transformational educator requires critical thinking to help students mature in discernment, understanding, and wisdom.

3. The transformational educator allows time for students to ponder the goodness of God. Awe, gratitude, thanksgiving, and their love for God are welcomed and not stifled. A penitent student is not told, "It's OK," but is allowed to grieve their offence to God.

4. The transformational educator values the individual person as God uniquely made them to be.

5. The transformational educator encourages students to generate products reflective of their own originality.

6. The transformational educator creates as classroom milieu that fosters students and teachers being known and knowing one another. In a variety of ways, the students understand that when it is done unto the least of these, it is done unto Jesus.

7. The transformational educator fosters demonstrations of intimacy with God and others. Concern for others and expression of feelings is welcomed.

8. The transformational educator helps students recognize and comply with right and wrong. Admitting wrongdoing, asking forgiveness, seeking reconciliation, and restoration are practiced in the educational setting.

Questions to consider:

1. As teachers, how do we cultivate a recognition and respect in our students for the fact that all people are made in the image of God?

2. Reflect upon a time when, as a result of your lesson, students were in awe of what God has made.

3. Have you ever had a student thank you for not accepting their subpar work?

Resources for further exploration:

Francis Collins's *The Language of God* (2006)

Section 3

Children Are Born with a Sinful Nature

Someone said that the reason we discipline our dogs is so we can love them. Sounds profoundly unbiblical and transactional instead of the unconditional love we aspire to in our human relationships. But I admit the statement has much truth ... and not just for dogs but for our children too. Undisciplined children are simply not pleasant to be around. God gives wisdom to parents and those in authority who seek wisdom in disciplining children.

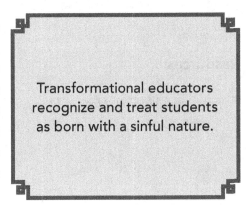

Transformational educators recognize and treat students as born with a sinful nature.

Why would a parent who is older, wiser, stronger, and more resourced choose to tolerate their child's rebellion, disrespect, disobedience, and defiance?

a) They don't know what to do about the child's behavior.
b) They have a mistaken view/understanding of the role of the child and the parent.
c) They are too tired and/or busy to take the action they know is needed.
d) They fear losing the child's affection.
e) They feel sorry for the child and feel permissiveness somehow makes up for the child's misfortune.
f) What other reasons?

Consider the teacher's role in the life of a child. Parents have a responsibility to educate their child. While they cannot set aside this God-given responsibility, they can and do share it with teachers in a delegated fashion. Do teachers also struggle with the same dilemma of how to love and discipline a child? Are there teachers who do not particularly like a student because of the student's behavior? We know that teachers are leaving the teaching profession in unprecedented numbers in the US and abroad because of disruptive student misbehavior.

While being image bearers of God, our students (and, of course, ourselves) are sinners. It's a paradox; we are created in the likeness of God yet are so unlike God in our sinful attitudes and behaviors. As Romans 3:23 reminds us, "all have sinned and fallen short of the glory of God." When teachers understand that students are "little bundles of sin, made in the image of God," they will be ready to correct, discipline, and nurture the image bearing capacity of the student, even knowing that their discipline is a way of loving the student.

Questions to consider:

1. Do you truly believe in the power of the gospel to transform a sinful nature? What of your sinful nature has been transformed?

2. What would your students say is the reason you correct and discipline them?

Resources:

Scorners and Mockers: How to Dampen Their Influence in Your School by Rick Horne

Section 4

Repentance and Reconciliation

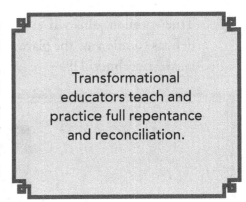

Repentance, forgiveness, and reconciliation are at the core of transformation. It is indeed a powerful and Spirit-laden experience to repent, to receive forgiveness, and to be reconciled to another. I personally and intimately experience God's pleasure when practicing forgiveness and reconciliation and believe such is very close to His heart. The following practices I derived from other sources through the years and incorporated into practice of repentance and reconciliation:

> Transformational educators teach and practice full repentance and reconciliation.

- When I know I have sinned against another person, I must prepare myself to be reconciled. Sometimes this may involve help from a wise person, extra time in meditation and prayer, or reading.
- In confession, it's important to identify specifically what I did and how it affected the person. The apology is not "sorry you were hurt" but confessing that my actions caused the hurt.
- If there are witnesses to the offense, I need to confess in front of them or make sure they are aware of my confession. This may mean that I ask forgiveness from one student while the class is listening because the class was present when I offended the one.
- If my confession to the person will in any way cause more harm to them, then I must put their need in front of my own and not go to them. It must be victim centered, not me centered.
- When approaching other people in repentance, I must not expect them to confess their contribution to the problem or expect them to forgive me. I am taking responsibility for my sin without any expectations from them.
- Repentance involves restitution, which serves as a concrete indication of a willingness to make things right. Restitution may involve my finances, my time, my reputation, or whatever amends are necessary.
- I know I have truly repented when I can commit the same offense again and don't, and I don't even want to because my heart has been changed.

Questions to consider:

1. What practices would you add to the list above? Do you disagree with any of them?

2. How are humility and forgiveness related? Or are they related?

Section 5

Unlocking Who God Made the Student to Be

True vocation joins self and service, as Frederick Buechner asserts when he defines vocation as "the place where your deep gladness meets the world's deep need. (Buechner, 119)

The Dream Team

What kind of work do think God made you to do instead of what do you want to be when you grown up?

At the school I directed were three kindergarten teachers and a teacher's aide who were so awesome that I eventually started referring to them as the dream team. They were not your stereotypical bubbly, fresh-from-college kindergarten teachers but rather mature women who, while being superb teachers of five-year-olds, were especially gifted at sharing their wisdom, care, and support with parents of their students. I had one friend who said she volunteered in the class each week just so she could observe and learn about being a godly parent from her child's kindergarten teacher. These teachers saw their ministry as wider than the education of five-year olds; they ministered to everyone God put in their path.

> The transformational educator's work is unlocking the image of Christ in each student to become all God intended him or her to be.

One time when visiting a kindergarten class, I observed the teacher interviewing the child of the day. The child of the day was determined by a rotating schedule (everyone had a turn at it) and had special privileges during the day, such as being the line leader and currier for messages to the office. As part of the morning meeting, the teacher called the child of the day to the front of the class and interviewed the child so the classmates could know more about him or her. One interview question hit me as simple but quite profound. She asked the child, "What kind of work do you think God may have created you to do?" This wording replaced the usual question of "What do you want to be when you grow up?" The implications of her wording of the question hit me on a several levels:

Implied: The child belonged to God and had his or her identity in *belonging to God* versus raising children with no grand sense of identity or belonging. It chips away at the "I am alone and meaningless," a perspective that is wreaking havoc on the Western society.

Implied: God creates people with a bent toward different gifts and interests for His purpose versus children not seeing their unique creation with a purpose.

Implied: An expectation to work. God designed work/occupation. It was present before the Fall, as Adam and Eve had the privileged occupation of tending the garden. Being a homemaker, a financial manager, teacher, a student, a salesperson, a caretaker for the elderly, all these are from and for God. Work is not the bad stuff that you have to do when you can't play video games, watch TV, or play soccer.

Implied: Education is not just for the future, as if students are passively in training for eighteen years, then suddenly expected to become active followers of Jesus in all areas of their lives.

By observing and getting to know their students, transformational educators help students imagine how God made them and for what purposes. Cultivation is a descriptive word for this process. Through reflection and listening prayer, teachers will be instruments in helping students uncover their God-ordained lives.

More about instructional methods that help unlock how God made the student can be found in section 5 of chapter 6.

Questions to consider:

1. When and how did you know that God created you as an educator?

2. What practices do you do that help students realize God's purposes for their lives?

3. What effect does a having a Christian identity have on meaning and purpose in life?

Section 6

Teaching with a Student's Age in Mind

Although research into childhood development is extensive and comprehensive, especially in the cognitive, social-emotional, and physical domains, comparatively less research exists in the area of moral and spiritual development. Just as a teacher would not teach quadratic equations in a kindergarten math curriculum, neither would she teach that same class about the complexities of the Holy Trinity in Bible class. Young students can amuse us with their misunderstanding of the Bible, and they can also astound us with their astute spiritual insights.

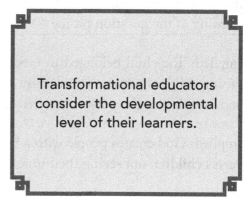

Transformational educators consider the developmental level of their learners.

Terri asked her Sunday school class to draw pictures of their favorite Bible stories. She was puzzled by Kyle's picture, which showed four people on an airplane, so she asked him which story it was meant to represent.

"The flight to Egypt," said Kyle.

"I see. And that must be Mary, Joseph, and baby Jesus," Miss Terri said. "But who's the fourth person?"

"Oh, that's Pontius, the pilot." [6]

Just as theorist have chartered stages of cognitive, moral, language, physical, socioemotional development, James Fowler described a stage theory for spiritual development. In his 1981 book *Stages of Faith*, James W. Fowler developed a theory of six stages that people go through as their faith matures. The basic theory can be applied not only to those in traditional faiths but also those who follow alternative spiritualities or secular worldviews.

Children are innately spiritual. I believe this from scripture and from observation. Children are not empty vessels needing to be filled by adult religious instruction. Likewise, adult students without much religious training aren't spiritually void either. They often have astute observations, and their questions can drive straight to the core of meaning and value in our faith.

We intuitively know when teaching the young learner the story of creation, of Noah's ark, of Jonah in the belly of a fish, that to include the scientific arguments about origins, or processing with them the ethics of mass drownings during the flood, or the angst of similar stories in other cultures about a man being swallowed and regurgitated by a fish is simply not developmentally appropriate or necessary.

At the same time, we do not want to leave our learners at the developmental level of a six-year-old when they question the clues pointing to different origin accounts, discover stories similar to the Bible in ancient literature, or contemplate the ethics of several biblical accounts that cast God as committing genocide. They can be the beginning of significant faith issues if covered over or tamed into submission. Cognitive development opens different needs in the adolescent and older student. The Bible can raise some difficult dilemmas. Current Christianity is relying upon a rationalism that demands airtight constructs. It has not always been this way. Christian faith through the centuries has engaged doubt and questions as part of a deep and meaningful faith. It is imperative that teachers engage the students' questions and doubt, even if it involves doing research together with the teacher or acknowledging, "I do not know the answer to your question."

The Bible Invoking Wonder

Imagine a circle of children sitting on the floor and a storyteller sitting among them with quality props made from natural materials to accompany the story. Without a lot of manufactured excitement or introduction, the storyteller begins the storytelling by using the props to create curiosity, frequently saying, "I wonder …" The story is then told, almost verbatim from modern language scripture, with the props serving as a significant aid to the storytelling. Once complete, a period of silence allows the children to contemplate. Instead of a series of binary questions hammering home a moralistic lesson for which the children must parrot an answer; the storyteller initiates a series of more "I wonder" questions and statements. The wondering questions may be concrete, such as "I wonder what would have happened if …" or as open-ended as "I wonder what causes you fear." After the storytelling and open discussion, the children are invited to do whatever they need to do with the story. A feast (usually juice and crackers) follows with the adults and children talking among themselves. After the feast, the children are dismissed to make choices about what to do with the art supplies, props from other Bible stories, dress-up costumes, books, and so on. This description is from a program called *Godly Play*. There are teachers and programs like it by other names or no name at all. It addresses six aspects of children's spiritual development:

Nye (2009) proposed six conditions that nurture relational consciousness in programs of spiritual formation for children: space, process, imagination, relationship, intimacy, and trust.

1. Space. Nye proposed that the space (the physical, emotional, and auditory space) in which the nurture of relational consciousness takes place is important for communicating a sense of value for spirituality, for the children in the space, and for the relationships they are building with the teacher, their peers, and with God.

2. Process. In order for relational consciousness to flourish, Nye proposed there must be a focus on process as opposed to product.

3. Imagination. In order for relational consciousness to flourish, Nye proposed that children need to be encouraged to use their imaginative faculties.

4. Relationship. Relational consciousness as defined by Hay and Nye (2006) is rooted in relationships, so it follows that attending to relationships must be an explicit part of its nurture.

5. Intimacy. Nye proposed that in order to experience and express relational consciousness, intimacy is required.

6. Trust. Trust is defined in this context by Nye as less about the kind of trust needed for intimacy and more about the trust the adult leader has for the children and for spirituality.

Must you always have an answer?

> A huge trust is bestowed on teachers by parents of younger learners and by the trust of all learners. The norm is for teachers to present the Bible according to what is wise in their own eyes. And most people would say, of course a teacher would present the Bible according to how he or she understands the Bible to be. I doubt anything written here can change that, so another approach is to pose some questions that students ask for which transformational teachers need to be equipped to engage with students ... notice I did not say "answer." I did not say questions which transformational teachers need to be able to answer because, quite frankly, teachers may not be able to answer some questions with integrity. The teacher may need to respond with a simple, "I do not know the answer to that question" or "I am wrestling with that myself." *A transformational teacher must be the safest of all people for a learner to entrust spiritual questions and admit doubt.* Contrary to our current practice of Christianity where "certainty" is lauded and having the answer to defend the faith (apologetics) is a required course in Christian schools, a historic glance at our faith did not demand certainty. (Enns)

Questions to consider:

1. Do the stage theories reflect biblical truth or not? Do stage theories account for the cycles that some people have in their faith?

2. Do you think transformation and the spiritual developmental stages are related? If so, how?

3. How do you interface with the student with significant doubts or unbelief? Are you a safe person with whom to discuss these doubts? Would your student feel rejected if he or she announced atheism?

Resources:

Children's Spiritually: What It Is and Why It Matters by Rebecca Nye (Church House Publishing, UK)

Godly Play: https://www.godlyplayfoundation.org/

Journal: what, if anything, from studying this chapter will you embrace or incorporate?

CLOSING PRAYER

Beloved Father,

Thank You for making us educators, and thank You for the students entrusted to our care. Help us love our students the way You love us. Help us see them as You see them. Equip us to effectively teach them according to the way You made them and with sensitivity to their age. May they bow down before You as their Lord and Savior and live an abundant life.

CHAPTER 8

SACRED WOUNDS OR MEANINGLESS SCARS

The Lord gave and the Lord has taken away; may
the name of the Lord be praised.

—Job 1:21

In a Barna research study, a cross-section of Americans were asked, "If you could ask God one question and knew he would give you an answer, what would you ask?" More than any other question, they answered, "Why is there so much pain and suffering?" (OmniPoll 1999).

The common rationale is:

- God is all-loving, so God loves us.
- Authentic love seeks the good of those who are loved.
- Suffering is not good; therefore, God does not want us to suffer.

> The transformational educator prepares students for and shepherds students through suffering.

Or another version:

- God is all-powerful.
- God can prevent, reverse, or destroy whatever causes us to suffer.
- Therefore, God would not allow us to suffer.

Or the Epicurean paradox:

Is God willing to prevent evil, but not able?
Then he is not omnipotent.
Is he able, but not willing?
Then he is malevolent.
Is he both able and willing?
Then whence cometh evil?
Is he neither able nor willing?
Then why call him God?

Or for the current audience:

If God is all powerful, he cannot be all good. And if he's all good, then he cannot be all powerful. (*Batman v. Superman: Dawn of Justice*)

The question of God and suffering is indeed a troubling question and one that derails many churched people when faced with a crisis. This theme is one of the most important for educators to prepare for when cultivating ground for transformation. The essential question is, will suffering result in despair and a meaningless scar on life, or will it be a wound that transforms so positively that it is considered sacred?

Unfortunately, answers such as the ones that follow are not helpful:

- "God wanted another angel in heaven."
- "God takes the best for Himself."
- "Only the good die young."

When people make such comments, I think they're trying to express that God is at work in our lives, that God guides us and is leading us along the way. Unfortunately, this language can also represent God as cruel, as one who inflicts pain on His own creation for His personal benefit. Nothing could be further from the truth about God's character.

There is much our students need to understand about suffering and God's character. Are we preparing them for their dark moments? Are we preparing them "to offer comfort to those in any trouble with the comfort we ourselves have received from God" (2 Corinthians 1:3–4)?

Transformational educators cultivate a theology of suffering that equips students to expect suffering, to trust God while walking through it, and to be transformed by suffering.

Questions to consider:

1. Have you ever addressed a student questioning why God allows (or causes) suffering? If so, what did you say?

2. As a sufferer yourself, what did people say or do that you found to be unhelpful or irritating?

3. Why do you think a chapter on suffering is included in a handbook about transformational education?

Section 1

Suffering Is Real

This chapter uses suffering as a broad term for all kinds of pain, disappointment, adversity, grief, and trauma. Think about all the things that cause people to suffer. We all know someone personally who has suffered in one or more ways, with that person sometimes being us. "In Christ"—that's our identity, and it is marked by our participation in suffering.

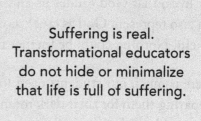

Suffering is real.
Transformational educators do not hide or minimalize that life is full of suffering.

Look at the list of types of suffering and think of any others not listed. Think of ways in which you or someone you know has been transformed in some way by suffering.

- death
- unplanned pregnancy
- miscarriage
- addiction
- broken relationship
- bullied
- divorce
- accident
- being deceived
- natural disaster
- persecution
- terminal illness
- hunger
- rape
- failure
- handicapping
- sickness
- injury
- poverty
- loneliness
- role or identity change
- pet dying or disappearing
- dashed dreams
- infertility

- suicide of a loved one
- child disappoints you
- dark night of the soul
- loss of a job or business
- imprisonment of a loved one
- spiritual deconstruction
- war
- separation from a loved one for a length of time
- being violated
- loss
- financial ruin
- betrayal
- mental illness
- captivity

A disheartening task would be to look at the statistics on the types of suffering listed above for children, for teens, and for adults. Of course, the stats would differ from country to country—contrasting, among other things, the nature of first world and third world suffering. Transformational educators, with consideration given to the age and region of their students, seek to be equipped by learning about the signs, resources, and interventions for the suffering they will encounter. Teachers in West Africa may emphasize training in how to work with traumatized children, whereas teachers in northwest United States may emphasize suicide prevention. Although the signs, resources, and interventions may differ by region and age, the fundamental biblical understanding remains constant.

Suffering Starts Early in Life

The urge to protect children from experiencing or being exposed to others' suffering is probably universal. Unfortunately, even young people encounter pain and disappointment and can benefit from teachers who comfort them as well as help shape their understanding of suffering.

- Grandparents die.
- Parents fight and sometimes divorce.
- Beloved pets die.
- Children are not spared suffering even when adults choose to not address it.

Preparing teachers to address pain and suffering with their students is *not* to:

- chasten the good intentions of parents and teachers who want to shield children from suffering
- suggest parents and teachers prematurely force children to confront the evil and suffering that exists at a distance and will become real soon enough

It is to encourage teachers and parents to prepare children developmentally with a biblical understanding of suffering and to walk with children through pain when they are facing it.

A Sacred Wound Story

A university student with a good family background and much going for her made a mistake. She referred to it as "cutting corners" in her Christian walk, the consequence being an unwanted pregnancy. Unlike most university seniors, she chose to give life to the baby and selected a family to raise him. At the time of the baby's birth and even years later, she refers to the decision to give birth and release for adoption as the hardest and most painful decision in her life. She said it also reset her life in a positive direction and made her strong and thankful. The painful experience turned out to be a blessing in disguise. Really? How can such a hard, emotionally wrought decision like releasing a baby for adoption also be a positive life changer? Nearly three decades later, she is faithfully and humbly walking with God, enjoying a family of her own, and still strengthened in the relationship with God wrought through the painful experience of giving life. The unwanted pregnancy became a sacred wound for this faithful woman.

How many of you know cancer survivors who say that struggling through the illness was horrific, while also saying they would not exchange the experience for anything in life? They testify of thankfulness for the personal development that the suffering produced. The cancer was a sacred wound.

How many people, upon losing a job, think the world ended, only to discover it was a blessing in disguise?

On the other hand, not all suffering yields stories like those just shared. Some people react to suffering with bitterness, resentment, and despair. Suffering resulting in meaningless scars will be explored later in this chapter in section 6 on ressentiment.

The Pornography of Death

Psalm 90:12 says, "Teach us to number our days that we may get a heart of wisdom."

Is talking about death as taboo as pornography used to be? Think of how death is represented in our culture, and more importantly how death is, as Matt McCullough (2018) astutely points out, a taboo topic. In our day and time, we rarely see death portrayed as it usually happens— aging bodies that die a natural death. Death is sensationalized in the media, as he states: "Too often where death shows up in popular culture, it belongs to a fantasy world. It's newsworthy. It's tragic. It's psychopathic or maybe apocalyptic. But one way or another, death is exotic. It's something that happens to someone else" (McCullough 2018).

This avoidance of discussing or portraying the reality of death seriously inhibits our own acknowledgment that death happens to us and those we love. It's not fictious. Facing our finiteness not only breeds a quality of life but a quest for understanding what lies beyond life as we know it. As McCullough states, "In our time and place, where death is often banished from polite company, we will struggle to experience the beauty and power of Jesus because we've numbed ourselves to the problem he came to solve ... this honesty can lead us to Jesus, to a clearer view of his beauty and power, to a deeper awareness of his life-giving relevance to everything we face. We need to overcome our detachment from death so that we can enjoy a deeper attachment to Jesus" (McCullough 2018).

With this recognition of the error in making discussion of natural death a taboo topic, the transformational educator will proactively seek opportunities to help students understand a Christian view of death.

Transformational educators may:

- directly teach on the subject
- selectively read literature or watch films that address natural death
- ask students to journal about it
- explore what faithful Christians who are facing the end of life have to say

Spiritual Suffering Is Real

The process of transformation itself can cause suffering. A new spiritual perspective or insight can cause cognitive dissonance, leaving a person very unsettled. Is this new insight a heresy or a breakthrough like how Martin Luther must have felt when God revealed grace to him? We live in a time of religious certainty with little tolerance of uncertainty or exploring issues of faith. The believer often suffers alone in silence with a cry for God to clearly put forth what is true.

> Spiritual transformation always includes a disconcerting reorientation. It can either help people to find new meaning or it can force people to close down and slowly turn bitter ... Change happens, but transformation is always a process of letting go, living in the confusing, shadowy space for a while. Eventually, we are spit up on a new and unexpected shore. (Rohr 2020)

The falling apart of something that once was certain and comforting is a cause of suffering. This spiritual deconstruction is something that transformational educators need to be aware of and equipped to address as the numbers of young people leaving the church are at higher numbers than ever according to Pew Research. (et.al., In U.S., Decline of Christianity Continues at Rapid Pace 2019) (et.al., In U.S., Decline of Christianity Continues at Rapid Pace 2019).

Many of these departures are preceded by suffering, confusion, loneliness, shame, and a sense of betrayal related to their faith or participation in a church or paragroup organization.

What can educators do about spiritual suffering?

- Faithfully pray for students who are in the process of faith deconstruction.
- Help students know that faith shifting does not have to be an all or nothing proposition. Students may reject tenets of faith that they were taught as absolutes, while moving on to new understanding of what Jesus and the Bible intended.
- Create an open atmosphere for asking questions and expressing doubt.
- Directly teach from scripture how Jesus addressed doubt and sincere questions from His followers.
- Pursue a loving relationship with students who reject faith, always leaving open a door for them to share about their beliefs.

Research

Harriot, Extine, Hall, and Pargament (Harriot, 2014) research concluded the following:

- a greater awareness of God was related to resolving a spiritual struggle with a greater sense of closure and appreciation for the struggle's purpose.
- greater awareness of God's presence was related to both spiritual and emotional growth. Participants reported feeling stronger in their faith and in their ability to relate well with themselves and others after the struggle.
- greater awareness of God's presence was positively associated with measures of social and emotional well-being.
- as participants reported more awareness of God in their lives, they indicated a clearer understanding of life's purpose. Rather than searching for meaning in life, they more strongly indicated that they had found it. (Harriot 2014)

Resources for children:

I Miss You: A First Look at Death

The Invisible String

ida, ALWAYS

Sun Kisses, Moon Hugs

God Gave Us Heaven

The Memory Box: A Book about Grief

Someone I Love Died

Our Tree named Steve

Gentle Willow: A Story for Children about Dying

Badger's Parting Gifts

When I Feel Sad

Resources for adults:

Richard Rohr's *Falling Upward: A Spirituality for the Two Halves of Life* and other work by Richard Rohr

Tim Keller's *Walking with God through Pain and Suffering*

Philip Yancey's *Where Is God When It Hurts*

Questions to consider:

1. Assuming educators want to prepare students for suffering while also protecting them from the fear and anticipation of suffering, how does a teacher strike the correct balance between the two?

2. What role does a parent have in how a teacher prepares young students for suffering?

3. Why is faith deconstruction on the rise?

Section 2

A Biblical View of Suffering

Suffering can be a huge stumbling block when it comes to faith in God. People who normally don't give God a second thought are quick to cast blame on God when they experience or witness tragedy of some sort. Even more disconcerting is those who identify as Christians suddenly disavowing God when disaster strikes. I believe this is rooted in false understanding of scripture and God's purposes. Examining the whole counsel of scripture on suffering is important, especially because an incorrect understanding of

> Transformational educators communicate the breadth of biblical truths about going through suffering.

suffering is often rooted in erroneously claiming a subset of scripture as the entire message. An example is found in Mark 11:24, "Therefore I tell you, whatever you ask for in prayer, believe that you have received it, and it will be yours." These verses have been used to assert that by *believing* we can determine the outcome of prayer. Does this mean God is obligated to obey what we pray? Will God heal the sick child because we believe strongly enough that this will be what God does? Without taking the entire body of scripture into account, people have understood that prayer will be answered according to their desires, and they dismiss God when that is not what happens. Even Jesus prayed about suffering, and God did not answer as Jesus wanted. However, Jesus was willing to submit. "Abba Father," he said, "everything is possible for you. Take this cup from me. Yet not what I will, but what you will" (Mark 14:36). As modelled by Jesus, we pray for our desire with our posture always being to submit to God's perfect plan for us. Does it matter to a person that Jesus suffered too?

Activity #8-1

Here are a few of the many scriptural passages that teach us about suffering. Meditate on the verses below, asking God to communicate to you an understanding of suffering. Write a brief summary of your biblical understanding of suffering.

And the God of all grace, who called you to his eternal glory in Christ, after you have suffered a little while, will himself restore you and make you strong, firm, and steadfast. (1 Peter 5:10)

So that no one would be unsettled by these trials. For you know quite well that we are destined for them. (1 Thessalonians 3:3)

Dear friends, do not be surprised at the fiery ordeal that has come on you to test you, as though something strange were happening to you. (1 Peter 4:12)

He causes his sun to rise on the evil and the good and sends rain on the righteous and the unrighteous. (Matthew 5:45)

For just as we share abundantly in the sufferings of Christ, so also our comfort abounds through Christ. (2 Corinthians 1:5)

Praise be to the God and Father of our Lord Jesus Christ, the Father of compassion and the God of all comfort, [4] who comforts us in all our troubles, so that we can comfort those in any trouble with the comfort we ourselves receive from God. (2 Corinthians 1:3–4)

Not only so, but we also glory in our sufferings, because we know that suffering produces perseverance; perseverance, character; and character, hope. (Romans 5:3–4)

I consider that our present sufferings are not worth comparing with the glory that will be revealed in us. (Romans 8:18)

The righteous person may have many troubles, but the Lord delivers him from them all. (Psalm 34:19)

For our light and momentary troubles are achieving for us an eternal glory that far outweighs them all. (2 Corinthians 4:17)

Who shall separate us from the love of Christ? Shall trouble or hardship or persecution or famine or nakedness or danger or sword? (Romans 8:35)

Therefore, since Christ suffered in his body, arm yourselves also with the same attitude, because whoever suffers in the body is done with sin. (1 Peter 4:1)

But even if you should suffer for what is right, you are blessed. "Do not fear their threats; do not be frightened." (1 Peter 3:14)

Carry each other's burdens, and in this way you will fulfill the law of Christ. (Galatians 6:2)

For it has been granted to you on behalf of Christ not only to believe in him, but also to suffer for him. (Philippians 1:29)

He was despised and rejected by mankind,
a man of suffering, and familiar with pain.
Like one from whom people hide their faces
he was despised, and we held him in low esteem. (Isaiah 53:3)

"Whoever does not take up their cross and follow me is not worthy of me." (Matthew 10:38)

To this you were called, because Christ suffered for you, leaving you an example, that you should follow in his steps." (1 Peter 2:21)

For just as we share abundantly in the sufferings of Christ, so also our comfort abounds through Christ. (2 Corinthians 1:5)

At this, Job got up and tore his robe and shaved his head. Then he fell to the ground in worship and said:
"Naked I came from my mother's womb,
and naked I will depart.
The Lord gave and the Lord has taken away;
may the name of the Lord be praised." (Job 1:20–21)

God suffers.

Jesus suffers.

We suffer.

Activity #8-2

Read the last chapters in the book of Job in the Bible (take your time to savor this magnificent book, beautifully written with mounds of truth for our benefit).

Write down a one-sentence summary of what God says about human suffering.

Write down a one-sentence summary of how Job responded to what God shared with him about suffering.

What has reading, or rereading, Job meant to you?

> Could there possibly be something about suffering that a benevolent God knows, and we do not? Do we assume that if we cannot see for ourselves a reason for God's actions or lack thereof, then there is not any such reason, or possibly conclude that God is not good? (Keller 2013)

> We can forget that we are humans and delude ourselves into thinking that we can transcend our tiny place in the human drama and see from on high, as God sees. (Enns, The Sin of Certainty 2016, 17)

> Jesus Christ did not suffer so that you would not suffer. He suffered so that when you suffer, you'll become more like him. The gospel does not promise you better life circumstances; it promises you a better life. (Keller 2013)

What can a teacher do?

This section addresses a biblical view of suffering and some problems with misappropriating scripture. Having a correct apologetic regarding suffering is essential, especially for transformational educators to help students construct this foundation before the adversity strikes. How does a teacher construct this foundation? Overt, direct instruction is a great start for environments that provide the time and permission for such a theological study of suffering. Other ways are practicing mindfulness by examining conversations, literature, local and global events, sermons, blogs, and so forth to evaluate the content and insert questions or comments that will highlight a biblical view. Opportunities arise when the class is processing a personal or corporate loss, such as the students sharing about a family death, or a report showcases genocide or starvation. Already having a biblical foundation is very important because once the adversity strikes, a suffering student may feel more cared for, be more influenced by, and more changed by the compassion and love demonstrated by his or her teacher during the crisis than from the explanations or Bible verses about suffering. Although the student's questions (How could a loving God allow this to happen?) may appear to be a doctrinal concern, it often is an exclamation not inviting a response. Sharing theology and scripture may not be as transformational as listening, hugging, weeping with, and providing for the sufferer's basic needs. This is when the teacher hopes the student has

> Already having a foundation is important because once the adversity strikes, a suffering student may feel more cared for, be more influenced by, and more changed by the compassion and love demonstrated by his or her teacher during the crisis than from the explanations or Bible verses about suffering that come out of the mouth.

studied and embraced the biblical understanding of adversity so the focus can be on grieving well and lamenting.

Questions to consider:

1. What key truths would you say to students about a biblical response to suffering?

2. How would you be proactive in preparing students for suffering?

Section 3

The Source of Suffering

Sin was the entryway of suffering into the world. Commonly referred to as the Fall, human rebellion against God and wanting to be God instead of worshipping God ushered in suffering. God's love for us led to His act of reconciling us through Jesus Christ. Because of His great love for us, God had a plan for sin through redemption by His Son, Jesus Christ. You may read more in chapter 6 about the creation-Fall-redemption-restoration metanarrative of the Bible.

> Transformational educators help students understand that even though the Bible gives a variety of reasons people suffer, it also makes clear that we may never know the cause or purpose of a specific suffering we experience.

The Bible gives several examples of suffering being attributed to a specific source or cause. In the famous suffering story of Job, we also see that God may never reveal to us the cause or purpose for our suffering. When one scriptural reference is determined to provide the comprehensive answer to the question of suffering, then untruths will result. This happened in biblical times when Job's friends were certain that Job's suffering was due to his sin. Scripture says that our sin may be the cause of suffering, but it also gives other reasons not related to sin. After all, Christ suffered immensely, and He was without sin. It is imperative that the full Bible is used to understand a variety of sources/causes of suffering, including the fact that we may not ever know the why of suffering.

Do the exercise below to see some of the variety of biblical reasons for suffering.

Activity #8-3

Match the type of suffering to the scripture.

Types of suffering:

1. As a result of the Fall, humans rebelled against their Creator, and all the creation was affected
2. Because of our actions, a consequence
3. As God's discipline
4. A tool for pruning our lives, a means of growth, to turn us from sin
5. As the result of persecution
6. To know Christ more fully
7. Suffering for the sake of the church

Scripture source:

    A. John 15:20: "Remember what I told you: 'A servant is not greater than his master.' If they persecuted me, they will persecute you also. If they obeyed my teaching, they will obey yours also."

    B. Second Timothy 3:12: "In fact, everyone who wants to live a godly life in Christ Jesus will be persecuted."

    C. Colossians 1:24: "Now I rejoice in what I am suffering for you, and I fill up in my flesh what is still lacking in regard to Christ's afflictions, for the sake of his body, which is the church."

    D. Hebrews 12:6: "Because the Lord disciplines the ones he loves, and he chastens everyone he accepts as his son."

    E. Philippians 3:10: "I want to know Christ—yes, to know the power of his resurrection and participation in his sufferings, becoming like him in his death."

    F. Psalms 32:3–5: "When I kept silent, my bones wasted away through my groaning all day long. For day and night your hand was heavy on me; my strength was sapped as in the heat of summer. Then I acknowledged my sin to you and did not cover up my iniquity. I said, "I will confess my transgressions to the LORD.' And you forgave the guilt of my sin."

    G. Galatians 6:7–9: "Do not be deceived: God cannot be mocked. A man reaps what he sows. 8Whoever sows to please their flesh, from the flesh will reap destruction; whoever sows to please the Spirit, from the Spirit will reap eternal life."

    H. Genesis 3 reference—the entire chapter.

Questions to consider:

1. Should we even try to give a cause or explanation for suffering?

2. Explain the difference between a natural consequence for sin and God's punishment.

Section 4

Prayer and Suffering

If the following two verses were the only two you read, what would you conclude about prayers?

> "If you remain in me and my words remain in you, ask whatever you wish, and it will be done for you." (John 15:7)

> "If you believe, you will receive whatever you ask for in prayer." (Matthew 21:22)

Transformational educators help students understand the scriptures regarding the asking and receiving of prayer.

When looked at together like this, these verses seem to suggest that if we ask God for something, He will give it to us. So, if we pray for someone to be cured from heart disease, then God will do it? Do your students believe this? What happens to the Christian who prays and the loved one they prayed for died? Do they question God's goodness? Do they question the purpose of prayer? Do our students know that other scriptures give a different view of asking God? Elijah prayed that he would die, but God made him live longer (1 Kings 19:4). Paul asked three times for his "thorn in the flesh" (2 Corinthians 12:8) to be taken away, and it didn't happen. *Even a prayer by Jesus was denied.* Jesus asked for "this cup to be removed" (Luke 22:42) when He was in the garden, yet He was still crucified. Thank God that prayer was not granted!

We name it, and God gives it—simple as that. God is subservient to our wants and desires. I call it the cosmic sugar daddy view of God. Often, even if unintentionally, we present this view to our students. Even our Bible studies and textbooks sometimes seem to shore up this view, possibly by citing some of these scriptures mentioned above. However, just a few verses later, scripture says we are to ask in His Name. Seven times in the upper room discourse, He says, "in my name," which implies "in His will" or only what He would ask, which is the clear teaching of James where we quote 4:2, "You do not have because you do not ask God" without verse 3 (you ask with wrong motives) and verse 15, "You ought to say, 'If it is the Lord's will.'" This is different from a prayer to a cosmic sugar daddy.

The challenge for the transformational educator is to help students pull together a unified view of prayer from the Bible. It is not a simple task, but left undone, it leaves room for a student to take one verse about prayer and latch onto it as the only way to understand God's response to prayer.

A Story about Getting It Wrong

While visiting in the elementary classroom of a wonderful school in another country, I observed a classic example of how Christian schools can inadvertently discount suffering. It involved a misuse of scripture. The competent teacher was teaching a story from a Christian school curriculum used by many schools. Half the story was taught the day before I observed, but I gathered the story involved the characters being unhappy about a big hole in the ice covering a lake. On the day of my observation, the story continued with two young girls fleeing for their lives from a pack of wolves, praying as hard as they could for God to save them. Fortunately, while chasing the girls, the wolves fell into that hole in the ice, preventing the imminent attack. The girls were safe. Exciting story, but the moralizing at the end painted a deficit picture of prayer, God, and life. The moral of the story was *if you pray, God will do exactly what you ask*, and everything will be all right. Prayer to God means getting what you want, including a way to avoid suffering.

However, the whole counsel of scripture and the experience of life simply does not say we get everything we want by praying for it.

- Sometimes the wolves do catch the girls.
- Sometimes children do die.
- Sometimes our fervent prayers are not answered in the way we requested.

In Summary

Suffering is a part of life and is to be expected. Nowhere in the Bible is our happiness and contentment cited as the purpose of life. Life's purpose is to glorify God and that alone brings our deep contentment.

God is not the source of suffering; sin entering the world is the source of suffering.

God often does not reveal why He allows suffering, but He clearly shows us that it is not rooted in a lack of His love for us.

Jesus' work on the cross in reconciling us to God demonstrates God's complete love for us.

God promises to be with us when we suffer.

Questions to think about:

1. Does the fact that Jesus suffered make a difference to our students?

2. What are you prepared to say to a student of any age who says he or she prayed to God and God did not answer?

3. How do you answer a student who asks you, "How could a loving God do this?"

4. What are other scriptures people use to deny that Christians will suffer?

Section 5

Lament

What is lament? Lament is crying out to God about pain and suffering—both personal and corporate. It's not just weeping or whining; it is a form of prayer and is distinctly Christian because it is laced with hope that God will hear and respond. It is trusting God, and it draws us into the confidence that God is sovereign. Lament combines sound theology with authentic emotions.

> A transformational educator models and introduces students to lament.

> So that you do not grieve like the rest of mankind, who have no hope. (1 Thessalonians 4:13)

> To cry is human, but to lament is Christian. (Vroegop 2019)

As I write this, lament is very real to me. Although unscathed, I am reeling from observing an abundance of suffering. People are dying from COVID; one business after another in my hometown is closed, and people have lost jobs due to the fallout from COVID-; the facts of brutality, inequality, and hatred based on race smack me in the face; fires rage on the West Coast; hurricanes batter the gulf shores; politicians treat one another like dirt; and we don't trust anything. And this is just America, not considering all the countries that were already hurting before dealing with COVID-issues. I have not been sick, known anyone who died from COVID-19, and have not lost my job. I've been spared from poverty, hunger, racial and ethnic discrimination, hurricanes, and fires. This survivor's guilt has me asking God why I have been spared and others not. So I wonder why I am so sad about all that is happening when I am doing quite well. This season of unusual global suffering has burdened me, and like so many others, I am mourning the brokenness of the world while crying out with hope and trust that God is God. This is lament—something the psalmist described and something worthy of the attention of transformational educators.

An invitation to lament from N.T. Wright:

> Christianity Offers No Answers About the Coronavirus. It's Not Supposed To.

> No doubt the usual silly suspects will tell us why God is doing this to us. A punishment? A warning? A sign? These are knee-jerk would-be Christian reactions in a culture which, generations back, embraced rationalism: everything must have an explanation. But supposing it doesn't? Supposing real human

wisdom doesn't mean being able to string together some dodgy speculations and say, "So that's all right then?" What if, after all, there are moments such as T. S. Eliot recognized in the early 1940s, when the only advice is to wait without hope, because we'd be hoping for the wrong thing? ... Rationalists (including Christian rationalists) want explanations; Romantics (including Christian romantics) want to be given a sigh of relief. But perhaps what we need more than either is to recover the biblical tradition of *lament*. Lament is what happens when people ask, "Why?" and don't get an answer. It's where we get to when we move beyond our self-centered worry about our sins and failings and look more broadly at the suffering of the world. It's bad enough facing a pandemic in New York City or London. What about a crowded *refugee camp* on a Greek island? What about Gaza? Or South Sudan? It is no part of the Christian vocation, then, to be able to explain what's happening and why. In fact, it *is* part of the Christian vocation *not to be able* to explain—and to lament instead. As the Spirit laments within us, so we become, even in our self-isolation, small shrines where the presence and healing love of God can dwell. And out of that there can emerge new possibilities, new acts of kindness, new scientific understanding, new hope. New wisdom for our leaders? Now there's a thought. (Wright 2020)

Yes, that is a thought, N. T. Wright, and this thought is at the core of transformational education: "What were we saved for?" We are commanded and empowered by the Holy Spirit to make a difference for good in this broken world. We are to sift through the ashes of destruction and brokenness to repair the ruins in the name of Jesus. We teach so that students will know how to find vaccines for COVID-19, so students will nurse the sick from the ravages of the pandemic, so students will act out of compassions toward those stricken by hurricanes and fires, so students will be peacemakers and champions of racial justice, so students will go into the world to tell the hopeless about Christ and how much God loves them. The kingdom of God is now, and our business is to faithfully restore it to God's intentions.

T.S. Eliot expressed the dark night of the soul so well that I find it troubling.

Second Quarter from T. S. Eliot's *East Coker*

I said to my soul, be still, and wait without hope,
For hope would be hope for the wrong thing: wait without love
For love would be love of the wrong thing; there is yet faith
But the faith and the hope and the love are all in the waiting
Wait without thought, for you are not yet ready for thought:
So the darkness shall be the light, and the stillness the dancing ...
In order to arrive at what you do not know
You must go by the way which is the way of ignorance ...

Activity #8-4

Write your own lament and consider the advisability of having your students also write one. One way to start would be to read psalms of lament. Start with Psalms 10, 13, 22, and 77.

Graham Hill (Hill 2020) provides a template of nine steps of lament. As you write your lament, you may choose to write a paragraph or two on each point:

1. Cry out to God (your address to God)
2. Complaint (your anger, pain, heartache, or sadness)
3. Affirmation of Trust (your remembrance of God's presence in your past)
4. Petition/Request (your deepest desire)
5. Additional Argument (anything more, why God should intervene)
6. Rage against Your Enemies (bringing your enemies before God)
7. Assurance of Being Heard (what you need to feel heard)
8. Promise to Offer Praise to God (the promise you can offer to God)
9. Assurance (the attribute of God you are thankful for in the moment)

The end of all lament: "He will wipe every tear from their eyes. There will be no more death or mourning or crying or pain, for the old order of things has passed away" (Revelation 21:4).

Questions to consider:

1. Is T. S. Elliot's poem about waiting consistent with a biblical view? Why or why not?

2. Select a psalm of lament and identify which of the nine steps of lament from Graham Hill it addresses.

3. How would you explain the difference between personal sadness and biblical lament?

Section 6

Why Does God Allow Suffering?

In his book *Walking with God through Pain and Suffering* (Keller 2013, 28), Tim Keller uses comparison of different worldviews to explain various approaches to suffering. Notice the aspects of these worldviews that camouflage a Christian view.

> The transformational teacher challenges student to embrace the mysterious aspects of suffering because they know God promised to walk with us, God is trustworthy, and God has a good plan for those who follow Him.

Moralism. Suffering stems from failure to live rightly. There are many versions of this view, but they all involve obeying god(s), a moral code, and so on, which leads to life going well. We control it. Karma is the purest form of moralism—"suffering in the present days pays for sins in the past."

Self-Transcendent. Suffering comes from unfulfilled desires, and the solution is to get rid of these desires. Death is an illusion, and the belief is that one lives on in their family. These desires come from the illusion that we are individual selves.

Stoics. Classical thinkers believe suffering makes you stronger. It forges character so is therefore good.

Secularist. Because this present life is all there is, the goal is to make it as happy and free of suffering as possible. Meaning in life is to have the freedom to choose the life that makes you most happy—no room for suffering. "That means that when facing unavoidable suffering, secular people must smuggle in resources from other views of life, having recourse to ideas of karma, or Buddhism, or Stoicism from the classical era, or Christianity, even though their beliefs about the nature of the universe do not line up with those resources" (Keller 2013, 17).

Fatalism. In fatalism, people are called to heroically endure suffering. Sufferers are to embrace one's destiny nobly. Fate, destiny, and life circumstances are seen as set by the stars, supernatural forces, doom of the gods. In Islam, the inscrutable will of Allah (surrender to God's mysterious will without question has been one of the central requirements of righteousness). "In all these cultures, submission to a difficult, divine fate without compromise or complaint was the highest virtue and therefore the way to find great meaning in suffering" (Keller 2013, 13).

Dualistic. Dualism calls sufferers to put their hope in the future, pie in the sky by and by. Just endure for now, and when you die, all will be great.

According to Keller (2013) all the above-mentioned views of suffering have the following in common:

- expect suffering, it is part of human existence
- suffering can help them move toward the main purpose in life whether it be spiritual growth, the mastery of oneself, achievement of honor, or the promotion of good" (p. 19)
- the key to rising and achieving in suffering is something they must take the responsibility to do. They must put themselves into a right relationship to spiritual reality.

From the Christian perspective, all of these cultures of suffering have an element of truth. Sufferers do indeed need to stop loving material goods too much. And yes, the Bible says that, in general, the suffering filling the world is a result of the human race turning from God. And we do need to endure suffering and not let it overthrow us. Secularism is right to warn us about being too accepting of conditions and factors that harm people and should be changed...But, as we have seen, from the Christian view of things, all of these approaches are too simple and reductionist and therefore are half-truths. The example and redemptive work of Jesus Christ incorporates all these insights into a coherent whole and yet transcends them. (Keller 2013, 30)

Question to consider:

1. Give examples you have observed of non-Christian philosophies creeping into Christian reactions to suffering.

2. Which philosophy do you think inserts itself the most into Christians' understanding of suffering?

Section 7

Ressentiment

Ressentiment is a scholarly word for what I refer to as hopeless cynicism. The challenge for transformational educators is to identify and address the academic content and classroom discussions that may seed ressentiment.

> Transformational teachers know that suffering can evoke cynicism, despair, and bitterness. Transformational teachers demonstrate God's loving grace and discerningly help students understand suffering and the meaning of Godly forgiveness.

Peter Berger expressed, "Every culture has provided an explanation of human events that bestows meaning upon the experiences of suffering and evil. Because of this deep inner compulsion, every culture either must help its people face suffering or risk a loss of credibility. When no explanation at all is given -when suffering is perceived as simply senseless, a waste, and inescapable -victims can develop a deep undying anger and poisonous hate that was called ressentiment" (Keller 2013, 14).

Definition of ressentiment: https://www.dictionary.com/browse/ressentiment: "any cautious, defeatist, or cynical attitude based on the belief that the individual and human institutions exist in a hostile or indifferent universe or society."

Have you been around someone stuck in bitterness? Not pretty, is it? Bitterness results from a wound that was not dealt with well. It festered instead of healed. Two people can receive the same affliction, and one will blossom in Christ, and the other will bitterly leave their faith. I remember a church friend whose elderly dad died a peaceful death at eighty-eight years. She furiously denied a God who would allow such a horrible thing to happen. Contrastingly, I also remember a friend whose only son died in a car wreck and whose husband asked for a divorce a few days later. She grieved, clung to God through it all, and for decades afterward was a woman who reflected the attractive character of Christ.

Suffering is not automatically beneficial. We can allow a wound to heal or fester. Festered wounds are arguably the main reason people reject God. In a world where all people are destined to experience affliction, it is imperative we challenge students to heal and even be transformed by wounds.

Discuss or think about someone you know who has become bitter as a result of suffering. Why do some people experience growth and insight from suffering while others become bitter and abused by it? Is it possible that one's view of suffering shapes the outcome of the sufferer and that teachers could help shape those views?

Addressing ressentiment in our students:

- Teach and model forgiveness (see next section).

- Point out bitterness, defeatism, and cynicism when observed in a student and explore the basis of it if the student is willing.

- Use literature or media to showcase ressentiment's damage and ways to overcome it.

Section 8

Forgiveness and Suffering

Suffering, for many people, is caused by another person or persons. If there is not forgiveness, the pain can fester into bitterness. Of course, bitterness then intensifies the suffering. The problem is that forgiveness requires a change of heart, and the person cannot fool himself or herself. Forgiveness is not to be confused with accepting the offense that caused the pain. It never says the offense was OK. Rather, forgiveness involves giving the offender over to God, as He said, "Vengeance is mine" (Romans 12:19). It requires trusting God and looking at the offender as if he or she was the person God intended them to be. It is still hard but worthy of the prayer and counsel of wise people to help break free from the bondage of unforgiveness. Most importantly, God commands us to forgive.

> No one wants to be bitter. It sneaks up on us. Bitterness is unforgiveness fermented. The more we hold onto past hurts the more we become drunk on our pain and the experience can rob us of the joy we can find in anything. (Popcak 2019)

Examine the questions below to see if they add benefit to knowing how bitterness can be transformed.

"Bitterness is unforgiveness fermented" (Popcak 2019).

Counselling about forgiveness questions:

1. Can you identify whether the person maliciously and purposefully hurt you, or did he/she act out of their own selfish need/desire without you being the actual target?
2. Could you have contributed in some way to your offender treating you as he/she did? Was the offense retaliatory?
3. Can you name ways in which your bitterness has harmed you? Has it distanced you from God?
4. Could you forgive your offender if you think about him or her as if they were the person God intended him or her to be?
5. Can you mentally turn that person over to God to restore him or her and allow yourself to be free from the hold that person's behavior has on you?
6. Could you, with a peaceful and sincere heart, give your offender a gift or say something positive to him or her?

Questions to consider:

1. Have you moved closer to God or away from God in your personal suffering?

2. Does your theology of suffering need to be tweaked? If so, in what way(s)?

Resources for further exploration:

Healing the Wounded Heart by Dan Allender

Section 9

What Can We Practically Do?

"When you pass through the waters, I will be with you; and when you pass through the rivers, they will not sweep over you. When you walk through the fire, you will not be burned; the flames will not set you ablaze. For I am the Lord your God, the Holy One of Israel, your Savior ... Do not be afraid, for I am with you." (Isaiah 43:2–3, 5)

> Transformational teachers help students develop a biblical understanding of suffering, which fosters growth and change through hardship based on trusting God as opposed to fostering alienation from God.

A Story about Hope in Suffering

When she was three years old, my dear niece approached me with the pronouncement that "Jesus has two dogs." She responded to my probing by saying that the two dogs belonging to Jesus were her recently deceased pet and the deceased dog that had been her mother's and my pet for seventeen years. I really like this story. My three-year-old niece got it, and, no, I am not talking about some biblical defense about pets in heaven. What I believe is that my niece expressed a developmentally appropriate, biblical understanding of suffering, one grounded in hope and truth. She understood that the beloved pets were dead and gone, but she did not despair because Jesus had them in His tender care.

As transformational educators, our message about suffering is to abide in Christ through suffering, to glean the truths only given to the brokenhearted, and to thank and trust God for His enduring faithfulness. Our message is not to avoid suffering at all costs, to manage suffering through distraction or avoidance, or to deny the existence or power of pain.

> As transformational educators, our message about suffering is to abide in Christ through suffering, to glean the truths only given to the brokenhearted, and to thank and trust God for His enduring faithfulness. Our message is not to avoid suffering at all costs, to manage suffering through distraction or avoidance, or to deny the existence or power of pain.

Much of the Western world addresses the problem of pain by encouraging sufferers to manage their suffering devoid of God by participating in activities, such as starting a new hobby, engaging a counsellor, exercising, getting away on a retreat or vacation, or participating in a support group. Keller (2013, p. 225) points out, "Most books and resources for sufferers today no longer talk about enduring affliction but instead use a vocabulary drawn from business and psychology to enable people to manage, reduce, and cope with stress, strain, or trauma." Our job as transformational educators is to influence the narrative of "managing suffering" to the biblical picture of "abiding with God" through the suffering. God does not desert us; He is actually transforming us as we yield to Him during the affliction. The pain alone is not what transforms, as we know that sometimes people respond to suffering with bitterness. But our yieldedness allows God to strengthen, mold, teach, restore, and essentially change us. We must encourage our students to go deep with God when enduring hardship—to pray, obey, reflect on the scriptures, and trust God with all their heart (Isaiah 43:19).

Practices of transformational teachers related to suffering:

1. Pray that God would use you as His instrument in understanding and ministering to suffering.
2. Clarify scripture that may confuse a student about the reality of God's responses to our prayers about suffering.
3. Teach students the Bible's directive about enduring suffering.
4. Plan your responses to the difficult questions students may ask related to God and suffering.
5. Help students pray boldly and persistently, trusting God with those for whom they pray.
6. Be on the lookout for comments, stories, lyrics, or anything that tries to avoid, hide, or minimalize the fact that life includes suffering and make the correction for the students as needed.
7. Allow open discussion and grieving by students (and yourself!).
8. Expose students to literature, art, music, and drama that addresses suffering from Christian truth.
9. Teach students to lament.
10. Learn to identify and correct the subtle errors in understanding suffering that are embedded in both Christian and secular communication.
11. Practice being "a peaceful presence" with a sufferer; "rejoice with those who rejoice and mourn with those who mourn" (Romans 12:15).

Seek out professional development in areas of suffering common to the students you teach.

Learn about your students' backgrounds and seek out specific recommendations for identifying problems and interfacing with them. Some communities around the world have high suicide rates. Learn to identify the signs that someone may be considering such and how to do a suicide assessment. Another example is the recent research on bullying, which provides information for educators on how to address this type of suffering. Different cultures have unique concerns for which the educators must seek out information on how to identify and intervene if appropriate (e.g., child bride, incest). For example, in many educational settings around the world, classrooms are full of traumatized students. Transformational educators in such regions should receive training to prepare themselves on how to care for traumatized students.

Educators care for traumatized students by ...

- not ignoring the traumatic event(s) but by engaging with the student when he or she brings it up. Listen, answer questions, and offer comfort. If the student senses you are not open to talking about the event, then he or she may not do the processing or receive the comfort that can assist in the healing.
- providing a consistent, stable, and predictable routine. When changes are expected, let the student know ahead of time. It is important for them to know someone is in control.
- letting the abused person initiate touching or physical contact, then reciprocating. For people, especially children, who have been sexually or physically abused, touching and affection may elicit fear and discomfort.
- noting that after a trauma, the victim predictably will reenact (e.g., in play, drawing, behaviors) or avoid (e.g., being withdrawn, daydreaming, avoiding other children) and will be physiologically hyperreactive (e.g., anxiety, sleep problems, behavioral impulsivity). Keep a record of these occurrences to discern whether there is a pattern or something that routinely incites the post-traumatic symptoms. Be understanding and comforting, while also explaining limits and consequences for behavior (not physical punishment).
- providing the child with age-appropriate information so that their environment is known, predictable, and understood. Without factual information, the traumatized child will speculate, often anticipating much worse outcomes than what awaits.
- giving the student choices that communicate that the student has some control over things in his or her life. Trauma is rooted in someone or thing having control over the victim. Even giving the student the choice to comply with your request or choose the consequence is promoting the student's sense of control.
- protecting the student. Notice when certain interactions or activities incite or retraumatize the student and restructure activities or routines that habitually trigger the student.

CLOSING PRAYER

Holy God, because You are perfect, holy, and loving, and because You so greatly suffered for us, we look to You when we observe or experience suffering. Help us to be steadfast in believing Your loving care for us. Help our students to trust You as they suffer. Free us from cynicism and bitterness. Let us clearly see You walking with us through suffering. Mold us and make us after Your will.

Amen.

REFERENCES

2000. ""The Great Cost to Follow Jesus"." *http://theshovel.net.* January 1.

2019. *Program for Performance of Handel's Messiah.* Durham, N.C., December 3.

n.d.

Armstrong, Thomas. n.d. *multiple Intelligances.*

Augustine. 2003. *Enchiridion 117, trans. J. F., Shaw in Philip Schaff ed., Nicene and Post-Nicene Fathers First Series Vol 3.* Peabody, MA: Hendrickson Publishers.

Beech, Geoff. 2015. *Christians As Teachers, What Might It Look Like?* Eugene Oregon: WIPF& STOCK.

Boa, Kenneth. 2001. *Conformed to His Image.* Grand Rapids: Zondervan.

Bonhoeffer, Dietrich. 1963. *Dietrich Bonhoffer The Cost of Discipleship.* New York: Simon & Schuster.

Brantley, Garry K. 1995. *"Train Up a Child"--What Does It Mean?*

Bratt, James D. 1998. *Abraham Kuyper: A Centennial Reader.* Grand Rapids: Wm. B. Eerdmans Publishing.

Browning, Elizabeth Barrett BrowningKerry McSweeney | Oct 15, 2008. 2008. *Aurora Leigh (Oxford World Classics).* Oxford: Oxford University Press.

Brummelen, Harro Van. 2002. *Steppingstones to Curriculum, A Biblical Path.* Colorado Springs: Purposeful Design.

Bruner, Jerome S. 1966. *Cultural of Education.* Cambridge: Harvard University Press.

Buechner, Frederick. 1983., *Wishful Thinking: A Seeker's ABC.* San Francisco: Harper.

Durance, George, interview by Helen Vaughan. 2019. *Defining Transformational Education* (January 24).

Enns, Peter. 2016. *The Sin of Certainty.* San Fransisco: Harper One.

—. 2016. *The Sin of Certainty: Why God Desires Our Trust More Than Our "Correct" Beliefs.* Dunmore, Pa.: HarperCollins PublishersDunmore, Pa.

et.al., Gregory Smith. 2019. "In U.S., Decline of Christianity Continues at Rapid Pace." *www.pewresearch.org.* October 17. Accessed 10 7, 2021. https://www.pewresearch.org/religion/2019/10/17.

—. 2019. "In U.S., Decline of Christianity Continues at Rapid Pace." *pewresearch.org/religion.* October 17. Accessed October 2021. https://www.pewresearch.org/religion/2019/10/17/acknowledgments-38/.

Evertson, C.E. 2013. *Classroom Management for Elementary Teachers.* Boston: Pearson.

Evertson, Carolyn E. & Emmer, Edmund T. 2013. *Classroom Management for Elementary Teachers*. Boston: Pearson.

2015. *Farlex Dictionary of Idioms. © 2015 Farlex, Inc,*. Huntingdon, Pa.: Farlex Inc.

Foster, Richard. 2001. *Streams of Living Water: Celebrating the Great Traditions of Christian Faith*. San Fransisco: Harper One.

Fowler, James. 1981. *Stages of Faith: The Psychology of Human Development and the Quest for Meaning*. San Franscisco: HarperOne.

Garde, Allison. 2017. *Dappled Studies*. February 26.

Graham, Donovan L. 2003. *Teaching Redemptively; Bringing Grace and Truth Into Your Classroom*. Colorado Springs: Purposeful Design Publications.

Graham, Donovan L. 2003. *Teaching redemptively; Bringing Grace and Truth into Your Classroom*. Colorado Springs: Purposeful Design Publications.

Graham, Donovan. 2003. *Teaching Redemptively :Bringing Grace and Truth into Your Classroom*. Colorado Springs: Association of Christian Schools Internation.

Haas, Peter. n.d. *The Contemplative Prayer*.

Haas, Peter Traben. 2013. *Centering Prayers, A One-Year Companion for Going Deeper Into the Love of God*. Brewster, MA: Paraclete Press.

Haidt, Jonathan. 2005. "Wired to Be Inspired." *Greater Good Magazine*, March 1: 1.

Harmel, Kristin. 1999. *Teachers' Nonverbal Clues Affect Student's Performance*. January 25. www.sciencedaily.com/releases/1999/01/990122130911.htm>.

Harriot, Valencia, Extine, Julie J., Hall, Todd W. Hall, and, Pargament Kenneth I. 2014. "Awareness of God's presence, well-being and responses to spiritual struggle." *Society for the Psychology of Religion and Spirituality Newsletter*, October.

Hatfield, elaine: Cacioppo, John T.: Rapson, Richard L.,: Clark, Margaret S. (Ed),. vol.14. "Emotional and social behavior." *Review of personality and Social Psychology* 151-177.

Henderson, Roger. 2008. "Kuyper's Inch." *Pro Rege;Vol.36: No.3* 12-14.

Herndon, Eva. 2018. *WHAT ARE MULTIPLE INTELLIGENCES AND HOW DO THEY AFFECT LEARNING?* Grand Rapids, Michigan, February 6.

Hill, Graham Joseph. 2020. *How to Write a Lament*. April 9.

Jacobs, Geroge M., Lee, Gan Siowck,& Ball, Jessica. 1997. *Learning Cooperative Learning Via Cooperative Learning*. San Clemente: Kagan Cooperative Learning.

Johansson, Calvin M. 1988. *Music & Ministry:A Biblical Counterpoint*. Peabody, Massachusettes: Hendrickson Publishers.

Keller, Timothy. 2008. *Prodigal God: Belief in an Age of Skepticism*. new York: Penguin Group USA.

—. 2013. *Walking With God Through Pain and Suffering*. London: Hodder & Stoughton Ltd.

Kinneman, David. 1990. "Only 10% of Christian Twentysomethings Have Resilient Faith." *Research Releases in Faith and Christianity*, Septmeber 24.

Klassen, Harold. 2005. "The Visual Valet." *transforming teachers.org*. October 27. https://transformingteachers.org/en/articles/biblical-integration/general/42-visual-valet.

Lewis, C.S. 1952. *Mere Christianity*. New York: Macmillan Publishing Co.

Lewis, CS. 2001. *The Weight of His Glory*. San Francisco: Haprper One.

Lund, Lisa. 2018. *Predicting Divorce: The Four Horsemen of the Apocalypse*. July 8.

Lyons, Gabe. n.d.

Mahoney, Kelli. 2019. "Overview of Spiritual Disciplines and How They Work." *Learn Religions*. June 25. lesrnreligions.com/what-are-spiritual-disciplines-712414.

Manning, Brennan. 2009. *The Furious Longing of God*. Colorado Springs: David C. Cook.

n.d. *Matter*. https://matterapp.com/skills/storytelling.

McCullough, Matt. 2018. "The Pronography of Death." *The Rabbit Room*. September 19. https://rabbitroom.com/?s=&akismet%5fcomment%5fnonce=5c397abdc8&ak%5fjs= 1538398217228&%5fajax%5flinking%5fnonce=dbdddd3fb6.

Miller, Sharon Miller. 2019. ""Why Niceness Weakens Our Witness"." *Christianity Today*, August 5.

n.a. n.d. *What is Project Based Learning*. https://www.magnifylearningin.org/what-is-project-based-learning#:~:text=%20What%20.

n.d. 2003. *Introduction in Nonverbal Communication*. October 16. http://www.phys.ksu. edu/-zhrepic/gened/nonverbalcom/non.

Nye, Rebecca. 2009. *Children's Spirituality, What It Is and Why It Matters*. London, UK: Church House Publishing.

1999. *OmniPoll*. Barna Research Group.

Pace, Heather. 2019. ""Don't trust Your Christianity"." *The Gospel Coalition*, August 7.

Palmer, Parker. 1998. *The Courage to Teach, Exploring the inner landscape of a teacher's life Jossey-Bass Publishers, San Francisco, 1998 (p. 5)*. San Francisco: Jossey-Bass Publishers.

Pearcey, Nancy. 2008. *Total Truth*. Wheaton: Crossway Publishers.

Perry, Bruce D. n.d. "Principles of Working with Traumatized Children." *teacher.scholastic. com/professional/bruceperry/working_children.htm*.

Peterson, Lani. 2017. "The Science Behind the Art of Storytelling." *Harvard Business Publishing*. Nivenmber 14. https://www.harvardbusiness.org/the-science-behind-the-art-of-storytelling/.

Popcak, Gregory. 2021. "Five Steps to Begin Overcoming Bitterness." *Catholic Exchange*, March 5: 1.

—. 2019. "Five Steps to Overcoming Bitterness." *The Catholic Exchange*, March 28.

Pratt, Richard L. 2000. *Designed for Dignity*. Harmony Township, New Jersey: Presbyterian and Reformed Publishers.

Pratt, Richard L. Jr. 2000. *Designed for Dignity: What God Has Made It Possible For You To Be*. Harmony Township, New Jersey: Presbyterian and Reformed Publishing Co.

—. 2000. *Designed for Dignity: What God Has Made It Possible for You to Be*. Harmony Township, New Jersey: Presbyterian and Reformed Publishing Co.

Riesen, Richard A. 2002. *Piety and Philosophy:a Primer for Christian Schools*. Phoenix: ACW Press.

Rohr, Richard. 2020. ""Change in Inevitable" Wisdom in Times of Crisis." July 5.

—. 2020. *A Healing Process*. September 10.

Rohr, Richard. 2017. "A New Reformation Monday from Richard Rohr's Daily Meditations." *Richard Rohr's Daily Meditation*. Albuquerque, New Mexico: Center for Action and Contemplation, October 12.

—. 2011. *Falling Upward: A Spirituality for the Two Halves of Life Truth*. San Francisco: Jossey-Bass.

—. 2017. *Just This*. Albuquerque: CAC Publishing.

Roska, Kiely Todd. 2021. *The Porter: At the Threshold of Hopitality*. https://www.benedictinecenter.org/the-porter/.

Rowe, Mary Budd. 1987. ""Wait Time: Slowing Down May Be a Way of Speeding Up." AMERICAN EDUCATOR." *American Educator*, Spring: 38-43, 47.

Scriven, Michael & Paul, Richard. 1987. "Define Critical thinking." *8th Annual International Conference on Critical Thinking and Education Reform*. The Foundation for Critical Thinking.

Settecase, Joel. 2019. *seven-worldview-questions*. May 18. https://thethink.institute/articles/seven-worldview-questions.

Sire, James W. 2009. *The Universe Next Door*. Downers Grove: Intervarsity Press.

Smith, David I, and John Shortt. 2002. *The Bible and the Task of Teaching*. Nottingham, UK: The Stapleford Centre.

Smith, David I. 2018. *On Christian Teaching: practicing faith in the classroom*. Grand Rapids: Wmilliam B. Eerdmans Publishing Company.

Smith, David I. 2009. "On Viewing Learners as Spiritual Beings: Implications for Language Educators." *CELEA vol.1, No.1 5*.

Smith, James K. 2009. *Desiring the Kingdom:Worship, Worldview, and Cultural Formation*. Grand Rapids: Baker Academics.

Stines, Sharie. 2015. ""The Power of Unconditional Positive Regard" blog-The recovery expert 8 Nov 2015." *the recovery*. November 8. https://therecoveryexpert.com.

Stott, John K.W. 2012. *Basic Christianity*. Wheaton: Intervarsity Press.

Swaner, Lynn E. 2016. *Professional Development for Christian School Educators and Leaders :Frameworks and Practices*. Accessed August 9, 2022. https://www.acsi.org/thought-leadership/professional-development-for-christian-schools.

n.d. *Teaching for Transformation*. https://cace.org/wp-content/uploads/2020/09/TfT-brochure.pdf.

The Great School Partnerships. 2015. Aoril 6. http://www.edglossary.org/scaffolding/htgives.

Tomlison, Carol. 2017. *How to Differentiate Instruction in Academically Diverse Classrooms*. Alexandria: ASCD.

Traben, Haas. Peter. 2013. *Centering Prayers., A One-Year Companion for Going Deeper into the Love of God*. Brewster, MA: Paraclete Press.

Vanderslice, Kendall. 2019. *We Will Feast*. grand Rapids Michhigan: Eerdman's Publishers.

Vaughan, Helen Purgason. 2019. "elements of transformational Education." *Annual Meeting of CATE*. Horsham, England: none. 2.

Vroegop, Mark. 2019. *Dark Clouds, Deep Mercy: Discovering the Grace of Lament.* Wheaton: Crossway.

Wallace, Jim. 2013. *On God's Side, What Religion and Politics Hasn't Learned About Serving the Common Good.* Grand Rapids: Brazos Press a division of Baker Publishing Group.

Wax, Trevin. 2011. *Counterfeit Gospels: Rediscovering the Good News in a World of False Hope.* Chicago: Moddy Publishers.

Wenger, Etienne. 1998. *Communities of Practice: Learning, Meaning, and Identity.* Cambridge: Cambridge University Press.

Worldview?, What is a Christian. n.d. *gotquestions.*

Wright, N.T. 2020. "Christianity Offers No Answers About the Coronavirus. It's Not Supposed To." *Time magazine,* March 29.

Zimbardo, George M. Slavich and Philip G. 2012. *Transformational Teaching:Theorectical underpinnings, Basic Principaes, Core Methods.* New York City, N.Y., July 24.

FACILITATOR'S GUIDE

THE HANDBOOK OF TRANSFORMATIONAL EDUCATION

The following *Facilitator's Guide* is a suggested blueprint for how a person could facilitate professional development using *The Handbook of Transformational Education*. It includes what content to prioritize, suggested learning activities, questions, and proposed evaluation and reflection times. This experience of having a facilitator and a group of educators go through the book together is referred to as a Sojourn. Sojourn is not intended to be a traditional teacher training but rather an experience of discussion, asking questions, reflection, prayer, and building relationships with participants.

The best preparation for facilitating a group is to have participated in one. It is imperative that the facilitator be very familiar with the handbook. If possible, the ideal group is comprised of colleagues working at the same place. After finishing the Sojourn, they could continue to meet as a professional learning community; drawing upon their experiences of implementing what was addressed in *The Handbook of Transformational Education*.

The *Facilitator's Guide* begins with a list of preparations to do ahead of time. Without mention, this step should always include prayer and familiarizing oneself with the chapter. The room arrangement is also mentioned and is usually desks that can be moved to face the facilitator and then easily turned to make groups of four participants. Ideally the desktops are flat and come together to make a work surface for the cooperative groups. Not to worry though, as people will creatively find a way to make a space to do the group work. What participants need to have with them is also listed—usually the handbook, a Bible, a journal, and paper and pencil to do tasks.

The handbook has statements that begin with "Transformational educators ..." Use these statements as your instructional objectives, your guide, and your benchmark for evaluation of learning. You may want to write them in some visible place at the beginning of each chapter.

At the end of the section or chapter are questions to consider. Always peruse these to see if you want to incorporate them into the group discussion or ask participants to journal their responses to the questions at the journaling time at the end of each chapter.

Define instructional objective: Instructional objectives are what a student can do or will know as a result of your teaching. They are not what the teacher does but are the specific, short-term, observable behaviors demonstrated by the learner as related to the teaching. They are commonly written in this format:

The learner will be able to (action verb) the (content to be learned).

Example: The learner will be able to write examples of how to correct ineffective praise.

Participants are abbreviated as Ps, and sometimes *transformational education* is abbreviated as TE

CHAPTER 1

INTRODUCTION

Prepare Ahead

Make name cards. Write each P's first name on a large, heavy-stock index card, folded longways. Use a bold permanent marker to write the name to make it as visible as possible. Make a card for yourself. Ps are to place these cards in front of them for the entire Sojourn.

Write out 2 Corinthians 3:3 and post it in the training area for the entire time.

Activity #1-1: collect the empty jar, stones, pebbles, and sand to do the object lesson.

Prepare to teach about Riesen's thoughts on Christian education.

Ensure each participant has a copy of the book, a journal, a Bible, and a pen.

Room arrangement: arrange seating for group instruction, which can also break into groups of four people for group work.

Welcome/Introduction of Ps

Welcome

Introduce yourself, highlighting your enthusiasm about TE.

Point out accommodations for comfort (toilets, refreshments, scheduled breaks).

Have Ps introduce themselves in a creative way of your choosing.

Overview of the Sojourn experience/schedule.

Go over p. VIII "How to Use This Book."

Introduction of Ps to One Another

Relationships are foundational to TE, so plan your welcome and introductions around how well the Ps may or may not know one another. For welcoming Ps who already know one another, plan a brief activity to set an informal, welcoming tone for the Sojourn. One idea is to sit in a circle and toss a ball or small object to another P to catch while you say a compliment about that person. That person then throws the object to a different P and says a compliment about them. This continues until everyone has been complimented.

For Ps who do not know one another, one idea is using the three-step interview cooperative learning found on p. 178.

Implement your preferred idea to establish an atmosphere of group engagement and trust.

Introduction

Section 1: Definition

Ask Ps to look at the cartoon on p. 2 and make comments. Ask if any person in the cartoon best represents what is meant by transformational education. Ask Ps to write down in their journal what they think transformational education means (this is for their eyes only; they can refer back to it after completing the book/Sojourn

Examine George's definition of transformational education on p. 3 and point out the following while inviting discussion.

- reference to *learning environments* and not only the *classroom*

Mention that education involves a *teacher* engaging a *learner*, so this definition broadly includes the teaching done by a youth worker, parent, sports coach, swim instructor, music teacher, language instructor, and so on.

- reference to every aspect of the environment and dimension of life and not just the academic work

Mention that factors other than the instructional objectives contribute to TE, such as the physical environment where the learning takes place, the emotional environment created by the way the teacher relates to the learner, even specific instructional methods, such as how questions are posed and responded to by the teacher.

- The goal is for the student *to embrace God's amazing design for him or herself.*

Read aloud p.3-4. George's definition emphasizes a biblical view of the learner as having a God-designed purpose and having unique attributes to be developed in order to fulfil that purpose.

- The emphasis on the abundant life is *not only for eternal life but also for the here and now.*

TE educators seek opportunities to introduce learners to the gospel and eternal life through Christ. However, the emphasis is not only on life after death but on the abundant life of Christ in the here and now.

- The emphasis is having an *impactful life,* not just for one's personal benefit.

Mention that TE is never just about mastering some learning objectives so the student can personally get ahead in life. It challenges the learner to understand how education equips them in fulfilling their purpose in God's kingdom and God's will being done on earth.

Read p. 3: "draw inspiration from the fact that transformational education communicates a rich and variegated message that is incapable of full and final definition." Ask Ps how they respond to the mutable/elusive nature of the definition. Ask how this affects the ability to measure how much students are actually being transformed.

Discuss these questions:

1. What strikes you about this definition of transformational education? Would you add or change anything?

Section 2: Imagine Being an Agent of Transformation

Examine the images on p. 5 of the stone cutters and explain imagination in the context of what we are imagining in terms of transforming lives through education.

Briefly talk through the ten examples of decisions that teachers make that contribute to transformation. Ask Ps for their own examples while discussing and indicate these will be developed further in later chapters.

Direct Ps to write their responses to the questions to ponder in their journals.

1. How much of your thinking about your teaching involves imagining yourself as a transformational educator?
2. Do you and your colleagues pray as if transformation truly depends on the work of the Holy Spirit?

3. Do any of the teacher decisions mentioned above reflect something for which you are gifted and have developed well?

Section 3: Transformed People Are Transformational

Read aloud 2 Corinthians 3:3. Ask Ps to memorize it during the training.

Emphasize that even though this training is trying to practically help teachers become transformational, the fact is their very *being* is used by the Spirit in transforming others.

Section 4: Schools a Biblical Concept?

Teach the reasoning for Christian schools not being a directly biblical concept Go over Reisen's reasons for the prominence of Christians' historical involvement in education. Ask for discussion and addition of other reasons.

Riesen's Reasons for Christian Education

The practical schooling fits in with the majority of life in that it is biblically "not enjoined nor forbidden but allowed." Most countries have laws requiring schooling for certain aged children, so it is practical for students to attend.

The ameliorative education is beneficial to individuals and communities; it is the essence of doing good works as instructed by the Bible.

The Imago Dei education. As created in the image of God, people are uniquely able to think and create. Education is all about challenging students to think and create.

Section 5: Are Transformational Education and Christian Education the Same?

Let Ps know this section requires much discussion and to be prepared to participate.

Do **Activity #1-1:** Divide Ps into groups of four and have them discuss the two questions below. A recorder/reporter should be appointed for each group to report back to the class.

Question 1: If the teacher is a Christian and there is prayer, weekly chapel, Bible class, biblical integration, and a biblical worldview, can we assume that the offering is transformational education? What more is there to add or leave off?

Question 2: What is Christian education?

After discussing the groups' responses to the questions above, use the contrasts chart on p. 19 to discuss whether transformational education and Christian education are the same.

Select these or other questions for discussion:

1. Do you agree that although schools are not a biblical construct, they indeed have a huge role in God's kingdom on earth? If so, name a few ways.
2. Do people who know the Bible better display evidence of more transformed living? What are some of the different ways of *knowing* the Bible?
3. What is the difference in worldview instruction and teaching from a specific worldview?
4. Discuss James K. Smith's question, "What if education wasn't first and foremost about what we know, but about what we love?"
5. How can teachers respect or honor a parent's role in the spiritual growth of their child?

Section 6: Transform, Not Only Reform

Define the difference between the terms *reform* and *transform*.

Ask Ps to give examples of transforming versus reforming.

Lead a discussion using the six questions below. Listen to Ps' answers to determine how much clarification you need to do in stressing the difference between reform and transformation.

1. Do we inadvertently teach our students that Christianity is a way of behaving?
2. How can we celebrate scripture memory, baptisms, acts of service, and so on in a way that points students to a life devoted to Christ and not simply as personal praise?
3. What experience(s) have you had with people of other cultures wanting to please you by complying with what they think you want?

Section 7: Teacher as Role Model

How does a teacher model that their "goodness" is not good enough and that he or she is broken and in need of a Savior?

Questions to consider:

1. How do you model for your students that you are a sinner in need of a Savior?

2. Do we inadvertently equate compliance with godly character?

3. Do we produce young people who, at least partially, believe they are *more spiritual* because they memorize scripture and listen to Christian music?

4. Apply the story of the prodigal son, Luke 15, to the idea of transformation being different from reformation.

Section 8: Reworking, Not Improving upon, Education

Read aloud the story of Hialte and Gizor. How did they transform religious practice of Ireland in that day?

Do the object lesson described below with filling the jars with stones, pebbles, and sand to represent teacher use of time in transformational education.

An object lesson may be a good way to illustrate this point that transformational education is not an addition of some spiritualized adornments (prayer, biblical connections to the lesson, chapel services) to what otherwise constitutes an education.

Object Lesson

Take an empty jar and add stones to fill the jar. Asks the students, "Is the jar full?" The students will likely say yes. The teacher then proceeds to take a handful of smaller pebbles and fill the empty spaces among the stones with pebbles. Again, the teacher asks, "Is the jar full?" The students are a little more hesitant this time but feel like the jar is pretty full at this point, so they say yes. Now the teacher fills the jar with even more fine sand.

Note that by gradations, you can put in stones, pebbles, and sand to fill a jar, *but you cannot do the reverse*. If you fill your jar up with sand first, there's no room for pebbles or rocks.

The demonstration can be used to illustrate the idea that a routine, unreflective dispensing of Christianized teacher behaviors can fill the jar quickly without giving the space (or energy, relinquishment, time, focus) for making divine connections with the Holy Spirit and students.

Sand represents biblically based lessons, chapel services, faculty devotions, monthly service projects, enforcement of appropriate student behavior. The focus can easily be filled with teacher activity that molds students instead of escorting them to the presence of God.

Pebbles represent our classroom or school policies and curriculum selection, which most likely were grounded in reflection and prayer initially but may have become routinized in implementation. Examples may be methods of measuring and reporting student progress, classroom-management plans, interpersonal time with students, and so on.

Stones represent our focus on the core threads of nurturing transformation, such as the teacher's prayer for transformation, personal practice of the spiritual disciplines, planning time and space conducive for students to interface directly with God, reflection on how we interact with students and colleagues, and how we discipline students.

Caution! It is quite easy to identify a problem and quite another thing to be a teacher on the front line, preparing and executing daily plans and caring for a classroom of students. The time to reflect, pray, and devote to transformational education is easier to imagine than to accomplish. If our focus is filled with sand, we will not have a space for pebbles or stones. My prayer is that reflectively going through this book will inspire, not discourage, teachers. The purpose is not to point fingers.

Section 9: Established Transformational Education Theory

This can be a brief section to point out that the term *transformational education* is used in a variety of ways.

1. Transformational education is a term used widely by people and meaning a variety of things.
2. Touch on the key points of the academic theorists Mezirow, Loder, and Nye.

Allow time for journaling on a topic you assign or whatever Ps choose to write.

CHAPTER 2

IT TAKES TWO, USUALLY THREE

Preparation

Materials: handbook, Bible, journal, paper and pencil/pen

Room arrangement: Arrange room conducive to full group discussion/lecture. The last activity is in pairs.

Prepare a short lecture on the idea of *friends of transformation*. If you need resources, look up "sacred wounds."

Instruction

Section 1: The Holy Spirit and Yieldedness

Explain these four key points:

- Teachers *don't* transform students.
- The Holy Spirit transforms.
- Students may deny the work of the Holy Spirit. A student may choose not to yield to God. This choice is inherent in God's nature as love. Love cannot demand or control; it must be given.
- Teachers *do* pray, nurture relationships, and create conditions that are conducive to transformation.

If any Ps have difficulty with this list, discuss how these points may be controversial among some Christian denominations; otherwise, do not discuss.

Emphasize transformational educators seek not only to see students come to faith in Christ but also to fulfill God's amazing design for their contribution to God's kingdom on earth.

Section 2: Asking God for Transformation—Prayer

After emphasizing the teacher's primary task of praying for transformation, ask Ps to share ways of praying that they find as effective or meaningful. Examples may be praying Bible verses, praying the Lection Divinia, praying for a student as you sit in his or her desk, prayer walking, and so on.

Give Ps time to silently read the "Praying with Students" bullet points. Once read, ask them to add any of their own that came to mind.

Praying with Students

1. Do not pressure students to pray out loud. Sometimes going around the circle for prayer can feel like pressure unless the teacher can effectively make it acceptable to pass.

2. Model spontaneous prayer. Stop whatever is being done to ask God for help, thank Him for a special blessing or answered prayer, or make a petition. Demonstrate that prayer can be a conversation with God at any time and any situation.

3. Be wary of students seeing prayer as giving God a wish list and making God into a cosmic sugar daddy. I observed people who struggled when God "didn't come through for them." Obviously, their view of prayer and understanding of God were misunderstood.

4. Help students learn spiritual language and habits, such as physical positions for prayer (e.g., kneeling, standing in a circle holding hands, or putting their palms together); praying the scriptures; Jesus's model prayer and His praise-thanksgiving-confession-petition outline for prayer; praying as a ministry, such as intercessory prayer; and so many more.

5. Teach and model prayer as a listening activity too and not just one sided from the student. Invite student to pray as a form of reflection and discernment in God's presence.

Section 3: Creating Conditions Conducive for Transformation

Ask Ps, "If the Holy Spirit is the transformer, how do we fit in as teachers?"

Read scripture that makes it clear that God includes us in His work. Ephesians 2:10 says, "For we are God's handiwork, created in Christ Jesus to do good works, which God prepared in advance for us to do."

Teach what is meant by creating conditions. Go over the four analogies (pp. 45-47) to shed light on creating conditions for something we cannot control but can nurture. Possibly ask Ps which analogy they think is best.

- getting to sleep
- growing crops
- doctors healing
- giving birth

Emphasize the process nature of transformation as well as significant moments that are transformational. Contrast this to the emphasis some give to a onetime decision for Christ or praying a sinner's prayer—once and done.

Section 4: What Comes after Belief? Nurturing Passion

Ask Ps for their favorite metaphor to describe teachers.

Explain that transformation is not just a behavioral change but is a complete change internally, as well as externally, in the student. The heart must be inhabited by Christ for transformation to be full. First the person recognizes and is overwhelmed by God's love for him or her. As love is reciprocated to God by the transformed person, God molds that person to love what God loves and choose what God chooses. Transformation cannot be imposed by a teacher, but a teacher can lead the student to Christ's presence. This is a very important concept to be developed and understood by Ps.

Read this quote to PS and ask for their responses:

> Worship is the "imagination station" that incubates our loves and longings so that our cultural endeavors are indexed toward God and his kingdom. Worship is about "formation" more than "expression." It is God himself meeting us to shape us into the kind of people who do His will, not just an outpouring of our sincere feelings about Him. (Smith 2013)

Section 4: Friends of Transformation

Discuss this concept of friends of transformation using applicable scripture and anecdotal examples.

Allow some time for Ps to share their own experiences of being transformed through one of the listed friends of transformation.

Have Ps discuss what and when students should or should not be insulated from hard experiences or truth. You may find a wide variety of opinion about this, especially as it relates to the age of the student. Discuss how the transformational educator helps the student benefit as much as possible from the friends of transformation.

Activity #2-1: After going over the steps to suicide assessment, have Ps pair off and actually go through the questions with their partner, with the partner making up responses that require the interrogation to continue.

End session with time for journaling on whatever topic you assign or whatever the participants may want to write.

CHAPTER 3

CORAM DEO OR FRAGMENTATION

Prepare Ahead

Room arrangement: Arrange four seats around one table so that Ps can see presenter and also turn to work together in a group using the table. Make sure the table is a flat surface where they can draw.

Materials: Ps should have a copy of the handbook, journal, Bible, and coloring paper and a set of colored markers

For activity #3-2, print one copy of the words below for every three Ps. Cut the words out and assemble in a small plastic bag. There should be one bag of words for every three participants. In the bag, include the directions. The Ps should be divided into groups of three with a flat work surface to place the strips of paper.

Directions for activity #3-2: Divide the words into two groups based on how they are alike or different in some way. After you have created the two groups, give a descriptive name for each group.

heart	private	feelings
secular	personal	values
morality	religion	subjective
scripture memory	mind	opinion
pastor	freedom	mind
facts	public	sacred
tolerance	objective	
engineer	multiplication facts	science

Section 1: Scripture Speaks That All of Life Is before the Face of God

Jesus proclaimed, "I am the way, the truth, and the life" (John 14:6). Profound! This scripture expresses the Christian worldview. God's living presence permeates all things, at all times, in all places. Knowing God's creation of and involvement in every aspect of life will change how we go about our daily lives. Our classrooms and kitchens, our grocery stores and cathedrals, our sports fields and baptismal fonts are all holy ground.

Do **Activity #3-1:** Meditate on the following scripture, asking God how to know Him through His creation; how to obey because of His established natural order; how to glorify Him through His works.

> The earth is the LORD's, and everything in it, the world, and all who live in it. (Psalm 24:1)

> For in him we live and move and have our being. (Acts 17:28)

> Do not conform to the pattern of this world but be transformed by the renewing of your mind. Then you will be able to test and approve what God's will is—his good, pleasing and perfect will. (Romans 12:2)

> So whether you eat or drink or whatever you do, do it all for the glory of God. (1 Corinthians 10:31)

> Whatever you do, work at it with all your heart, as working for the Lord, not for human masters, since you know that you will receive an inheritance from the Lord as a reward. It is the Lord Christ you are serving. (Colossians 3:23–24)

> Choose my instruction instead of silver, knowledge rather than choice gold, for wisdom is more precious than rubies, and nothing you desire can compare with her. (Proverbs 8:10–11)

> And this is my prayer: that your love may abound more and more in knowledge and depth of insight, so that you may be able to discern what is best and may be pure and blameless for the day of Christ. (Philippians 1:9–10)

> We demolish arguments and every pretension that sets itself up against the knowledge of God, and we take captive every thought to make it obedient to Christ. (2 Corinthians 10:5)

Do **Activity #3:2: Scripture Speaks That All of Life Is before the Face of God**

Ps are to read over these scriptures and write down key points about how God's presence in the world permeates everything:

The earth is the LORD's, and everything in it, the world, and all who live in it. (Psalm 24:1)

He is the Lord of every person, the planet, and all who resides on it.

For in him we live and move and have our being. (Acts 17:28)

All things depend on Him for existence; therefore, it is illogical to attempt to keep any aspect of life away from His oversight.

Do not conform to the pattern of this world but be transformed by the renewing of your mind. Then you will be able to test and approve what God's will is—his good, pleasing and perfect will. (Romans 12:2)

The apostle Paul appeals to his readers not based on adapting to culture but on the deeper level of critically scrutinizing with the mind. Prior to conforming to the world in our actions, we conform to the world in the mind. Therefore, the solution is not reforming our behavior but transforming our minds.

So whether you eat or drink or whatever you do, do it all for the glory of God. (1 Corinthians 10:31)

All the mundane, routine things we do, not just what we routinely consider spiritual acts, are to be done for God's glory.

Whatever you do, work at it with all your heart, as working for the Lord, not for human masters, since you know that you will receive an inheritance from the Lord as a reward. It is the Lord Christ you are serving. (Colossians 3:23–24)

Whether bathing a baby, removing trash, or performing intricate surgery, our service is to the Lord, and our effort should reflect the majesty of whom we are serving.

Choose my instruction instead of silver, knowledge rather than choice gold, for wisdom is more precious than rubies, and nothing you desire can compare with her. (Proverbs 8:10–11)

The wisdom of God is to be valued above anything else.

And this is my prayer: that your love may abound more and more in knowledge and depth of insight, so that you may be able to discern what is best and may be pure and blameless for the day of Christ. (Philippians 1:9–10)

Notice how love impacts knowledge and insight.

We demolish arguments and every pretension that sets itself up against the knowledge of God, and we take captive every thought to make it obedient to Christ. (2 Corinthians 10:5)

Notice how God calls us to be able to discern His truth so that we can demolish arguments and have minds wholly devoted to Christ.

Explain the metanarrative (pp. 73-75).

Do **activity #3:3:** Distribute coloring paper and colored markers for Ps to draw a poster.

Each participant draws a pictogram of the metanarrative. Ps divide their paper into four squares. In square one, they draw something to represent creation. In square two, they draw something to represent the Fall. Squares two and three are used for drawing a representation of redemption and restoration.

Chapter 3

Instruction

Introduce the chapter with Activity #3-1. Divide the Ps into groups of three and have each group sit around a table or flat surface where they can spread out and manipulate pieces of paper. Give each group one plastic bag with words and directions (see Prepare Ahead #1). Read the directions to Ps and make sure they know they can create *only two* groups with the words. Upon completion, ask the groups to explain the titles they gave to their two groups. Open a discussion, leading the Ps to understand the words are commonly divided to separate secular things from sacred things like these two groups:

List 1	*List 2*
morality	tolerance
pastor	science
personal	freedom
sacred	mind
scripture memory	facts
subjective	engineer
religion	public
pastor	objective
opinion	multiplication facts

Explain the terms *Coram Deo* and fragmentation. Explain how dualism has infiltrated Christian beliefs and schools.

Do together: Ensure Ps turn to p. 59 to see Browning's verse. Ask Ps what they think is being said and what they think about seeing and reverencing God in nature. Contrast the people who take off their shoes with the people who sit and pluck blackberries.

> Earth's crammed with heaven,
> And every common bush afire with God,
> But only he who sees takes off his shoes;
> The rest sit round and pluck blackberries.
> (Elizabeth Barrett Browning)

One interpretation is:

earth's crammed with heaven = creation as a manifestation of God

take off shoes = scripture on taking off shoes when on holy ground (Exodus 3:5)

the rest plucking blackberries = without the spiritual eyes to see God reflected in creation, the others see creation as a consumer would = for what it can provide them

Do **Activity #3:2: Scripture Speaks That All of Life Is Before the Face of God**

Distribute the five slips of scripture to five different Ps. Have them read the scripture out loud (possibly have them say how the verse speaks that all of life is before the face of God).

Section 1: Scripture Speaks That All of Life Is Before the Face of God

Jesus proclaimed, "I am the way, the truth, and the life" (John 14:6). Profound! This scripture expresses the Christian worldview. God's living presence permeates all things, at all times, in all places. Knowing God's creation of and involvement in every aspect of life will change how we go about our daily lives. Our classrooms and kitchens, our grocery stores and cathedrals, our sports fields and baptismal fonts are all holy ground.

Do **Activity #3-1:** Meditate on the following scripture, asking God how to know Him through His creation; how to obey because of His established natural order; how to glorify Him through His works.

> The earth is the LORD's, and everything in it, the world, and all who live in it. (Psalm 24:1)

> For in him we live and move and have our being. (Acts 17:28)

> Do not conform to the pattern of this world but be transformed by the renewing of your mind. Then you will be able to test and approve what God's will is—his good, pleasing and perfect will. (Romans 12:2)

> So whether you eat or drink or whatever you do, do it all for the glory of God. (1 Corinthians 10:31)

> Whatever you do, work at it with all your heart, as working for the Lord, not for human masters, since you know that you will receive an inheritance from the Lord as a reward. It is the Lord Christ you are serving. (Colossians 3:23–24)

Choose my instruction instead of silver, knowledge rather than choice gold, for wisdom is more precious than rubies, and nothing you desire can compare with her. (Proverbs 8:10–11)

And this is my prayer: that your love may abound more and more in knowledge and depth of insight, so that you may be able to discern what is best and may be pure and blameless for the day of Christ. (Philippians 1:9–10)

We demolish arguments and every pretension that sets itself up against the knowledge of God, and we take captive every thought to make it obedient to Christ. (2 Corinthians 10:5)

Section 2: The Sacred/Secular Split

Go over the examples of sacred/secular split on p. 64 and have Ps name others. Discuss what makes a Christian pie.

Section 3: Is Biblical Integration Really the Term We Mean to Use?

Show video clip or give examples of amusing biblical integration attempts.

Emphasize that transformational educator's focus is not to *tack on* a biblical truth.

Make the point that the term *biblical integration* is sometimes used interchangeably with a Christian worldview.

Section 4: Teaching from a Christian Worldview

Define worldview and then spend time examining and discussing the worldview charts on pp. 76-78.

Teach the metanarrative.

Do **Activity #3-4:** Ask Ps to draw a poster of the four stories in the metanarrative. Note that this instructional method ties into multiple intelligences by Howard garner discussed in chapter 6.

Ask Ps to give examples of how something they teach would lend itself to explanation from a Christian worldview.

Go over the two warnings on pp. 75-76.

Do **Activity #3-5:** Form Ps into groups of three people (try to have at least one doctrinally astute person in each group). Have the groups discuss and write out answers to the seven sets of questions on p. 77 from Joel Settecase. Come back together to discuss and to share examples of how these answers would impact your lessons.

Section 5: The Cultivation of Christians Learners

Discuss what a class looks like if students don't own a sense of purpose in their occupation as student. How could a teacher nurture student in assuming the significance of being a learner?

End this chapter by letting Ps select which of the discussion questions they want to discuss, and then discuss them as a group.

Give time to the Ps to journal or answer the questions.

CHAPTER 4

THE SWEET AROMA OF CHRIST OR BUG SPRAY

Prepare Ahead

Room arrangement: have table and chairs where four people can work in a group.

Materials: Ps will need their Bible, their journals, paper, and pen/pencil.

Select a method of restoration among offended parties to teach to Ps. The book recommends a website and one method.

Activity #4:1: Make a card for each "responsibility of a host" listed below. The four cards make a set that should be placed together in a plastic baggy. Make one set of cards for every four people.

1) A host welcomes.

How does the teacher welcome students to class? One of the biggest fears reported by students at the beginning of a new class is not knowing where the class is located. Welcoming on the first day of class involves helping students know they are in the correct location. The teacher welcomes students by being stationed at the entranceway to offer personalized greetings (handshakes, personal questions, smiles). This is a good time for the teacher-host to assess the current needs or emotional state of their student-guests. Name tags at the students' seats with a welcome sign on them or on the board is also a way of welcome. What other ways welcome students?

Instructional: Teacher-hosts are also in the position of welcoming students to a new sphere of learning, new ideas, and challenging tasks. Providing an atmosphere of acceptance and intellectual freedom allows the student-guests to learn and explore with a trusted teacher-host by their side.

2) A host introduces.

Who in your class already knows you or the other classmates? How do you plan to introduce yourself to the students and the students to one another? What teaching techniques, such as cooperative learning groups (see chapter 6), can you use to introduce and facilitate new relationships among the students? Some teachers train students to be a host or friend for new students. This student-host tells the new student what they need to know, helps the new student navigate the campus, and sits with them at lunch or snack time. The host-student also further acquaints the new student with classmates.

Are there other people you should introduce to the students? At the school I led, the kindergarten teachers always gave the students a tour of the campus with introductions to me and other administrative staff on the first day.

Instructional: Perhaps you are introducing your guests to a new subject, a new idea, a new author, or a new concept.

3) A host provides.

What do your students need to be responsible learners? Are their physical needs met, such as food, drink, adequate lighting, and temperature? How about the physical needs of correct desk and chair sizes, well-ventilated air, time to move and exercise after sitting or standing awhile? Are appropriate hygienic practices in place to prevent illness? Do they have the supplies and materials they need for class? One idea is to have a selection of school supplies from which students may borrow when they forget their own. This is also a great way to encourage students to contribute to the stockpile as members of a learning community who are looking out for one another. Teachers may keep snacks or other food items for students who forgot theirs or who may be feeling sick. Teacher-hosts often meet these needs by calling them to the attention of the parents or other school officials to address.

Instructional: How well are the students' academic needs being addressed? Has thought been given to advanced students who need greater challenges? Weaker students who need support? Does the teacher offer excellent classroom management so the student-guests have a safe and predictable place to learn?

4) A host serves.

Servant leadership is a concept and practice well known to transformational educators. Jesus taught this by washing His disciples' feet and by demonstrating a lowly stance throughout His life. The leader is to be one who serves, not glorifies himself. What are some ways that a teacher relinquishes privilege for the sake of serving their students in class? Research has demonstrated that observing someone being kind, unselfish or serving others inspires similar behaviors from those who observe (Haidt 2005).

Instructional: What ways are students allowed or encouraged to serve the teacher or classmates on academic tasks? Are peer tutors allowed or cooperative learning tasks utilized? Does the teacher promote the sharing of encouraging and celebratory words by classmates to other classmates regarding academic tasks? Teacher may have a bulletin board devoted to posting students' best work.

Section 4: prepare a way (either make strips pf paper with the scripture on them or call out scripture reference for Ps to find in their Bibles).

Section 3: prepare to explain Gottman's four markers of relationship failure.

Section 1: prepare to teach the sweet aroma of Christ origins from Roman wars (p. 84).

Prepare to explain the story of the porter on p.85-86

Prepare slips of paper with the steps for implementing praise found on pp. 85-86 or just assign one step to each participant for activity 4:5.

Chapter 4

Instruction

Section 1: The Hospitality of a Teacher

Open the chapter with this statement:

> The biblical Christ is winsome, beloved, and a friend of sinners. It seems the prophetic voice of Jesus was primarily against the religious leadership of the day. So why then are Christians often known to the masses for what they are against more than what they are for? Do we exude the sweet aroma of Christ in our classrooms or some type of the bug spray disguised as Christian piety?

Explain the "sweet aroma of Christ" origins from p. 84.

Note the difference between high-power distance cultures or informal classrooms. The point is whether the class is formal or more casual in how students and teachers relate. The students need to believe the teacher is *for them*.

Tell the story of the porter and ask Ps their favorite metaphor for a teacher (e.g., guide, sage, host, coach).

Do **Activity #4-1:** Divide into a group of four people. Each group gets a baggy with host cards. Each group member takes one "responsibility of a host" card. They read it and prepare to explain it to the group. Discuss the questions on the card or discuss how you, as a teacher, welcome, introduce, provide for, and serve the students.

Solicit from Ps ideas on how to make their classrooms hospitable. Compare to list on p. 88.

Section 2: The Necessary Practice of Spiritual Disciplines

Ask Ps to name some of the spiritual disciplines (p. 91) and share, if they wish, the ones that are particularly meaningful to them.

Discuss this quote "Love God and do whatever you want," credited to Augustine, probably paraphrasing from 1 John 4:4–12, which says, "Live according to your new life in the Holy spirit, and you won't be doing what your sinful nature craves."

Choose any of the questions on p. 92 to discuss with Ps.

Should you …

- maintain a formal stance in student relationships so they will respect you?
- not smile until Christmas?
- not reveal any personal information in the name of professionalism?
- not admit your errors to students so they will have confidence in you?
- disregard extenuating circumstances?

Section 3: Forming Loving Relationships

Tell Ps about Gottman's four markers of relationship failure research and make the application to nonmarital relationships, such as teacher to student, teacher to colleague, and so on.

Do **Activity #4-3:**

Apply Gottman's markers of relationship failure scenarios to school relationships between a teacher and students / other teachers / administrators or parents by giving examples and by having the Ps give examples. Depending on the class size, this may be done in smaller groups or all together as the class. (see p. 98.)

1. Example of criticism
   Example of an "I statement"

2. Example of defensiveness
   Example of taking responsibility

3. Example of a sarcastic statement posing as humor but is contempt
   Example of identifying the root of contempt and expressing it directly

4. Example of how a teacher can stonewall a student
   Example of how a student can stonewall a teacher

Do **Activity #4-4: Peacemaking**

Have Ps read Proverbs 18 silently and a make a list of principles relevant to settling disputes using one word or a short phrase to identity them. (Example: For verse 15, "listen to all sides" or "give due diligence to settling disputes.")

Have Ps read Matthew 18:15–17 silently and list steps for addressing grievances. From your experience, what happens when the offended person talks to everyone except the person who offended him or her?

Develop your own standard (steps you will do) for personally addressing offenses. Write it down to retrieve for implementation when you get offended. Compare your plan for addressing offense to your school's or team's policy. Adjust your own or recommend adjustments to your school's or team's grievance policy.

Discuss the participants' responses in the group.

Select a process for restoration that you want to teach. The book gives a website for one.

Section 4: Communication

Place the scripture below in front of the Ps (can be on a PowerPoint, a handout piece of paper, or located on p. 98 in the handbook.) Have them silently read the scripture and then ask Ps which of these scripture needs the most attention in their classrooms or workplace.

Second Timothy 2:16: "But avoid irreverent babble, for it will lead people into more and more ungodliness."

Colossians 4:6: "Let your speech always be gracious, seasoned with salt, so that you may know how you ought to answer each person."

Colossians 3:8: "But now you must put them all away: anger, wrath, malice, slander, and obscene talk from your mouth."

James 1:19: "Know this, my beloved brothers: let every person be quick to hear, slow to speak, slow to anger."

Ephesians 4:29: "Let no corrupting talk come out of your mouths, but only such as is good for building up, as fits the occasion, that it may give grace to those who hear."

Proverbs 10:19: "Sin is not ended by multiplying words, but the prudent hold their tongues."

Proverbs 12:18: "There is one whose rash words are like sword thrusts, but the tongue of the wise brings healing."

Proverbs 18:13: "If one gives an answer before he hears, it is his folly and shame."

Proverbs 18:2: "A fool takes no pleasure in understanding, but only in expressing his opinion."

Proverbs 25:12: "Like a gold ring or an ornament of gold is a wise reprover to a listening ear."

Proverbs 16:24: "Gracious words are like a honeycomb, sweetness to the soul and health to the body."

Luke 6:45: "The good person out of the good treasure of his heart produces good, and the evil person out of his evil treasure produces evil, for out of the abundance of the heart his mouth speaks."

James 3:5: "So also the tongue is a small member, yet it boasts of great things. How great a forest is set ablaze by such a small fire!"

First Timothy 5:1–2: "Do not rebuke an older man but encourage him as you would a father, younger men as brothers, older women as mothers, younger women as sisters, in all purity."

Teach the research on effective praise (p. 106).

Do **Activity #4:5:** Go over the tips for implementation of praise with the group by putting each tip on a single slip of paper and distribute the slips to Ps. Ps would take turns reading the tips and offering commentary or giving examples of the tip.

Tips for Implementation

a. Be nonjudgmental. Praise the student's accomplishment or behavior, not his or her achievement when compared with that of others.
   Example: "Doug, you really did a great job of being prepared for class today by bringing your pencils and notebook."
   Nonexample: "Doug, I'm glad you brought your supplies today like everyone else."

b. Avoid global positive statements.
   Example: "Wow, Keesha! You used several vivid terms in your paragraph to describe the story setting. Your use of adjectives has really increased."
   Nonexample. "Wow, Keesha! Great writing today!"

c. Be sincere and credible. Use statements that underscore the student's actual efforts and accomplishments. Make sure your voice and body language match the content of your message.
   Example: "Hector, you set up the multiplication problem correctly, placing all numbers in the appropriate columns. You are ready now to work on the next part of the problem."
   Nonexample: "Hector, you really did a great job solving your multiplication problems today."

d. Deliver immediate praise near the student for whom the praise is intended. Move around the classroom frequently so you note praiseworthy behaviors.

e.   Utilize a variety of verbal and written praise.

f.   Offer praise to several students at the same time. Or provide praise privately to avoid the embarrassment some students feel when being singled out in public.

g.   Evaluate and adjust praise.
     Is the praise effective? Do the students seem to like the attention?
     Do students maintain or improve the praised behavior?
     Do I offer each student some form of praise every day?
     Do I maintain a positive balance of positive and negative statements in my classroom?
     Do I include variety in my use of praise?

h.   Change the type, the way, or how often the praise is given based upon individual student responses or needs.

i.   Use frequent praise when new behavior and skills are taught. As the skill is mastered, this frequency should be gradually reduced to a more intermittent schedule.

Do **Activity #4-5** with the Ps: **Practice for Yourself**

Below, read the student behavior and the less effective praise statements the teacher makes regarding the behavior. Then rewrite the praise statements to make them more effective using the guidelines above. Notice the first one is an example to show you what to do.

Example:

1.   Jane scored an A on a math test.

Ineffective: You're smart Jane.

More effective: Jane, the extra time you put into studying resulted in an excellent grade.

2.   Jack shows you his artwork.

Ineffective: What a pretty picture, Jack!

More effective:

_____

_____

3. Lupe helps you hand out papers to the class.

Ineffective: You are so good, Lupe.

More effective:

_____

_____

4. After months of losing privileges due to not turning in homework, Mary turns in homework on time every day for a week.

Ineffective: At last, Mary, you are getting your work in on time.

More effective:

_____

_____

5. Sayeed scored two goals during the game.

Ineffective: You are a great player.

More effective:

_____

_____

Be wary of setting up opportunities where selfless service is overshadowed by the anticipation of receiving personal attention and benefit from service!

Discuss the other ways of honoring students and ask Ps to add more to those listed.

> Teach the verbal signs of listening:
>
> utterances
>
> brief verbal affirmation
>
> open and closed questioning
>
> reflection
>
> clarification
>
> summarization
>
> mentioning a similar situation

- *Paraphrasing*: "So you want us to build the new school in the style of the old one?"
- *Utterances*: "Uh-huh, yes, hmmmm."
- *Brief verbal affirmation*: "I appreciate the time you've taken to speak to me."
- *Asking open-ended questions*: "I understand you aren't happy with your new car. What changes can we make to it?"
- *Asking specific questions*: "How many employees did you take on last year?"
- *Mentioning similar situations*: "I was in a similar situation after my previous company made me redundant."
- *Notice people speaking*: A meeting facilitator encouraging a quiet team member to share their views about a project.
- *Summarize group conversations*: A manager summarizing what has been said at a meeting and checking with the others for agreement

Do **Activity#4-6: Role-Play Active Listening**

Ask two Ps to hold a conversation while the other Ps observe and write down all the indications of active listening they observe. Share the observations with the entire group. Ask for two other volunteers and do the exercise again as many times as needed for Ps to be able to actively listen and to notice when someone else is doing so.

Topics for Conversations Ideas

1. Any topic relevant to what the group has been experiencing in sojourn.

2. Talk about your fears of school as an elementary student.

3. Tell about your career or vocational dream.

4. Share about what someone did or said to you that made you feel proud.

5. Talk about your favorite teacher and what he or she did that made him or her a favorite.

CHAPTER 5

FIRE INSURANCE OR HIS KINGDOM PLAN

Prepare Ahead

Room setup: Place a whiteboard, chalkboard, or large paper where the facilitator can write words seen by all Ps in the presentation area.

Have tables with four chairs so that participants can divide into groups or turn chairs to participate in whole group sessions facing the facilitator.

Materials: Ps need their book, journal, Bible, paper, and pencil/pen.

Make a copy for each participant of the "Christian Job Description" or they can write in their book on p. 129.

Job Description for a Christian

Job title:

Effective date:

Location:

Position summary:

Answers to:

Supervises:

Relates to:

Qualifications:

Responsibilities:

Print the page below. Make a copy of the types of spiritual formation list and cut into strips with one type per slip. Place one sheet of strips in each plastic baggy. *Use for Activity #5:3.*

Spiritual Formation

Activity #5-3

Directions for Activity #5-3: In groups of four, take turns drawing one strip of paper and read it out loud to others in the group. Ps are invited to comment about it, possibly identifying their own preferences for spiritual formation.

1. *Relational spirituality.* As a communion of three persons, God is a relational being. He is the originator of a personal relationship with us. And our high and holy calling is to respond to His loving initiatives. By loving God completely, we discover who and whose we are as we come to see ourselves as God sees us. In this way, we become more secure to become others centered, and this enables us to become givers rather than grabbers.

2. *Paradigm spirituality.* This approach to spirituality centers on the radical contrasts between the temporal and eternal value systems and emphasizes the need for a paradigm shift from a cultural to a biblical way of seeing life. Experiencing our mortality can help us transfer our hope from the seen to the unseen and realize the preciousness of present opportunities. Our presuppositions shape our perspective, our perspective shapes our priorities, and our priorities shape our practice.

3. *Disciplined spirituality.* There has been a resurgence of interest in the classical disciplines of the spiritual life, and this approach stresses the benefits of these varied disciplines. At the same time, it recognizes the needed balance between radical dependence on God and personal discipline as an expression of obedience and application.

4. *Exchanged life spirituality.* The twentieth century saw the growth of an experiential approach to the spiritual life that is based on the believer's new identity in Christ. Identification with Christ in his crucifixion and resurrection (Romans 6; Galatians 2:20) means that our old life has been exchanged for the life of Christ. This approach to spirituality moves from a works to a grace orientation and from legalism to liberty because it centers on our acknowledgment that Christ's life is our life.

5. *Motivated spirituality.* People are motivated to satisfy their needs for security, significance, and fulfilment, but they turn to the wrong places to have their needs met. This approach emphasizes looking to Christ rather than the world to meet our needs. A study of scripture reveals a number of biblical motivators: fear, love and gratitude, rewards, identity, purpose and hope, and longing for God. Our task is to be more motivated by the things God declares to be important than by the things the world says are important.

6. *Devotional spirituality*. What are the keys to loving God, and how can we cultivate a growing intimacy with Him? This approach explores what it means to enjoy God and a trust in Him. We gradually become conformed to what we most love and admire and are most satisfied when we seek God's pleasure above our own.

7. *Holistic spirituality*. There is a general tendency to treat Christianity as a component of life along with other components such as family, work, and finances. This compartmentalization fosters a dichotomy between the secular and the spiritual. The biblical alternative is to understand the implications of Christ's lordship in such a way that even the most mundane components of life can become expressions of the life of Christ in us.

8. *Process spirituality*. In our culture, we increasingly tend to be human doings rather than human beings. The world tells us that what we achieve and accomplish determines who we are, but the scriptures teach that who we are in Christ should be the basis of what we do. The dynamics of growth are inside out rather than outside in. This approach considers what it means to be faithful to the process of life rather than one product to the next. It also focuses an abiding in Christ and practicing his presence.

9. *Spirit-filled spirituality*. Although there are divergent views of spiritual gifts, charismatics and noncharismatics agree that until recently, the role of the Holy Spirit has been somewhat neglected as a central dynamic of the spiritual life. This approach considers how to appropriate the love, wisdom, and power of the Spirit and stresses the biblical implications of the Holy Spirit as a personal presence rather than a mere force.

10. *Warfare spirituality*. Spiritual warfare is not optional for believers in Christ. Scripture teaches and illustrates the realities of this warfare on the three fronts of the world, the flesh, and the devil. The worldly and the demonic systems are external to the believer, but they entice and provide opportunities for the flesh, which is the capacity for sin within the believer. This approach develops a biblical strategy for dealing with each of these barriers to spiritual growth.

11. *Nurturing spirituality*. The believer's highest calling in ministry is to reproduce the life of Christ in others. Reproduction takes the form of evangelism for those who do not know Christ and edification for those who do. It is important to develop a philosophy of discipleship and evangelism and view edification and evangelism as a way of life; lifestyle discipleship and evangelism are the most effective and realistic approaches to unbelievers and believers within our sphere of influence.

12. *Corporate spirituality*. We come to faith as individuals, but we grow in community. A meaningful context of encouragement, accountability, and worship is essential to spiritual maturity, since this involves the others-centered use of spiritual gifts for mutual edification. This approach stressed the need for community, challenges and creators of community, the nature and purpose of the church, soul care, servant leadership, accountability, and renewal.

Chapter 5

Instruction

Section 1: What Is a Christian?

Ask Ps, "What is a Christian?" Go over the terms historically used to refer to those we now call Christian.

Do **Activity #5:1:** Write your definition of "in Christ" based on the sampling of scripture on p.128

Or:

Activity #5:2: Have them fill out the Christian job description (p.129) and then go over it as a group.

Lecture or discuss the book's section on what a Christian is and the questionable definitions that are often used.

Have 4 Ps take turns reading out loud the profound quotes on p. 130. Discuss if desired.

Section 2: What Is the Kingdom of God?

Have Ps silently read the scripture about the kingdom of God on p. 130. Once reading is concluded, ask Ps to call out descriptions of what the kingdom of God is. Write their responses down to be viewed by all.

Emphasize that the kingdom of God is here and now and not just after death.

Section 3: Grace and Counterfeits

Teach the concept of self-salvation and religion versus the gospel. You may want to use the prodigal son story from scripture to illuminate the hearts of the two sons.

Have Ps discuss and give examples of how they can help students understand the difference between biblical teaching and cultural norms chosen by you or the school.

Section 4: Cheap Grace versus Costly Discipleship

Do **Activity #5:3.**

Read Luke 14:28 and then have Ps reference p.142 on counting the cost. Have Ps silently read John Stott's view and the view expressed in "The Shovel" with this question in mind: "Which perspective of Luke 14:28 is correct?"

Section 5: The Parable of the Sower

Read the parable of the sower and discuss what the various soil types might look like in Ps' respective teaching assignments. Ask teachers to examine their thoughts about students representing the hard soil. Is it hard for them to see students not yielding to Jesus?

Section 6: What Makes a School a Christian School?

Discuss the assertion that values need a basis for their truth and require a sufficient basis for validation.

CHAPTER 6

HOW, NOT WHAT

Prepare Ahead

Room arrangement: ensure the seating arrangement allows both lecture / class discussion format as well as a quick way to assemble into groups of four Ps.

Materials: have a clock or timepiece to easily measure seconds and a copy of Bloom's taxonomy for every four Ps.

Activity #6-2: Make a copy of the sheet below. Cut the directions and each scripture into a strip of paper. Place the directions and strips into a plastic baggy. Make one baggy for each group of three people.

Directions: Pass the strips out. Go in a circle with one participant reading their strip to the group. Transformational educators practice instructional methods which foster positive caring relations in a community of learners. After one is read, the group can offer simple ideas of how to apply this to their class.

Ephesians 4:29: "Do not let any unwholesome talk come out of your mouths, but only what is helpful for building others up according to their needs, that it may benefit those who listen."

Proverbs 27:6: "Wounds from a friend can be trusted; but an enemy multiplies kisses."

Colossians 3:13: "Bear with each other and forgive one another if any of you has a grievance against someone. Forgive as the LORD forgave you."

Philippians 2:1–30: "Therefore if you have any encouragement from being united with Christ, if any comfort from his love, if any common sharing in the Spirit, if any tenderness and compassion, then make my joy complete by being like-minded, having the same love, being one spirit and of one mind. Do nothing out of selfish ambition or vain conceit. Rather, in humility value others above yourselves, not looking to your own interests but each of you to the interests of the others."

James 1:22: "Do not merely listen to the word, and so deceive yourselves. Do what it says."

Philippians 4:8: "Finally, brothers and sisters, whatever is true, whatever is noble, whatever is right, whatever is pure, whatever is lovely, whatever is admirable-if anything is excellent or praiseworthy-think about such things."

Prepare for napkin folding (activity #6:4):

Have a square, cloth napkin for each participant.

Make one copy of "Jordan's Napkin-Folding Directions" for each person.

Be prepared to give a variety of examples for how teachers differentiate instruction.

Objective: Students will correctly fold a napkin using Jordan's style.

Directions:

- Completely open the napkin in the shape of a square.
- Fold the napkin in half on the diagonal to make a right triangle.
- Take the vertices of the two acute angles so they meet the vertex of the right angle; crease to fold.
- The shape is now a square. Flip on the square over, careful that nothing comes unfolded.
- Fold in half again on the diagonal with the original right angle folding over to its opposite corner, creating a triangle.
- Fold the napkin with the two acute angles meeting each other and the center crease being the spine of the napkin.
- Place the napkin in an upright position.

Congratulations for folding a Jordan's style napkin.

Explain Bloom's taxonomy and have Ps practice making up questions from what they actually teach for each level in the taxonomy.

Prepare for activity #6:5: Distribute a copy of Bloom's taxonomy to each person and have Ps get in groups of four people. Have them select a movie or book familiar to everyone in their group. Have the group make up a question about the movie or book using each level of Bloom's taxonomy.

Prepare for activity #6:7: Print out one copy of the list below for every three Ps. Cut the phrases into individual strips and place in a plastic baggy with the directions.

Directions: Spread out the slips of paper statements so that all group members can read them. As a group, decide how to divide the statements into three groups based on how they are alike or different in some way. Think of a name to describe each of the three different groups.

Accept responsibility for your own behavior.

Bring all needed materials to class.

In class discussion, raise your hand; wait to be called on.

Lower your voices when the lights are switched off.

Place makeup work in the yellow basket.

Show respect for other people.

Use the restroom pass as needed when direct instruction is not being given.

Bring a positive attitude to class.

Place basketballs back on the cart.

Follow all directions correctly the first time.

Pass your papers to the right.

Show respect for other people's property.

Speak at appropriate times using appropriate voices.

Be in your seat and ready to begin when the bell rings.

Develop skills for lifelong learning.

Keep hands, feet, and objects to yourself.

Use a red pen to correct your homework in class.

Sharpen pencils before the beginning of class.

Think and make wise choices.

Use twelve-inch voices during cooperative group work.

Chapter 6

Instruction

Activity #6-1. Have Ps write their responses to the self-assessment on pp. 154-155. Have them star the top three they would like to discuss as a group.

Explain to Ps the difference between the how and what. Discuss the idea that scripture is relevant to how we teach, although scripture is not a handbook on pedagogy. Smith: "The challenge of being a Christian who teaches is not just a matter of spotting when to say Christian things, or of being a kind person, but of figuring out what might be the 'pattern of this world' to which we are conforming and being transformed."

Section 1: Jesus as a Teacher

Use the narrative in this section to lead a discussion about how (as opposed to what) Jesus taught. Ps familiar with scripture can construct this section by giving examples of how Jesus taught. People less familiar with scripture may need the facilitator to give examples of Jesus's pedagogy. Point out that, whereas scripture is not a handbook on pedagogy, it gives examples of Jesus's methods.

Section 2: Content versus Pedagogy

Have Ps share their description of Christian education.

Have Ps think about how teachers can be transformational in their teaching methods.

Ideas: Examine the scriptures, ask students for feedback, examine traditions, study the research, pray for discernment, receive input from colleagues, be a student of your students, reflect on your pedagogy, and trust God to direct your teaching. The ideas in this module are not sacrosanct; use your mind as God designed to see that which is good. Then apply it in your classroom as a transformational educator.

Section 3: The Hidden Curriculum

Explain "hidden curriculum."

Do **Activity #6-2** with Ps divided into small groups for discussion. If you like, bring the groups together to discuss.

Do **Activity #6-3:** Discuss with a colleague (pairs) the hidden curriculum in response to the list below. They are on p. 163 in the book.

1) When we teach about the evils of other people's sin, but we ignore our own sin, such as gossip, pride, envy, the idol of appearances.
2) When we consistently ignore certain school rules but demand other rules are followed.
3) When we require that students meet deadlines but return graded work whenever we get around to it.
4) When most historical topics we teach are about war.
5) When students are asked to act differently, or we act differently when someone is observing the class.
6) When we give tokens to students for complying with expectations.
7) When the teacher can have warm coffee or cold water in class, but the student cannot.
8) When learning is exclusively centered on "Will it be on the test?".
9) When assessment of learning is based on competition (highest grade) versus meeting instructional objectives.

Section 3: Recognizing and Teaching Students as God Made Them to Be

Lead Ps in a discussion about the cartoon and Brantley's (and numerous other scholars') explanation of "train up a child."

Do **Activity #6-4.** Give each Ps a square cloth napkin and a set of the directions for folding napkins using pyramid style. Tell Ps to fold the napkin according to the directions without looking at anyone else's work or asking the teacher for help. Observe their work to be able to comment upon it later. After Ps have had sufficient time to try to fold the napkin, tell them to put the napkin away and simply observe you folding the napkin as you comment on what you are doing each step of the directions. Next, ask the Ps to take their napkins and *follow you one step at a time* as you fold the napkin as a class, according to the directions. (You will likely have to correct as few Ps who want to work ahead on their own.) To master the folding for yourself ahead of time, watch a YouTube demonstration: https://www.youtube.com/watch?v=Ab7dg3EhZo8.

After having done the napkin folding together, with you demonstrating, ask the students to try it on their own while you circle among them giving help and correction. If necessary, do the exercise again until all Ps can complete it on their own successfully.

Process the exercise by having Ps discuss their feelings and reactions during various stages of the exercise. Were some Ps better at this than others? Why? What may this exercise say about good pedagogy and the teacher's role? What teaching practices would this discourage (e.g., "read the chapter and answer the questions," "read the explanation and do the problem set," not allowing students to assist each other in learning).

Read Carol Tomlison's definition of differentiation and examine the chart of the many ways it is implemented. Allow Ps to share, and you also share questions and comments while studying the chart.

If Ps are practicing teachers, lead a discussion on ways they already implement differentiation and the constraints of it. If not, go over multiple examples of ways differentiation can be implemented.

Divide Ps into groups of three and have them come up with three different ways to teach a concept using multiple intelligences.

Section 4: Instructional Techniques Conducive to Transformation

Reiterate the idea that these techniques seem to foster some characteristics conducive to transformation but that transformation is never a technique. Ps must use discernment.

Tell Ps that you are going to ask a question and then use a timer to mark three seconds. Say, "How long is three seconds?" Using a timer, wait three seconds before saying, "That's three seconds."

Explain *wait time*, emphasizing that it is a well-researched construct.

Do **Activity #6-5:** have students take out pencil and paper and ask them to write their responses to the questions on the Griney Grollers Thinking Skills Test.

Write the following sentence so that all Ps can see it:

The griney grollers grangled in the granchy gak.

Call out the questions below and have Ps write their responses.

1. What kind of grollers were they?
2. What did the grollers do?
3. Where did they do it?
4. In what kind of gak did they grangle?
5. Place one line under the subject and two lines under the verb.

After writing their answers, call the out the questions for the Ps to answers orally. All the answers should be uniformly correct.

Either ask or share that the point of this exercise is to show that students can make 100 percent on a test without having learned anything. Low-level questions and information require very little from a learner.

Just for fun and imagination, ask Ps the two questions below:

In one sentence, explain why the grollers were grangling in the granchy gak.

If you had to grangle in a granchy gak, what one item would you choose to have with you and why? Be prepared to justify your answer.

Lead into your presentation on Bloom's taxonomy (base your presentation on how familiar the Ps already are with Bloom's taxonomy). Have Ps practice making up a question from various levels of Bloom's taxonomy and having the group tell them if it is correct or not.

Do **Activity #6:6:** Distribute a copy of Bloom's taxonomy to each person and have Ps get in groups of four people. Have them select a movie or book familiar to everyone in their group. Have the group make up a question about the movie or book using each level of Bloom's taxonomy.

Point out that greater familiarity with the action verbs of the taxonomy will lead to greater use of them in writing lesson objectives and the use of higher-level questions during instruction.

Pretest the group by asking how many Ps are already familiar with the cooperative learning techniques mentioned in this session. Adjust accordingly. Explain cooperative groups by using them throughout the training and referring to this section as you do so. If you are not using all the chapters in this book, go through the research and the samples of cooperative groups given in this section.

Be sure to mention all the methods of this section. This is a practical section and will take much time. Consistently make connections as to how these methods may foster transformation.

Section 6: Assessing Learning: Doers or Hearers Only

Ask Ps to brainstorm reasons teachers give tests while the facilitator writes their responses so all can see. Compare their responses to van Brummel's list on pp. 183-184. Lead a discussion about positive and negative criteria for assessing students.

Section 7: Classroom Management for Image Bearers

Ask Ps for reason(s) why a transformation educator should have a well-managed classroom. Discuss the reason on p. 187 of how well-managed classes result in increased learning, which benefits students' preparation for their contributions to God's kingdom on earth.

Differentiate between classroom management (definition below) and discipline (what happens after a student breaks a rule).

> Classroom management consists of *teacher behaviors* that produce high levels of *student involvement* in classroom activities, *minimal* amounts of student behavior that *interfere* with the teacher's or other students' work, and *efficient* use of *instructional time*. (C. E. Evertson 2013)

Discuss each italicized point in the definition above. Note that classroom management is not just compliance or being quiet but requires student involvement in the activities.

Do **Activity #6:7**.

Ask groups to share how they divided the slips of paper. Discuss their lists as a way to introduce the idea of *rules* as different from *procedures* as different from *goals*. Check for understanding by asking Ps for examples of rules, goals, and procedures.

Explain that these rules and consequences for are elements of a classroom discipline plan. The teacher designs the classroom management plan before classes begin and teaches it to students on the first days of school.

Activity #6:8

Have Ps write their own classroom management plan for:

    Rules:
    Consequences:
    Procedures:
    Goals:

CHAPTER 7

THE STUDENT: IMAGE BEARER, BUNDLE OF SIN, OR MASS OF TISSUE

Preparation

Get a copy of *You Are Special* by Max Lucado or *Les Miserable* by Victor Hugo.

Prepare how you will explain unconditional positive regard.

Prepare your explanation of biblical repentance and reconciliation.

Google and print a chart of James Fowler's stages of faith development to use in section 6.

Chapter 7

Instruction

Section 1: God's Beloved Children

Read Max Lucado's *You Are Special* or an excerpt from Victor Hugo's *Les Miserable* where the priest intercepted the arrest and gave the silver to Jean Valjean.

Explain unconditional positive regard.

Discuss the questions to consider on p. 199.

Section 2: Students Are Made in the Image of God

Ask Ps to explain what being made in the image of God means.

Have Ps do **activity #7:1** and allow for discussion if desired.

Section 3: Children Are Born with a Sinful Nature

Prompt Ps to share their personal views about being born with a sinful nature and about disciplining students. The handbook or sojourn is based on the understanding that we are born with a sinful nature, which is to be disciplined based on biblical principles. This is contrary to many educators' views, and this distinction may need to be addressed.

Have Ps answer, "What would your students say is the reason you correct and discipline them?"

Section 4: Repentance and Reconciliation

After explaining the practice of biblical repentance and reconciliation (p. 205), ask Ps to volunteer at role-playing the following:

Scenario A: The class got rowdy when your computer would not work for you to access the lesson for the day. As you frustratingly worked on your computer, the class got rowdier and rowdier. You lost your cool and punished the entire class out of anger.

Scenario B: It was the final straw from the biology teacher next door as she refused to correct students for blatant violation of phone usage.

Section 4: Unlocking Who God Made the Student to Be

Write out *"What kind of work do you think God may have created you to do?"* and *"What do you want to be when you grow up?"* Ask Ps to share the differences they see and the implications of these two varied statements. Share any you want to add or that the book mentions.

Discuss what impact knowing there is a purpose for their life may have for students both now and in the future.

Section 5: Teaching with a Student's Age in Mind

Ask Ps to share amusing stories they have heard young children say that reflect their faith or misunderstandings of biblical language or meaning.

Give Ps time to examine Fowler's stages of faith chart. Have Ps discuss these questions:

1. Do these stages reflect biblical truth or not? How or how not?
2. Do you think transformation and the spiritual developmental stages are related? If so, how?
3. What can a teacher do to help students trust asking questions and sharing doubts about their faith?

CHAPTER 8

SACRED WOUNDS OR MEANINGLESS SCARS

Preparation

Put each verse below on a strip of paper to be distributed to Ps for **activity #8-1.** Have a dry mark board or large chart paper and marker to write down elements of a biblical view of suffering.

> And the God of all grace, who called you to his eternal glory in Christ, after you have suffered a little while, will himself restore you and make you strong, firm and steadfast. (1 Peter 5:10)

> So that no man may be disturbed by these afflictions; for you yourselves know that we have been destined for this. (1 Thessalonians 3:3)

> Beloved, do not be surprised at the fiery trial when it comes upon you to test you, as though something strange were happening to you. (1 Peter 4:12)

> He causes his sun to rise on the evil and the good and sends rain on the righteous and the unrighteous. (Matthew 5:45)

> For just as we share abundantly in the sufferings of Christ, so also our comfort abounds through Christ. (2 Corinthians 1:5)

> Praise be to the God and Father of our Lord Jesus Christ, the Father of compassion and the God of all comfort, who comforts us in all our troubles, so that we can comfort those in any trouble with the comfort we ourselves receive from God. (2 Corinthians 1:3–4)

Not only so, but we also glory in our sufferings, because we know that suffering produces perseverance; perseverance, character; and character, hope. (Romans 5:3–4)

I consider that our present sufferings are not worth comparing with the glory that will be revealed in us. (Romans 8:18)

The righteous person may have many troubles,
but the Lord delivers him from them all. (Psalm 34:19)

For our light and momentary troubles are achieving for us an eternal glory that far outweighs them all. (2 Corinthians 4:17)

Who shall separate us from the love of Christ? Shall trouble or hardship or persecution or famine or nakedness or danger or sword? (Romans 8:35)

Therefore, since Christ suffered in his body, arm yourselves also with the same attitude, because whoever suffers in the body is done with sin. (1 Peter 4:1)

But even if you should suffer for what is right, you are blessed. "Do not fear their threats; do not be frightened." (1 Peter 3:14)

Carry each other's burdens, and in this way you will fulfill the law of Christ. (Galatians 6:2)

For it has been granted to you on behalf of Christ not only to believe in him, but also to suffer for him. (Philippians 1:29)

He was despised and rejected by mankind,
a man of suffering, and familiar with pain.
Like one from whom people hide their faces
he was despised, and we held him in low esteem. (Isaiah 53:3)

I want to know Christ—yes, to know the power of his resurrection and participation in his sufferings, becoming like him in his death. (Philippians 3:10)

Whoever does not take up their cross and follow me is not worthy of me. (Matthew 10:38)

To this you were called, because Christ suffered for you, leaving you an example, that you should follow in his steps. (1 Peter 2:21)

For just as we share abundantly in the sufferings of Christ, so also our comfort abounds through Christ. (2 Corinthians 1:5)

At this, Job got up and tore his robe and shaved his head. Then he fell to the ground in worship and said:
"Naked I came from my mother's womb,
and naked I will depart.
The Lord gave and the Lord has taken away;
may the name of the Lord be praised." (Job 1:20–21)

Prepare what you will say to teach section 4.

Chapter 8

Instruction

Section 1: Suffering Is Real

Examine the list of ways people suffer on pp. 216-217. Can Ps add any? Discuss or think of ways in which you or someone you know has been transformed in some way by suffering.

Prepare Ps for this chapter by discussing the following concerns related to suffering:

- increasingly high rates of suicide, indicating a lack of emotional resiliency and a hopeless despair
- increasingly high rates of anesthetizing suffering through drugs, alcohol, running away, denial, and ending relationships versus the hard work of restoration
- terrible theology that assumes God should not allow suffering or that people suffer because they lack faith or all suffering is God's punishment
- reasons for refusing to walk through suffering ourselves or to walk with hurting family/ friends or even strangers

Make Ps aware of the delicate balancing act of dealing with suffering:

- not to chasten the good intentions of parents and teachers who want to shield children from suffering
- nor to suggest parents and teachers prematurely force children to confront the evil and suffering that exists at a distance and will become real soon enough
- but to encourage teacher and parents to teach a biblical view of suffering and walk with children through the pain of suffering they are facing

Section 2: A Biblical View of Suffering

Do **Activity #8-1** on pp. 223-224 of matching scripture with reasons people suffer

Read Richard Foster's quote about God's hiddenness on pp. 223-224 and ask the group to discuss these questions:

> What are you prepared to say to a student of any age who says he or she prayed to God and God did not answer?

> How do you answer a student who asks you, "How could a loving God do this?"

Discuss the suggested practices of transformational teachers related to suffering and their students.

1) Clarify scripture that may confuse a student about the reality of God's responses to our prayers about suffering.

2) Help students pray boldly and persistently, trusting God with those for whom they pray.

3) Be on the lookout for comments, stories, lyrics, or anything that tries to avoid, hide, or minimalize the fact that life includes suffering, and make the correction for the students as needed.

4) Allow open discussion and grieving by students (and yourself!) about suffering.

5) Expose students to literature, art, music, and drama that addresses suffering from Christian truth. Name some examples and use this time for teachers to help one another.

Section 3: A Biblical Response to Suffering

Do **Activity #8-2** (p. 224). Do with the full group together.

Distribute pieces of paper, with one of the verses below on each piece, until none are left (meaning Ps may have more than one paper with the scripture). Go around the room, having Ps read aloud the verse on the paper and make a comment if they want to. After the scriptures are read, ask Ps to name some points that define a biblical view of suffering. Write them on a large chart as they are said. (For example, Christ suffered, not all prayer is answered with healing or cessation of the problem, suffering can mold you more into God's desired person, don't be surprised by pain and suffering, our own suffering enables us to comfort others who suffer, we can have hope for the future, and, of course, Job's response, "Blessed be the name of the Lord.")

Do **Activity #8-3** (pp. 227-228). Read chapters 38–42 in the book of Job in the Bible (take your time to savor this magnificent book, beautifully written with mounds of truth for our benefit).

Write down a one-sentence summary of what God says about human response to suffering.

Write down a one-sentence summary of how Job responded to what God shared with him about suffering.

What has reading, or rereading, these chapters from Job meant to you?

The source of suffering and the end of suffering are critical points for Ps to understand, as they serve as the root of much misunderstanding about the God who they accuse of causing suffering.

Go over the ways people deny suffering.

Section 4: Prayer and Suffering

Ask Ps, "If the following two verses were the only two you read, what would you conclude about prayers?"

> "If you remain in me and my words remain in you, ask whatever you wish, and it will be done for you." (John 15:7)

> "If you believe, you will receive whatever you ask for in prayer." (Matthew 21:22)

Teach the key points made in this section, including that Jesus, Paul, and others had prayers not answered according to their request.

Lead a discussion on these questions to think about:

1. Does the fact that Jesus suffered make a difference to our students?
2. What are you prepared to say to a student of any age who says he or she prayed to God and God did not answer?
3. How do you answer a student who asks you, "How could a loving God do this?"
4. What are other scriptures people use to deny Christian suffering?

Section 5: Lament

Define lament and compare it to other kinds of sadness.

Have Ps do **Activity #8-4:** Write your own lament and consider the advisability of having your students also write one. See p. 234.

Read both NT Wright's comments and T. S. Elliot's excerpt from *East Coker*. Ask Ps for their reactions and how this goes along with transformational education.

Section 6: Why Does a Loving God Allow Suffering?

Read the Epicurious paradox and ask Ps if they have ever had to address it with students.

Go over the worldviews listed on p. 235 and how they would be expressed in comments people may make about suffering and death. It is worthwhile to help Ps understand how to identify comments that may reflect an underlying worldview because this may open the door to discuss Christian belief.

Section 7: Ressentiment

Ask Ps, "Does suffering always work to bring about personal growth in people? Do you know of situations where the result of suffering was bitterness?"

Define ressentiment.

Teach the six questions about forgiveness on p. 239 and discuss as desired.

Section 8: Forgiveness and Suffering

Ask Ps to think of a person they struggled to forgive—either in the past or someone they are currently struggling to forgive. Go through each of the counselling for forgiveness questions and ask Ps to think about their answers in light of the person they need to / needed to forgive. After completing the questions, ask Ps to share insights and other comments.

What can we practically do?

Read each statement below and ask Ps to give a thumbs-up or thumbs-down based on whether it is true. Follow this with a discussion of how teachers have embedded these truths in their teaching and relationships with students.

> God created, sustains, and loves the people He created; we are not random, meaningless, or unloved.

> Suffering originated when sin entered the world.

> Suffering is awful, and the Bible recognizes the need for tears and lament.

Jesus can empathize with our suffering because He suffered deeply in every way that we suffer.

We do not always know why suffering happens, but we know it is not always a rewards/consequence scenario.

God can take what was intended for evil and suffering and turn it into good.

We have a choice. Suffering can either makes us bitter or change us for the better.

Journal: What can teachers practically do to help students understand suffering and minister to them while they experience it?

Conclude your sojourn by taking a look at all the transformational educators—statements statements which are boxed throughout the handbook. Ps may ask for more explanation on any of them.